THE ZUNIS OF CIBOLA

THE ZUNIS OF CIBOLA

C. Gregory Crampton

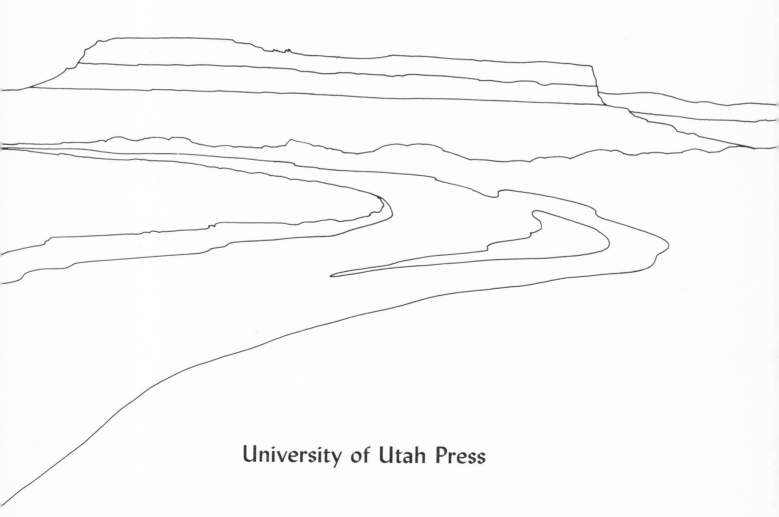

University of Utah Press

Copyright © 1977 by C. Gregory Crampton
International Standard Book Number 0-87480-120-6
Library of Congress Catalog Card Number 77-072586
Printed in the United States of America

Second printing 1979

To the Zuni People

Contents

Illustrations

Preface

An oven at Pescado

For well over five hundred years the Zuni people have supported and maintained themselves, perpetuated their society and culture, and preserved their unique identity. This they have done against substantial environmental odds and in the face of successive challenges from Indian neighbors and from Spain, Mexico, and the United States. This book is a history of that remarkable achievement. Living in western New Mexico, the Zuni Indians, who now number over five thousand, are perhaps best known to the outside world as the original inhabitants of the "Seven Cities" in the land of Cíbola, sought in the mid-sixteenth century by the Spaniard Coronado. They are also well known through the works of numerous students who have found in the Zunis' peaceful and friendly ways, and intricate ceremonial life, much of absorbing interest.

Anthropology, first, and history, second, predominate in the writing about Zuni. Following the work begun by Cushing, literally hundreds of anthropological studies have been published. Far less attention has been given to Zuni archeology or prehistory. For the most part, the historians, following Bandelier's lead, have confined themselves to the Spanish period prior to the Pueblo Revolt, a time span of but a hundred and forty years. It is a pleasure to be able to note that recently the Zunis themselves have begun the publication of their own literature. *The Zunis: Self-portrayals*, a volume of stories taken from oral tradition and translated by Alvina Quam, was issued in 1972.

I have attempted here to outline the history of the Zuni people from late prehistoric times to the present. There have been few guidelines to follow but I am grateful to those who have set down oral tradition, drafted documents, written articles, dictated reminiscences, and prepared learned papers, for providing me a mass of material from which to build my own work. Insofar as the sources would permit, I have used them to bring out the Zuni side of things, to catch the Zuni perspective on the Zunis' own past. That a non-Zuni can successfully undertake such a task may well be debated. My brief would be that sympathetic objectivity should move one away from the more serious pitfalls toward a measure of success. My own bias in the matter seems implicit in the Dedication.

The hardy cultural vitality of the Zuni people and their remarkable historical continuity have been a neglected story but an inspirational one, worthy of a wide audience, that should have special interest in today's world.

I am indebted to many people and institutions for assistance given to me in the Zuni country, in correspondence, in libraries and archives, in research and editing, and in interviews and in the routine of manuscript preparation. I gratefully thank all of these people, named and unnamed, for their help. The interpretation I have placed upon the material coming from all sources is altogether my own. The basic research and writing for this book were completed in 1974.

At the Zuni Pueblo I received kind assistance from Governor Robert E. Lewis and his council and their administrative staff, and from Quincy Panteah, Albert Natachu, Alex Seowtewa, Gordon Peywa, Alvina Quam, Katie Poblano, Sam P. Poblano, Rufina Dutukewa, and Olivia Dutukewa.

The following persons assisted in many different ways: Eleanor B. Adams, Mary Jane Anderson, Virginia W. Anderson, Phyllis Ball, Katherine Bartlett, Jon R. Barton, Deward Bond, Fr. Clair Boudereaux, O.F.M., Daphne Ann Bowen, L. W. Butler, John M. Cahoon, Ruth M. Christensen, Curtis D. Cook, Marguerite B. Cooley, Dr. Helen M. Crampton, Margaret Currier, Professor Robert W. Delaney, Dr. Carl Schaefer Dentzel, Mike Doran, Gertrude R. Elsmore, Octavia Fellin, Bert Fireman, Dr. Bernard L. Fontana, John Gray, Carmelo Guadagno, Helen R. Hadley, Richard E. Hart, Gerald A. Huntley, Juanita C. Huntley, Dr. Myra Ellen Jenkins, Michael Kan, John M. Kitchen, Rev. Don Klompien, Fr. Niles Kraft, O.F.M., Robert M. Kvasnicka, Rebecca H. Latimer, Dr. Alexander J. Lindsay, Jr., Julianne H. Nielsen, Arthur L. Olivas, Dr. Floyd A. O'Neil, John D. Sylvester, Dr. Sandra C. Taylor, Jerry Tuttle, Dr. S. Lyman Tyler, Bernard J. VanderWagen, Mrs. Gertrude VanderWagen Wall, Michael Weber, and Dr. Stephen Williams.

These institutions lent assistance in background research: Arizona Historical Foundation, Arizona State University, Tempe; Arizona State Museum, University of Arizona, Tucson; Bancroft Library, University of California, Berkeley;

Boston Public Library; Brooklyn Museum, Brooklyn, New York; Bureau of Indian Affairs, Southern Pueblos Agency, Albuquerque, New Mexico; Center of Southwest Studies, Fort Lewis College, Durango, Colorado; Department of Library and Archives, State of Arizona, Phoenix; Duke Indian Oral History Project, American West Center, University of Utah; El Morro National Monument; Gallup Public Library, Gallup, New Mexico; Huntington Library, San Marino, California; Library of Congress, Washington, D.C.; Los Angeles County Museum of Natural History; Marriott Library, University of Utah, Salt Lake City; Museum of the American Indian, Heye Foundation, New York City; Museum of New Mexico, Santa Fe; Museum of Northern Arizona, Flagstaff; National Anthropological Archives, National Museum of Natural History, Smithsonian Institution, Washington, D.C.; New York Public Library, New York City; Northern Arizona University, Flagstaff; Peabody Museum, Harvard University; Sacred Heart Cathedral, Gallup, New Mexico; Southwest Museum, Highland Park, Los Angeles; State of New Mexico Records Center, Santa Fe; University of Arizona Library, Special Collections; Utah State Historical Society, Salt Lake City; Western History Department, Denver Public Library; and the Zimmerman Library, University of New Mexico, Albuquerque.

The sketches appearing at the chapter headings are from Victor Mindeleff, "A Study of Pueblo Architecture: Tusayan and Cibola," in the *Eighth Annual Report of the Bureau of Ethnology, 1886–87* (1891).

A word about usage: The Spanish spelling with the tilde — "Zuñi" — is no longer used by the Zuni people and I have consistently followed their preference except in quoted matter. In the spelling of the names of the ancient Zuni villages and certain other place names — Kechipbowa, Towayalane, etc. — I have followed the usage established in 1970 by the government of the Zuni Pueblo.

C. Gregory Crampton

Chapter I

The Ancient Past Lives

A Zuni chimney

At the outset let me say that in all the New World there are few places where the feel of history is stronger than it is in the Zuni pueblo. A personal view, of course, but many others have felt the same way. If you would know the Zuni Indians, visit them in their own land. Here where there are great reaches of space, where earth and sky meet in pleasant rhythms of line, the people still live close to the environment which has nurtured them for centuries. If your visit is in the summer, you can see for days on end the silhouette of the old pueblo standing out against a blue sky enlivened by perfectly spaced cotton-puff clouds.

Enter the village and follow ways and walk past walls known to generations of Zunis and their visitors — Spanish padres, Rocky Mountain trappers, army surveyors, zealous missionaries, and inquiring students. The houses in the pueblo still adjoin one another, though they are of only one story now. You can reach the flat roofs of many of them by following individual paths or by climbing stairways.

From the vantage of the rooftop look off to the southeast where Towayalane, the sacred mountain and refuge of the people in earlier times, dominates the landscape. Bisecting the pueblo is the Zuni River, frequently nothing more than a rivulet of water in a bed of glistening sand. Close at hand, a kiva ladder, a television aerial, and the cross of the Catholic church seem to compose a single picture.

Perhaps as you stand on the rooftop a ceremonial dance will be held in the plaza below. Who, from the outside world, has not been moved to awe by the dances — the masked figures, the elaborate dress and ritual, the shuffling feet, the turtle rattles that sound like falling rain? The dancers do not play to the few villagers watching, or to the tourists, but to the gods who are expected to bring rain and good health. To see these things is to be touched by the ambience of the pueblo; history becomes real. Here the ancient past lives.

Talk to the people. Enjoy their pleasant, friendly faces, soft voices, and gentle ways. Visitors since Coronado's time have found them gracious and hospitable. Commenting on this a Zuni said recently, "My grandfather was a great man. He taught me words of wisdom. A few weeks before he died, he told me: 'Be generous to your people, love your people, help your people and be courteous not only to your people, but to the people that come your way.' " [1]

"And what of the ceremonial dances?" you ask.

"Today as we live in the present ways of our people, we live also within the realm of our ancestors, for we are sustained through the rituals and beliefs of long ago. We live in accordance with the ways of our people, which bring life, blessings, and happiness." [2]

In their land the Zuni Indians live in contentment. They feel less need for worldly goods than those less fortunately placed. They live in harmony with the land though it is a harsh land with little rain. They are self-sufficient and self-sustained. Their vivid mythology and the constant rhythm of their ceremonial life hold them together and bring them happiness. They seem to grow stronger with the passage of time.

These people for centuries have suffered the impact of the alien, selecting what they wish from other cultures but never losing sight of their own traditions or their own identity. The quality and the power of their way of life have made the vicissitudes of living easier for them. They are an enduring people who look at the world with friendly eyes.

If you want to know where the Zuni country is, pick up a map of western New Mexico and eastern Arizona. Locate Gallup, Grants, and the little town of Quemado, in New Mexico, and Springerville, Holbrook, and Ganado, in Arizona. A line connecting these points would describe a wide circle. At the center is the Zuni Indian Pueblo, one of the most historic communities in North America. Though Zuni Indians now occupy only the center part of this big circle of country, the threads of their history extend into the peripheral areas and even beyond. Neighboring Indians — the Navajos and the Pueblos of Laguna and Acoma—occupy some of the outer reaches of this area, too. Mexican-Americans

---

[1] Alex Seowtewa (1971, 13).

[2] *In* Quam, trans. (1972, 181).

in some numbers and Anglo-Americans, noticeably strong in the railroad towns of Grants, Gallup, and Holbrook, complete the ethnic composition of the circle.[3]

The historic heartland of the Zunis falls within and takes up most of the basins of the Zuni River and Carrizo Creek, tributaries of the Little Colorado River. These head on the Pacific side of the Continental Divide, the ridge which separates the waters flowing to the Gulf of Mexico and the Gulf of California. The ancient homelands of the Zunis are along the middle reaches of the Zuni River where their cultural ancestors lived for centuries. Near the settlements and villages left by the ancient people, the Zuni Indians built compact villages of multi-storied houses. These were the towns seen and lived in by Coronado and his men and called by them the "Seven Cities" in the land of Cíbola.

For the last three hundred years, most of the Indians have lived in a single village, the Pueblo of Zuni. Within the boundaries of the small, rather cramped reservation are smaller farming villages at Pescado, Nutria, and Ojo Caliente, which were established probably in the eighteenth century but which in more recent years have been occupied only during the time of planting and harvest, if at all.[4] Beyond the boundaries of the reservation there are ancient sites and areas, sacred points and shrines, and places of pilgrimage central to Zuni life and history.

The Zuni country is a wedge-shaped segment of the southeastern part of the Colorado Plateau, a vast expanse of tablelands and mesas, cliffs and canyons covering parts of four states — New Mexico, Arizona, Utah, and Colorado. The whole is a masterpiece of erosion, created through many geological ages by the waters of the Colorado River system.

The Zuni sector of the plateau, bounded on the east by the heights of the Continental Divide, extends from the Zuni Mountains south over a broad table-

---

[3] Vogt and Albert, eds. (1966), report on a major study conducted in the Zuni region by Harvard University. The "comparative study of values in five cultures" was begun in 1949 and completed in 1955. The "cultures" involved were Navajo, Zuni, Spanish-American, Mormon, and Texan. Oddly enough, some place names, and even some geographical names, in the report are thinly disguised: Gallup becomes "Railtown," Ramah becomes "Rimrock," etc. Zuni, however, remains Zuni! In appendix 1, Vogt and Albert give seven pages of publications emanating from the project. The resulting field research and dissertations helped more than ten scholars qualify for the doctor of philosophy degree. The bibliography is a valuable reference. See the technical study by Kluckhohn, Strodtbeck, and others (1961).

To Cushing (1885) the Zunis broadly described the boundaries of their lands which extended far beyond the limits of the present reservation.

[4] The Zuni names for the farming villages, and English translations, are given in Hodge, Hammond, and Rey, eds. and trans. (1945, 294).

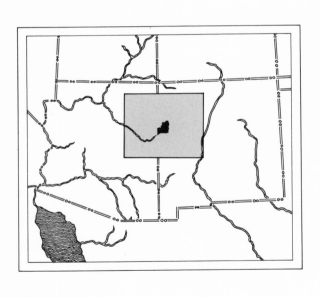

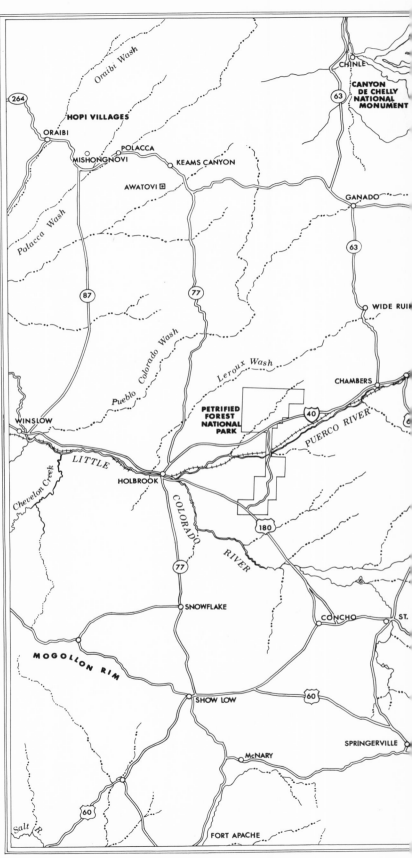

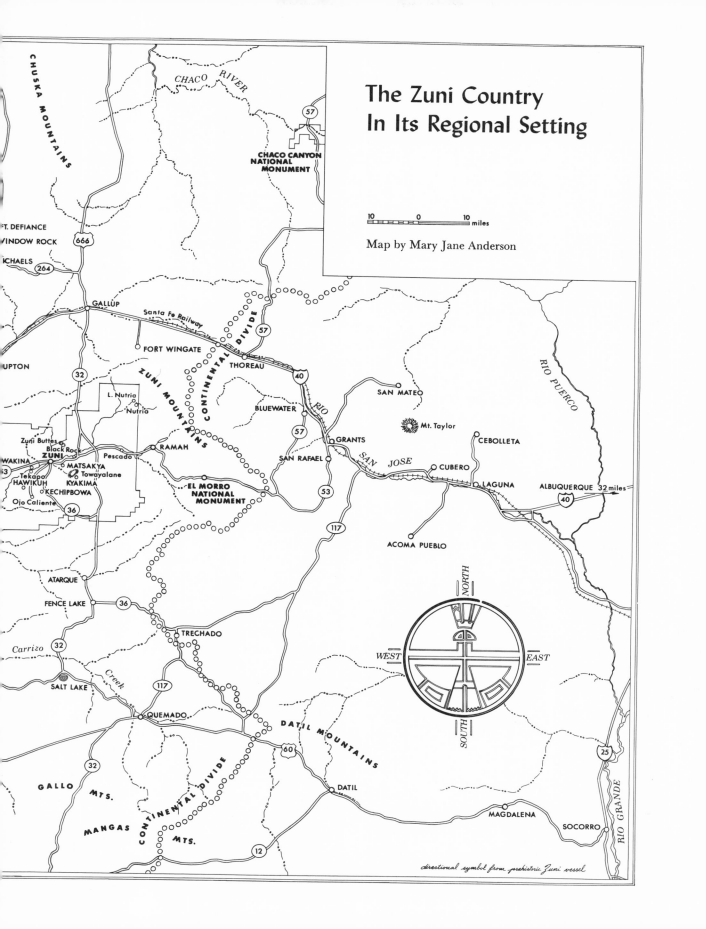

The Zuni Country
In Its Regional Setting

10   0   10 miles

Map by Mary Jane Anderson

CHUSKA MOUNTAINS

CHACO RIVER

57

CHACO CANYON
NATIONAL
MONUMENT

FT. DEFIANCE

WINDOW ROCK

ICHAELS   264

666

GALLUP

Santa Fe Railway

57

FORT WINGATE

THOREAU

40

SAN MATEO

UPTON

32

CONTINENTAL DIVIDE

ZUNI MOUNTAINS

L. Nutria

Nutria

BLUEWATER

RIO

Mt. Taylor

57

CEBOLLETA

Zuni Buttes

Black Rock

ZUNI

WAKINA

MATSAKYA

Towayalane

Pescado

RAMAH

GRANTS

SAN RAFAEL

SAN JOSE

CUBERO

Tekapo

HAWIKUH

KYAKIMA

53

LAGUNA

ALBUQUERQUE   32 miles

Ojo Caliente

KECHIPBOWA

36

EL MORRO
NATIONAL
MONUMENT

40

117

ACOMA PUEBLO

RIO PUERCO

ATARQUE

NORTH

FENCE LAKE

36

WEST

EAST

Carrizo   32

TRECHADO

Creek

117

SALT LAKE

SOUTH

QUEMADO

DATIL MOUNTAINS

32

60

GALLO   MTS.

CONTINENTAL DIVIDE

DATIL

MAGDALENA

SOCORRO

RIO GRANDE

25

MANGAS   MTS.

12

directional symbol from prehistoric Zuni vessel

land to the Mangas and Gallo mountains, outlying sections of the Mogollon Rim. The Zuni Mountains, actually the eroded remnants of a seventy-mile-long elliptical upwarp, a blister in the earth's crust, form the most prominent topographical feature of the region. The central mountain mass, which from a distance appears as a rounded, pine-topped ridge, is not spectacular, rising above nine thousand feet in elevation in only a few places.

The landscape around the lower, peripheral slopes of these mountains is more striking. Millions of years ago when pressures deep in the earth began to hump up the surface, the massive beds of sedimentary strata covering the area were uplifted and tilted. Through the geological ages these beds eroded and retreated away from the central core (of hard precambrian granite and schist), forming a series of cliffs and valleys surrounding the base of the upwarp. The softer strata, eroding easily, formed gentle slopes and valleys; the hard, resistant rock formed lines of cliffs. These great cliffs, ablaze with color, are the crowning elements of superlative beauty in this desert land. One conspicuous landmark is the line of red cliffs of Wingate sandstone extending for fully seventy miles east from Gallup.

Even more colorful than the Wingate is the Zuni sandstone, best seen along the southern and western bases of the Zuni Mountains where it is exposed in massive cliffs and bosses of brilliant, variegated colors. Colorings run from creamy white to red but they appear in no distinctive or characteristic pattern. Alternating bands of red and white distinguish some of the boldest exposures. Dutton, who named the formation in 1884, compared the banded colors to the stripes on the American flag: "The white looks as if it had been painted with pot and brush upon a uniform smooth red surface." [5]

History attaches to the Zuni sandstone. If you follow either of the two main forks of the Zuni River, the Pescado and the Nutria, which head on the western slopes of the Zuni Mountains and on the adjoining tableland, you may see beautiful exposures of the formation, witnesses to hundreds of years of human history.

---

[5] C. E. Dutton, whose prior studies of Utah's high plateaus and the Grand Canyon are classics in geographical literature, wrote the first substantial study (1885) of the Zuni Mountains and of Mount Taylor, the volcanic area adjoining it to the northeast. Dutton found little in the landscape of this region to match the glories of other sections of the Colorado Plateau, but he saw much to admire in the Wingate and Zuni sandstones (pp. 136–37). Dutton referred to the Zuni Mountains as the Zuni Plateau. C. B. Hunt (1967, chap. 14) and Fenneman (1931, 317–27) describe the physiography of this section of the Colorado Plateau and its origins. Foster (1958) has prepared a guidebook to make regional geology meaningful to the highway traveler. A somewhat similar publication was issued by Darton and others (1915) for the convenience of travelers on the Santa Fe Railway; see pp. 98–105.

On the Pescado is the jutting promontory of El Morro, the site of one of the homes of prehistoric peoples and the rock face upon which travelers for centuries have inscribed their names. Progressing westward from El Morro you can admire the banded cliffs of the formation near the little Mormon town of Ramah. A few miles away at the Zuni farming village of Nutria, on Nutria Creek, you can see the Zuni sandstone almost standing on edge, the most colorful formation in steep Nutria monocline, its serrated edge rising sharply four hundred feet or more above the general surface.

For several miles west of Ramah and Nutria, Pescado and Nutria creeks flow through fairly wide, shallow valleys bordered by low mesas topped with piñon and juniper. At the confluence of the two streams the character of the country changes radically. You are surprised to see the familiar Zuni sandstone dipping, or sloping, in directions opposite to those upstream at El Morro and at the Nutria monocline. In ages past a flexure, a gentle folding in the earth's surface, had occurred here. The fold, which followed north–south lines (extending as far north as Fort Defiance), depressed the strata on the eastern side and raised them on the western but, except for the folded area itself, the beds on either side retained a comparatively horizontal position. With the passage of long periods of geological time the Zuni River gradually eroded the strata west of the fold, leaving exposed a line of nearly perpendicular cliffs of Zuni sandstone.[6]

Thus, as you travel from the confluence of the Nutria and the Pescado downstream along the Zuni River toward the pueblo, you see the ascending slopes of the sandstone through which the river has cut a narrow notch — the "Gates of Zuni," or "Zuni Pass." When you are through the pass, you notice that the strata have regained a nearly horizontal position. By the time you reach the pueblo, nine miles from the confluence, you are out in an open valley surrounded on three sides by brilliant cliffs of plain, variegated, and banded Zuni sandstone.

Three miles southeast from the pueblo stands Towayalane, or Corn Mountain, sacred to the Zunis and central to their mythology and history. Isolated by erosion from adjacent sections of the formation, it towers a full thousand feet above the valley. Nearby, Horsehead, Cheama, and Galestina canyons, opening out on the plain, reveal dramatic walls. To the north, twin mesas of lower elevation, capped by the two Zuni Buttes, dominate the skyline. To the south, less spectacular cliffs and mesas recede to the horizon. Off to the west and south-

---

[6] Dutton (1885, 145–48) briefly explains the geological fluctuations in the Zuni sandstone.

west of the pueblo the Zuni River, its bed often bone dry, flows through open country all the way to the Little Colorado. Piñon and juniper give way to sagebrush and bunch grass. The wide vistas on every side are interrupted here and there by stream-side bluffs, an occasional butte, rolling hills and low, sharp-edged mesas.

The remainder of Zuni country, less important historically, may be described briefly. The Mangas and the Gallo mountains at the southern extremity are a few feet higher than the Zuni Mountains. The wide seventy-mile-long tableland, covered in places with lava and grown over with piñon and juniper, is some two thousand feet lower than the two mountain masses it separates. Carrizo Creek and the southern branches of the Zuni River drain these heights. Although the western escarpment of the tableland has been intricately eroded by these streams, there are few canyons. Instead, cliffless washes and open country dominate the landscape. Carrizo Creek, seldom more than a dry wash, enters the Little Colorado through a wide valley not far below the mouth of the Zuni River.

One of the important geographical features of the southern area is the Zuni salt lake located in the Carrizo Valley about forty-five miles south of the pueblo. This shallow spring-fed body of water, which contains salt of excellent quality, is situated at the bottom of a circular crater-like depression about a mile in diameter. The remarkable appearance of the lake, glistening and brilliant white in the sun, is enhanced by two black volcanic cinder cones rising from its waters.

The lake appears in the mythology of the Zuni Indians, having been known to them for centuries. They come here on pilgrimages to perform certain rites and also to gather salt for domestic and ceremonial use.[7]

Like so much of the Colorado Plateau, the Zuni country is high desert, all of it well over five thousand feet high, though seldom does it rise above nine thousand feet. The Zuni Pueblo itself stands at about 6,300 feet above the sea. At this level the days in the summer months are warm to hot but nighttime temperatures may drop as much as forty, even fifty degrees. The winters are cold, with below-zero readings common — sometimes twenty and thirty below. Desert means arid, dry. Most of the precipitation comes in two seasons: winter brings snow; and summer, rain. Spring and fall are dry.

---

[7] Darton (1905) has reported on the geology of the Zuni salt lake. See Cushing (1896, 352–55) for a discussion of the prehistoric uses of this salt, and M. C. Stevenson (1904, 58–60) for mythological significance.

But there is little rain and little snow. Precipitation of twelve to thirteen inches, perhaps, will fall on the Zuni Pueblo in any one year. This is the annual average computed over a number of years. Twelve inches is scarcely enough to keep the Indians' crops growing and alive. Those years when the water falls below average threaten life itself. Then, too, precipitation is uneven. How often has the anxious farmer watched a summer rain drench a mile-wide strip of open desert leaving his field dry and parched? Sometimes there is too much rain. A cloudburst on the desert, if there is little or nothing on the surface to hold the water, can either wash out a field or cover it a foot deep with mud.

There are precious few springs and few streams of living water in the Zuni heartland. The highest sections receive the most precipitation and produce water for the few permanent streams. Springs may have their sources in the same places. Groundwater comes from falling rain and snow, but in this land the water does not flow very far from its source. The quantity is small, though for centuries limited irrigation has been practiced. Life depends on a few ribbons and patches of green. To truly remember the Zuni earth, Kroeber wrote, you must see it from the summit of Towayalane. "If in addition, one be privileged to see distant rainstorms travel among the still sunshine, he will know the world the Zuni heart dreams of as well as the one its body walks." Under the Zuni sky the Indians for centuries have lived by farming. Yet through most of their history, the sky itself, productive of so little rain, has posed for them one of life's most constant problems.[8]

It is an old problem. Archeologists say that climatic conditions were much the same as today when the first men wandered through the Southwest nine thousand years ago or more. However, these pioneers were wanderers. They were not rooted to the soil. They moved in small bands with the seasons, hunting, collecting, and gathering, and they were probably not plagued by lack of water except in times of general drought. After the passage of many millennia, the culture of the earlier peoples began to change through the assimilation of new ideas from Mexico. The most important, agriculture based on the growing of corn, squash, and beans, turned the foragers into farmers.

---

[8] Vogt and Albert, eds. (1966, 42–43), give precipitation statistics for the Ramah area over the years from 1923 to 1950. The average annual precipitation for those years is 13.35 inches. The average for the Zuni Pueblo, about three hundred feet lower in altitude, is given as 12.43 inches! Some of the thoughts expressed in Chapter 1 were formulated while reading Calvin's *Sky Determines* (1965). Kroeber's paragraph on the view from Towayalane is from his "Zuñi Potsherds" (1916c, 29).

Having achieved a reliable food supply, some early Southwesterners turned to sedentary ways. With leisure time on their hands they gradually developed cultural traditions which became distinctively their own. One such was the Anasazi culture which rose along the middle reaches of the San Juan River, spread into adjoining parts of Utah, Colorado, New Mexico, and Arizona, and reached a classical stage of development from about A.D. 1000 to 1300. Sophistication in arts and crafts distinguished the culture and we may assume that there was a rich ceremonial life closely linked to the growing of crops on which life depended. Great communal towns — pueblos — capable of housing hundreds of persons were built at Mesa Verde, Kayenta, Chaco Canyon, and elsewhere. Very early in the classical age, and only a few miles from the Zuni Pueblo, the Anasazis built an imposing religious center, the "Village of the Great Kivas," so-called from the large ceremonial chambers found there.

Late in the thirteenth century, for causes not yet fully understood, the Anasazis, who had built so well, suffered a decline and the classical age ended. They abandoned their northern towns and settlements, fields and farms, and moved south to the upper tributaries of the Little Colorado, to Hopiland, and to the Rio Grande where they blended with the people already established in those areas. They continued living much as they had in the past, building large, compact towns of many-storied houses. Probably for defensive reasons nearly everyone preferred the security of urban living; few built individual homes in the country.[9]

In the upper basin of the Little Colorado the Anasazis found it necessary to share the country with another group of sophisticated Southwesterners, that of the Mogollon culture. From their ancestral homelands in southern New Mexico and Arizona, and northern Mexico, these people had pushed into the Little Colorado region and were well established there even before the Anasazis reached their classical age. Just what happened as the two peoples mingled is not very clear. Quite possibly there was a blending and a sharing of ways and ideas. Perhaps, since the Mogollon culture gradually seems to have become predomi-

---

[9] There is no lack of published work on Southwestern prehistory. The extensive bibliographies in Wormington (1961) and McGregor (1965) attest to the vigor of research in this area. Baldwin (1963) is a short summary; Dozier (1970) is a recent synthesis. Extensive treatment is given in more general works covering the American hemispheres, e.g., Willey (1966), Jennings and Norbeck, eds. (1964), and Martin, Quimby, and Collier (1947).

nant, the Anasazis were expelled from the territory. Whatever the case, those who emerged from the amalgam were the prehistoric Zuni Indians.[10]

The pre-Columbian Zunis must have enjoyed a good life. They sprang from diverse backgrounds and therefore would, perhaps, have been receptive to new ideas borne to them through commerce and other contacts with alien peoples. Not that they were quick to change. Instead, exposure to foreign influence probably strengthened their belief in their own ways. Indeed, the Zuni language, unrelated to any other, emerged from prehistory apparently little affected by the tongues of neighboring peoples.[11] During the winter there was leisure time to listen to stories of the first beginnings — the origin legends. These beautiful stories tell of a time when the Children of the Sun led the ancestors of the Zuni people out of the underworld through four wombs of the earth. Then the ancestors went searching for the center of the universe — the middle place. After many wanderings and adventures they finally found the middle (called by the Indians *hepatina*) where they built the first village, Itiwana. The ancestors,

---

[10] In writing of Southwestern prehistory the historian must use such words as "probably" and "perhaps" with considerable frequency. Although the dating of prehistoric sites is quite exact, thanks to dendrochronology, the movements and activities of preliterate peoples, particularly of the earliest ones, as yet have been established only within broad and general chronologies. Some recent researches on the prehistoric origins of the Zuni culture stress the predominance of the Anasazi style — particularly the Chaco style — in the early periods and the growing predominance of the Mogollon in the later eras. Whether the Mogollon people actually predominated in the prehistoric Zuni amalgam has not been determined. I refer to recent articles by Reed (1955) and Rinaldo (1964) and the references given in n. 9 of this chapter. Roberts (1932) excavated and named the "Village of the Great Kivas." See also Roberts' report on the excavations at Kiatuthlanna (1931). Vivian and Reiter (1960) study the relationships of the great kivas of Chaco Canyon with those elsewhere.

[11] Since we have no documentation, other than archeological evidence, descriptive of late prehistoric Zuni life, I am taking a few liberties here in projecting knowledge of later conditions back to past times.

The Zunian language may have been the tongue of the Mogollon invaders. Some linguists have found certain similarities between Zunian and the Penutian language of California, but the connection is remote. See the *Zuni Dictionary* by Newman (1958). Newman (1965) introduces Zuni grammar and relates the ways in which anthropologists since 1879 have handled a difficult matter. See Bunzel (1935) on the Zuni language.

Archeological evidence, though, is not as complete as it might be. Mindeleff (1891), Fewkes (1891b), and Spier (1917a, 1917b) found prehistoric ruins all over the Zuni country, but few of them have been systematically investigated. Hodge, of course, excavated the ruins at Hawikuh, 1917–1923. The results finally have been reported by Smith, Woodbury, and Woodbury (1966). Roberts excavated the ruins at Kiatuthlanna (1931) and the Village of the Great Kivas (1932), and Woodbury (1956) dug the ruins on El Morro.

according to this legend, had reached the site of Halona, the present Zuni Pueblo.[12]

The Indians throve and grew prosperous. Their towns dotted the valleys of the Nutria and Pescado, though some of them were located in more easily defensible positions on the mesa rims. One of the largest, containing more than five hundred rooms, was built atop the lofty summit of El Morro. With the passage of time, probably for defensive reasons, El Morro along with the other settlements in these upper valleys was abandoned in favor of towns located at lower elevations downstream. Late in the prehistoric period there were but six, possibly seven, major towns. The largest were Halona (Zuni) on the Zuni River, Matsakya nearby, and Kyakima at the base of Towayalane. A few miles away to the southwest were Kechipbowa and Hawikuh. The Zunis were living in these towns when the Europeans invaded their land in 1539.

---

[12] The Zuni people themselves have compiled some of their own origin legends and creation myths. See Quam, trans. (1972). Cushing (1896), M. C. Stevenson (1904), Parsons (1923), Bunzel (1932b), and Benedict (1969) are the standard compilations.

Woodbury (1956) excavated the large ruin (he named it Atsinna at the suggestion of Zuni workmen) on top of El Morro. His report is a concise summary of Zuni prehistory emphasizing the late abandonment of at least a dozen pueblos along the Zuni River. Atsinna, he finds, was vacated late in the fourteenth century; its inhabitants moved in with their fellows to swell the population of the larger towns downstream. See also Woodbury and Woodbury (1956). On the Zuni names for the ancient, abandoned villages, see E. S. Curtis (1926, 195).

Chapter 2

Cíbola

A stone roof drain

To the Spaniards in America anything seemed possible after the fall of Anáhuac. Mexico, the capital of the Aztecs, with its pyramids and temples, sanctuaries and shrines, paved streets and plastered buildings, and the wealth and culture of its inhabitants, bedazzled the European invaders and set in motion a frantic twenty-year exploration of the New World by those who hoped to top the luck of Cortés. When Pizarro shortly subjugated the Quechua (Inca) realm in Peru, America became a wonderland where any dream might come true. Eager explorers mentally filled the lands beyond the horizon with glittering and wonderful things, their imaginations fired by the Indians who regaled the credulous Spaniards with many a tall tale. One of these — Eldorado, the Gilded Man — has come to symbolize man's quest for easy wealth. The Spanish capacity for illusion was ample indeed. Even a few old-world stories of strange and fabulous places were imported to the new world and interwoven with those told by the Indians. One such was the medieval legend of the Seven Cities.

Not long after the fall of the Aztecs, the first hints of a fabled northern country were heard in Mexico. The Aztecs themselves preserved a tradition which told that in the course of their migratory wanderings from the north they had lived for a time in a place where there were seven caves. Added to this was a fanciful story told to Hernán Nuño de Guzmán by an Indian slave. "Forty days march north of the Spanish settlements," he said, "there were seven large towns where precious metals were found in abundance. They were so rich that entire streets were given over to workers in silver."

Subsequently, in a brutal and ruthless conquest north along the Pacific coast, Guzmán failed to locate the land of the Seven Caves, or the Seven Towns; but he did advance the Spanish frontier to the upper limits of Sinaloa, where in 1531

an outpost was established at Culiacán. It was here, five years later, that Alvar
Núñez Cabeza de Vaca and three companions appeared. Having survived a
shipwreck on the Texas coast, they eventually worked their way across the continent, paralleling the present international boundary of the United States and
Mexico. The travelers had tales to tell. Among other things they reported having heard of a people, north of their route, who lived in "populous towns and very
large houses" and who traded turquoises and emeralds for the plumage of
parrots.

This may have been an allusion to the pueblos of Arizona and New Mexico,
which Cabeza de Vaca did not see. His report of things seen and heard on the
westward crossing appealed to the dreamers. Was this another report of the
Seven Towns Guzmán had looked for? Were the "populous" towns near the
Aztecs' Seven Caves?

The Spaniards remembered the medieval legend of the Seven Cities. This
told of a rich land or island in the Atlantic, which was sometimes called Antilia
and which was inhabited by Christians. Columbus had looked for Antilia and
bestowed the name on the islands of the Caribbean, though he found neither
Christians nor rich cities. "What of the mysterious lands of the north?" Spaniards in Mexico asked themselves. The recurring magic number "seven" suggested to some at least that the fabled Seven Cities might yet be found — in a
land perhaps richer than Mexico or Peru.

The report of Cabeza de Vaca provided the impulse for the northward quest-
ing to follow. The viceroy, Antonio de Mendoza, was most interested and in
1539 sent the Franciscan Friar Marcos de Niza up the west coast to make a
reconnaissance. With Marcos as guide was the Moorish Negro Estevan, or
Estevanico, one of the companions of Cabeza de Vaca. At a point in Sonora
Estevan went on ahead, promising to send back news of what he discovered.
Couriers, it was agreed, would carry back crosses — the larger the cross, the more
important the news.

Friar Marcos must have been agreeably surprised when, four days later,
several Indian messengers came in bearing a man-sized cross! They carried
important news from the Moor; he urged the friar to follow at once. Estevan
reported that he was only thirty days' journey from "seven very large cities"
located in a land called Cíbola. The people there were well dressed and lived in
multi-storied houses studded with turquoise. Beyond Cíbola, he had learned,
there were even more wonderful cities and provinces.

Marcos went on and soon reached the Indian village whose people had given Estevan the news of the wonders ahead. They confirmed to him what they had told the Moor, adding that the provinces, or kingdoms, beyond Cíbola were called Marata, Acus, and Totonteac.

The Seven Cities and the land of promise were at hand! Marcos hurried on, hoping to catch up with Estevan, but he never saw him again. He soon learned that the Moor had been killed by the Cíbolans. Cautiously, the friar went on to have a look at Cíbola. Finally, from an elevated position he came in view of a pueblo built on a low, narrow, rounded height of land overlooking a grassy plain. It was Hawikuh, one of the towns inhabited by the Zuni Indians. The date was early June 1539.

Before leaving the scene Marcos, with an arrogance characteristic of the crusading Spanish conquerors of America, erected a cross and then, in the name of the Spanish crown, "took possession" of the Seven Cities, and of Totonteac, Acus, and Marata. He named the newly discovered land the New Kingdom of San Francisco (*El Nuevo Reino de San Francisco*).

With "far more fright than food" Friar Marcos returned to Mexico where he was the hero of the hour. Enthusiastic audiences, convinced that the medieval Seven Cities had been found in the American wilderness, pumped the Franciscan for information. His narrative seems to have lost nothing in the telling. "It was a paradise on earth," Marcos said, "and the place I saw was larger than the City of Mexico." "Cíbola surely must be richer than Mexico," said his listeners. Who could question the veracity of a man of God?

The viceroy now enlisted a large force — three hundred horse and foot soldiers and hundreds of Indian allies — to explore the Seven Cities and the kingdoms beyond. In February 1540 all was ready at the rendezvous point at Compostela on the west coast. Mendoza himself appeared and launched the expedition with a "very eloquent and short speech." Placed in command was Francisco Vásquez de Coronado who, arrayed in shining armor, rode at the head of the column. Less conspicuous was the gray-robed Franciscan Friar Marcos de Niza, who went along as guide.

Coronado and an advance guard reached the environs of Cíbola early in July. Moving up the Zuni River, which they called the Rio Vermejo (Red River) because its waters were muddy and reddish, the Spaniards came in sight of the first of the Seven Cities — Hawikuh. Unwilling to let the invaders enter the pueblo, the Zuni Indians, armed with bows and arrows, clubs and stone knives, set up their defenses. But men on horseback, armed with harquebuses and crossbows, soon dispersed them, and the village was taken by assault.[1]

Hawikuh was a sickening disappointment to the Spaniards. "It is a little, crowded village," said the chronicler of the Coronado expedition, "looking as if it had been cramped all up together." There were no precious metals or stones, only a few turquoises. Was this the city richer than Mexico? Furthermore, Totonteac, Acus, and Marata appeared to be either unimportant or nonexistent. Much abuse was heaped on the head of Friar Marcos for his exaggerated report of Cíbola, and shortly he found occasion to return to Mexico.[2] But the Zunis had good stocks of corn and other food that the Spaniards "were most in need of" and the invaders took up residence in the pueblo, which they named Granada.

---

[1] Cabeza de Vaca's westward crossing, the preliminary exploration by Friar Marcos, and Coronado's *entrada* are some of the best known events in the early history of the Southwest. Bandelier's studies (1890b) of Cabeza de Vaca and Friar Marcos, and of Zuni up to 1700 (1892b) are basic works. Hodge and Lewis, eds. (1965), have brought together the narratives of Cabeza de Vaca and of Pedro de Castañeda, principal chronicler of the Coronado expedition; see also Winship (1896). Hammond and Rey, eds. and trans. (1940), have assembled and newly translated the basic primary documents touching on the Coronado adventure. Bolton (1949) is the fullest study on Coronado. Bancroft (1889), Bandelier (1893, 125–257), and Twitchell (1911–1915) are still useful.

In an elaborately annotated work Hodge (1937) describes in detail the succession of Spanish parties visiting Hawikuh up to 1692. Bandelier's (1892b) documentary history of Zuni to 1700 is an essential source. This is but a sampling of the literature devoted to the Spanish discovery and exploration of the Pueblo country. A list of the works cited in the above references would run to hundreds of titles. The bibliography of contemporary works on the Spanish Southwest to 1794 has been thoroughly described by Wagner (1967). Huff (1951) points out that Coronado may have interrupted certain summer ceremonies and that the battle of Hawikuh may have been a delaying action on the part of the Zunis. There is some indication that the Zunis in the mid-sixteenth century were using arrows dipped in rattlesnake poison. See Hodge (1924).

[2] Some scholars have insisted that Marcos never came near Cíbola. Hodge (1937, 112) examines the controversy. Bandelier (1892b) is a stout defender of the friar's veracity but Hallenbeck (1949) sides against Marcos. In a scholarly book Chávez (1968) examines the Franciscans' role in the Coronado expedition. Bandelier (1892b, 7–16) has examined the contemporary documents for some motive in the killing of Estevan; he was probably aggressive and demanding and aroused fear when he described the power of Spain. Bandelier (1890b, 154–55) repeats a Zuni folk tale related by Cushing to the effect that a "black Mexican" was killed because he was "greedy, voracious and bold." Cushing (1896, 326) states that Estevan was killed at the village of Kyakima. I venture the suggestion that Estevan may have audaciously interrupted a ceremonial and met the wrath of the Indians in so doing.

The word Cíbola appears to have been derived from the Zuni word Ashiwi (and variant spellings), the tribal range of the Zunis. The name Zuni was first recorded by Espejo in 1583. See the synonymy of the names in Hodge (1937, 128–30), and Hammond and Rey, eds. and trans. (1966, 225), for Espejo's reference to "Zuni, or Cíbola."

Coronado used this as his headquarters for four months while he explored the other cities of Cíbola and lands beyond.

He soon discovered that the other five or six Zuni pueblos were no more lustrous than Hawikuh. Soon, another land — rich, where also Seven Cities were reported — beckoned from the northwest. This, the Spaniards were told, was Tusayán — the Hopi country. Coronado sent Pedro de Tovar to reconnoiter. The Hopi towns were little different from those of Cíbola, maybe a little larger, but no richer. But the Hopis told the invaders that off to the west they would find a great river along which lived a race of tall people — giants! García López de Cárdenas looked into the report but failed to locate the giants, though the explorers were the first Europeans to see the Grand Canyon of the Colorado. At about the same time, Hernando de Alarcón, who had been sent by sea to cooperate with Coronado, was exploring the head of the Gulf of California and the lower reaches of the Colorado River.

Now from the east came news of the buffalo country, of another great river, and of the province of Tiguex, where there were more Indian cities. These of course were the Eastern Pueblos scattered along the Rio Grande. Coronado now moved his entire command thither, where he spent the next eighteen months in a fruitless search for another land as rich as Mexico.

Then, during the warm months of 1541, he was lured to the Great Plains in search of Quivira — sure to be the new El Dorado — but that, too, was a disappointment. Disillusioned, empty-handed, worn out and forlorn, the bedraggled expedition headed for home in April 1542. At Cíbola the corps rested briefly before starting out on the long trek to Culiacán where they were disbanded.

Some have called the Coronado expedition a failure. It was far from that! Coronado did not discover another Anáhuac but, while drunk on dreams of Cíbola, Tusayán, Tiguex, and Quivira, he explored and revealed the wonders of a vast region in North America new to Europeans. But it is true that the new land was a ruinous disappointment to Coronado, and his was the last of the grand military expeditions in North America to devote itself wholly to looking for the realms of fancy.

Yet the daring enterprise resulted in so many discoveries of practical interest that soon men were talking again about the "good country" Coronado's party had visited. Much of the talk came from those who had seen the land themselves. Pedro de Castañeda, writing twenty years or more later, prefaced his chronicle of the Coronado expedition with a regret that the new lands had been abandoned after their discovery. Few riches had been found, but, he said, it was "a good country to settle in" and one from which the Spaniards could continue to search the horizon for fabulous places. "Our hearts weep for having lost so favorable an opportunity," and, he adds, "we are all the time imagining and trying to find ways to get it back again."

What made it a "good" country in large part was the presence of the Pueblo Indians who lived by agriculture in towns and villages. They were an intelligent people of high cultural achievement who might well be incorporated into a colonial venture.

During their four months' sojourn in Cíbola, Coronado and his men had come to know the Zunis particularly well. Once in possession of Hawikuh, the invaders made no attempt to subdue the other Zuni towns and the Indians offered no further resistance. It appears from the documents that during this time the two peoples managed to live side by side in an atmosphere of friendliness bordering on cordiality. This was in sharp contrast to the situation at Tiguex where the excesses of the Spaniards won them the enduring enmity of the Eastern Pueblos. The Zunis enjoyed good relations with some of the "Christian" Aztecs in Coronado's retinue. When the Spaniards returned to Mexico, at least three of these Indians elected to remain in Cíbola.

The Spaniards learned that the Zunis, numbering perhaps three thousand, lived in a cluster of seven towns or villages, all located within a radius of seven or eight miles. The Spanish chroniclers made some brief notes about religious practices, about kivas, priests, and plumed prayer sticks, and added, "What they worship most is water." They described the Indians' dress — mantles of cotton and of rabbit fur, deerskin boots, buffalo robes, and dresses of maguey fiber. The Zunis raised corn, beans, and squash, and game was plentiful. Turkeys were raised for their feathers, and eagles were kept in captivity for the same purpose. Indians from afar came to Cíbola to trade: they brought parrot plumes from Mexico, shells from the California coast, buffalo hides from the Great Plains; from the Zunis they obtained excellent turquoise and salt.

Though the lack of wealth in the towns disappointed them, the Spaniards described the towns in detail — the multi-storied stone and adobe complexes of connecting rooms, the plazas and narrow corridors, and the flat mud roofs

supported by brush and timbers — and they praised the intelligence and industry of their builders.[3]

Back home in Mexico again, those who had been to the Zuni land remembered it as a good country; the information they brought back kept up interest
in the northern interior. The cartographers of the day helped keep alive a
legend too sweet to die. Long after Coronado returned home, the map makers,
using more imagination than accuracy, portrayed the country he had discovered
as the opulent "Seven Cities of Cíbola." Coronado's name for Hawikuh —
Granada — appeared on the maps also, usually as "Nueva Granada," a designation given as well to the entire region. Nearly all of the names of the places seen
and not seen, given by Friar Marcos and Coronado, were sprinkled about on the
contemporary maps. The publishers thus perpetuated the illusion of fabled
lands, and whetted men's thirst for the easy wealth in that good land on the
distant northern frontier.[4]

---

[3] The contemporary documents contain a substantial body of ethnographic data. See
Hammond and Rey, eds. and trans. (1940); see particularly the "Relación del Suceso,"
pp. 284–94, whose author observed that what the Zuni "worship most is water."

Given the very real language barrier, initial comunication between the Spanish explorers
and the Indians was not always satisfactory. Riley (1971) suggests the possibility that some
of the Indians met by Cabeza de Vaca, Marcos, and Coronado may have had some knowledge of Aztec, or Nahuatl, and other Mexican-Indian languages, thus easing communication
with the Spaniards' guides and interpreters.

[4] Wheat (1957–1963), vol. 1, chaps. 2–3, reproduces a number of sixteenth- and
seventeenth-century maps reflecting the use of Marcos' and Coronado's names by imaginative
cartographers. See also Wagner (1968). Marcos' name for the Zuni region — New Kingdom of San Francisco — seems to have been used little, however.

Chapter 3

The Good Country

A Zuni oven

Forty years elapsed before the foreigners returned to Cíbola. During that time the big silver bonanzas had been opened in Mexico at Zacatecas, Guanajuato, and elsewhere, and the succession of silver rushes that followed rapidly pushed the Spanish frontier northward to the headstreams of the Conchos River, a tributary of the Rio Grande. The most flourishing district on the Conchos centered around Santa Barbara in southern Chihuahua, then part of the province of Nueva Vizcaya. In the lively atmosphere of this frontier silver camp there was bound to be talk about the places to the north discovered years earlier by Cabeza de Vaca and Coronado, places now within reach, which had lost but little luster with the passage of time. An early return to the land of the Pueblos was assured when the Indians in and about the Chihuahua frontier fed the Spanish interest with reports of the wealth and high culture of the northern peoples.

The first *entrada* after Coronado's expedition was a small party led by Agustín Rodríquez, a Franciscan friar, and Francisco Sánchez Chamuscado. Intent on missionary endeavor as well as trade and exploration, the party left Santa Barbara in June 1581 and was in the field eleven months. Descending the Conchos and ascending the Rio Grande, the explorers toured most of the Eastern Pueblos. Before turning back they briefly visited Acoma and Zuni.

Of their discoveries, wrote diarist Hernán Gallegos, the valley "called Suni" was the best, since the suitable land was under cultivation and sown to corn. The Spaniards visited six of the Zuni towns and recorded the local names of each: Kyakima, Matsakya, Halona, Kwakina, Hawikuh, Kechipbowa. Hawikah, the largest, contained 125 houses. In all of the towns together, the visitors estimated there were 437 houses ranging in height from three to five stories, many of them containing eight rooms or more.[1]

The Spaniards may not have found gold plate on the walls but they did admire the Zuni stone houses — "amazing" said the chronicler of the Rodríquez–Chamuscado party. With their interesting plazas and passages and rooftop doorways reached by wooden ladders, the Indian homes, "whitewashed and painted inside and out," must have been an appealing sight. Probably the Zuni dwellings looked somewhat better than the visitors' own homes.

Indeed, the Spaniards must have admired the entire ensemble presented by the individual Zuni towns. Located on high or prominent places overlooking the wide valley of the Zuni River, they appeared in profile, from a distance, as low, truncated pyramids — exotic, picturesque, and alive.

The Spaniards used several names for the Zuni Indians and their country. Friar Marcos and Coronado and his chroniclers wrote of Cíbola and the Seven Cities. The latter term gradually faded away, however, and Cíbola remained as the name for the land — and Cíbolans for the people — for the next three and a half centuries. Then it, too, faded into disuse as the name Zuni, first used by Gallego (who spelled it Suni) and by Espejo in 1583, gradually replaced it. There are now some signs that Cíbola is coming back into popular usage.[2]

Within a year another group of Spanish explorers from the Chihuahua frontier had reached the Zuni pueblos. Antonio de Espejo, cattleman and entrepreneur, with a small party followed the trail up the Rio Grande blazed by Rodríquez and Chamuscado to rescue two friars left behind by that expedition, and to trade, prospect, and spy out the land for future settlements. After visiting some of the Eastern Pueblos, Espejo headed west and on March 14, 1583, reached the Zuni village of Matsakya. The Indians received the Spaniards hospitably, and during the next three and a half months some of Espejo's party moved in on the Zunis and, as Coronado had done years before, lived on food

---

[1] The essential primary documentation of the Rodríquez–Chamuscado and Espejo expeditions, 1581–1583, has been edited by Hammond and Rey (1966). An earlier edition of the Espejo narrative and other relevant documents appears in Bolton, ed. (1916).

[2] The names of the Zuni pueblos, to say nothing of the words Cíbola and Zuni, have been spelled variously through the centuries; the Spanish orthography has been worked out in a synonymy by Hodge (1937, 128–34), who is fully convinced that there were never more than six "cities" in Cíbola; see his article on the subject (1926). See also Hodge, ed. (1907–1910, 1015–20) and Swanton (1952, 346–48). In my own text I have followed the spelling of the several villages and other places in current usage by the Zuni tribe.

supplied by their hosts and in rooms placed at their disposal in Matsakya, Halona, and Hawikuh.

The most detailed account of the exploration was written by Diego Pérez de Luxán, one of Espejo's officers. Luxán has much to say about the Zuni lifestyle of the late sixteenth century. At Easter time the Spaniards witnessed the spring planting in the irrigated fields at Ojo Caliente near Hawikuh. These people are "great farmers," Luxán wrote. He took note of the kivas ("small prayer houses") and the dwellings built of sandstone, and he mentions weaving, clothing, and women's hair styles ("done up in large puffs").

In Luxán's words, the Zunis, though poor, were "industrious and peaceful" and "extremely healthy." The Spaniards saw no sick or crippled persons, but they did see "many old ones." Luxán thought that the Pueblos, both men and women, were very much like the Aztecs ("pure Mexican") in the way they "walk, cry," and live, but, he added, they were "neater" than the Mexican Indians.[3]

Judging from these reports, the Zunis were not offended by the Spanish attempts to propagate the faith among them. Well-built crosses, apparently erected by Coronado, were still standing in all of the pueblos. At Halona, Espejo found the three Christian Indians from Mexico — Andrés of Cuyuacán, Gaspar of Mexico, and Antón of Guadalajara — who had elected to remain behind when Coronado left Cíbola forty-one years before. It was not recorded how constant they had been in their devotion to Christianity. The Mexican Indians had married into the tribe and had forgotten most of the Spanish they had known and even their own language.

But the expatriates soon remembered enough Spanish to communicate fairly well and then they had some good stories to tell. They revived many of the tall tales Coronado had listened to. Off to the north and west there was a large lake, they said, where there were many towns inhabited by people who wore golden bracelets and earrings. Pedro de Tovar, one of Coronado's men, had gone to look for the lake, they declared, but it was sixty days' journey from Cíbola and he had run out of water before reaching it.

Tovar had found the Hopi villages, if not the golden lake, and now Espejo with part of his command headed for Tusayán. The Hopis were friendly and told their visitors of mines far to the west. Before returning to Zuni Espejo went

---

[3] Luxán's account is found in Hammond and Rey, eds. and trans. (1966, 153–212); another edition was issued by the same authors in 1929.

to look for these mines. After a long journey he finally found some disappointing prospects near Jerome in north central Arizona. Undaunted, the Spaniards returned to the Rio Grande to prospect in the land of the Eastern Pueblos. But they had no better luck there and finally headed back, reaching their home base in mid-September 1583 after an absence of ten months.

Despite the poor mineral outlook, the reports of Espejo's explorations, confirming those of Rodríquez and Chamuscado and of Coronado before them, were hailed with enthusiasm in the Chihuahua mining camps. Much interest was shown in the advanced culture of the Pueblo Indians, especially their dress and agriculture, religion and architecture. The pueblo villages reminded the Spaniards of the towns and cities built by the Aztecs. Moreover, the Pueblo people were "pure Mexican," or Aztec, in nearly everything they did, as Luxán reported. By the time the Rodríquez–Chamuscado and Espejo expeditions returned to Chihuahua the name New Mexico was being used to describe the Pueblo country from the Rio Grande to the Rio Colorado.[4]

It was as good a land as Coronado's men had said. Luxán thought that if mines were found Cíbola and Tusayán would be "the best land ever discovered." The mines were there, Espejo reported, "many rich mines," and he had ores at hand waiting to be assayed to prove the worth of those distant diggings. And beyond the mines, over the horizon, was the lake surrounded by towns inhabited by people who wore golden necklaces. There was still room to dream in that quarter. The myth of the Seven Cities had lost currency but the golden aura of Cíbola persisted.

Soon after Espejo returned, the Archbishop of Mexico remarked in a letter to the king that if all the reports about the northern country were true then it must be "another new world." The king had already decided to colonize New Mexico and after many delays he chose Juan de Oñate to do the job.

In January 1598 Oñate got under way. At the head of a large colonizing expedition he traveled up the Rio Grande through El Paso to the mouth of the Chama River, where he appropriated an Indian pueblo for his use as a capital and permanent headquarters, renaming it San Gabriel.[5]

---

[4] Espejo's report on the exploration, and Luxán's, together with other pertinent documents, are in Hammond and Rey, eds. and trans. (1966).

[5] The exploration and colonization of New Mexico by Oñate is one of the best-documented chapters in Southwestern history. Hammond and Rey, who have done so much to assemble and translate primary Spanish documents, have put together two large volumes — nearly twelve hundred pages — of the Oñate papers (1953). Another source of great interest

For the Pueblo Indians of New Mexico this was an ominous move. It was the first step in the Spanish conquest which meant that military, civil, and ecclesiastical controls were going to be imposed upon the Indians and that the available lands, water, and other resources would have to be shared with the colonists. However, given the strongly individualistic personality of the separate pueblos and of Pueblo culture, and the scarcity of arable land and other resources, the Spaniards were deceived if they thought Pueblo integration into their system would come easily and without conflict.

Once the colony was settled Oñate set out to explore the realm. He sent one expedition east to the buffalo plains while he, after some preliminaries, turned west to open a route to the South Sea, that is, to the Pacific Ocean. Oñate reached Cíbola on November 1, 1598, where he spent a week, most of it at Hawikuh. When the Spaniards entered the village, the Zunis showered them with corn meal, and then, as they had done in the past, treated their visitors to a bounty of corn, tortillas, squash, beans, and rabbits, and provided them with housing. They even invited the Spaniards to join in a communal rabbit hunt.

In the several pueblos the crosses were still standing and, Oñate noted, prayer sticks and corn meal were seen near them. The Christian Indians left behind by Coronado were dead now but one had left two sons. The visitors tried to talk to one of them, Alonso; he was competent enough in his mother's tongue but not his father's, and there was no communication.

While resting at Zuni Oñate sent a detachment under Marcos Farfán to explore the Zuni salt lake some forty miles south of Hawikuh. Farfán returned with an accurate description of the lake and reported that the entire surface was thickly encrusted with salt except for a place in the middle where spring waters bubbled up from unfathomed depths. One could walk over the crust without breaking it; to obtain samples it was necessary to use an iron bar or pickaxe. Farfán was much impressed. The salt was white and of "excellent grain." Not even the king of Spain enjoyed salt of such quality. The lake was a "marvelous thing," Farfán reported; he thought it was the finest saline in all the world.

Oñate did not reach the South Sea, but he did go on to visit the Hopi villages; from there a detachment under Farfán journeyed west to prospect for mines. The parties were reunited at Zuni but when the reinforcements necessary for the

---

is the history of New Mexico written in verse by one of Oñate's captains, Gaspar Pérez de Villagrá. It was first published in 1610. A prose translation was made by Gilberto Espinosa and edited by Hodge (1933).

longer trip to the coast did not arrive, Oñate turned back to his headquarters on the Rio Grande.

The Indians being friendly and hospitable, the Spaniards, during their sojourn at Zuni, learned much about their hosts and wrote about them in some detail. And of course, the Zunis learned much about their visitors — the implications of such words as "taking possession" and "conquest" and "pacification" were explained to them.

At Hawikuh, on one occasion, Oñate assembled the chiefs and some of the people from the six pueblos and told them that the Spaniards had come among the Indians to bring them knowledge of their God and their king upon whom depended their salvation and safety and that in view of this it would be fitting for them to swear obedience and become vassals of both God and the king. Should the Zunis do so, Oñate explained, they would be subject to the authority, commands, and laws of their king and "natural master," and should they fail to obey they would be punished.

Two men, "Negua homi" and "Atiz oha," who said they were the chiefs of the six pueblos, replied "with signs of contentment and harmony" that they wished to become vassals and render obedience. At least that is the way Oñate's secretary, Juan Velarde, reported the event. "In testimony of the truth" of the proceedings, he wrote, six Spaniards with their signatures witnessed the "Act of Obedience and Vassalage." The date was November 9, 1598. Pleased that he had dealt so successfully with the Pueblos and full of expectations, Oñate shortly wrote the viceroy and the king promising to give them in New Mexico a "new world," greater even than the New Spain given to old Spain by Cortés.

It was an easier promise to make than to fulfill. For one thing, the Indians began to chafe under the Spanish yoke when they learned something of the deeper meaning of "obedience and vassalage." The Pueblo of Acoma, eighty miles east of the Zuni villages, was first to learn this bitter lesson. When the Acomans killed thirteen Spaniards, half of the command of reinforcements Oñate was awaiting in Zuni, retribution was swift. In January 1599 Spanish forces stormed the four-hundred-foot-high mesa, home of the Indians, and laid it waste, killing many of the inhabitants. The survivors, made captive, were tried and sentenced: males over twenty-five to have one foot cut off and to serve in slavery for twenty years; males between twelve and twenty-five to serve in slavery for twenty years; women over twelve to serve in slavery for twenty years; two Hopi Indians caught in the fight to have the right hand cut off and then to be set free. Inasmuch as the Indians in public ceremony had previously pledged their obedience, they were now being punished not only for "their wickedness" but for "treason to his majesty," wrote Oñate in a letter to the viceroy.[6]

For the Spaniards, life on the distant and isolated frontier of New Mexico was anything but easy. The dawning of the seventeenth century brought no improvement and Oñate found himself plagued with dissension in his own colony. Although he had extended the king's dominion, like Coronado he had failed to locate fabled cities and rich mines, and he found himself falling from favor at court.

On a gamble, the governor decided to go west again to restore his flagging reputation. In that direction Espejo and Farfán had located mines. Moreover, he might discover a waterway by which New Mexico could be supplied from the Gulf of California or some other part of the Pacific coast, and he might find a strait connecting the oceans.

Ever mindful that the continent of North America stood as a barrier to commerce between Spain and Asia, the Spanish crown since 1492 had taken a lively interest in the geographical findings brought back by explorers of the northern wilderness. The great hope was for a sea-level water passage, a strait connecting the Atlantic and Pacific oceans, or in contemporary usage, the North and South seas. That such a passage existed few doubted. It even bore a name — Anián. Spain hoped to discover and fortify it in advance of any other European power. The rumor that Francis Drake in 1579 may have discovered the Pacific entrance of the Strait of Anián, claiming it for England, undoubtedly had something to do with Spain's decision to send Oñate to New Mexico.

Friar Marcos had been instructed to look for waterways and inlets opening toward the interior from either coast. Coronado had spent more time in the quest for Indian cities than in looking for straits, but at a point fifty miles east of the Zuni villages his party made an important geographical discovery. All the streams thus far, the men noted, flowed to the Pacific Ocean; beyond, they

---

[6] The basic documents on Oñate's adventure in New Mexico are in Hammond and Rey, eds. and trans. (1953). See particularly pp. 357–59, 393–97, 406–15, 428–88, 492–93, for Oñate's and Farfán's accounts of the expedition to Zuni and beyond, the "act of obedience and vassalage" by the Zuni Indians, and Oñate's letters to the viceroy and king dated March 2 and April 15, 1599, and the rebellion and brutal retribution at Acoma. Villagrá's *Historia*, strong on the Acoma rebellion, also contains material on Zuni not found in the other sources. See the prose translation by Gilberto Espinosa, edited by Hodge (1933), notably pp. 164–71, where Villagrá relates that the Spaniards were showered with corn meal at Hawikuh, and speaks of the communal rabbit hunt involving about eight hundred Indians.

flowed eastward to the Atlantic. Coronado's men had, of course, crossed and identified the Continental Divide. This meant that, between the latitudes of the basins of the Rio Colorado and the Rio Grande, no one would find a sea-level water passage connecting the oceans.[7]

However, Coronado's men had seen the Colorado at the Grand Canyon and Alarcón had explored the lower reaches of the rivers from the Gulf of California. Slowly, it began to dawn on those who concerned themselves with water passages that, failing a strait, the great rivers somehow might be used in the India trade. As the hope of locating a strait retreated before a succession of explorers, the idea of transcontinental travel by rivers took on greater currency.

But in the conjectural geography prevailing as the seventeenth century opened, the concept of a strait was still very much alive. And Espejo's lake, somewhere off to the west, where town dwellers wore golden bracelets and earrings, had not been forgotten.

To brighten up his tarnished image, Oñate was determined to clear up the geographical mysteries of the western country. With thirty soldiers and two Franciscan friars he left the Rio Grande on October 7, 1604, and started once more for the South Sea. Within a few days the party reached Zuni, where Oñate met with a friendly reception which recalled the one afforded him six years earlier. Friar Francisco de Escobar, diarist, was much impressed with Zuni hospitality which was "joyfully and courteously" renewed. The friar briefly described some of the superficial aspects of Zuni ways, and then added that of the six pueblos in the province four were then in ruins; he gave no explanation.

On leaving Zuni, Oñate's party took the now familiar route to the Hopi villages and to the mining country prospected earlier by both Espejo and Farfán. By way of the Bill Williams River the explorers reached the Colorado, which they named the Buena Esperanza — the Good Hope — an appropriate name in view of Oñate's desperate position. Then they descended the river to its mouth in the Gulf of California where Oñate took possession in the name of the crown.

From the Indians along the Colorado the Spaniards gathered a rich harvest of tall stories which Escobar preserved in his diary. He was told of some island dwellers who wore golden bracelets, of other people who subsisted on the odor of food, and of still others who slept under water or in trees. Knowing what would

---

[7] The Jaramillo narrative of the Coronado expedition, in Hammond and Rey, eds. (1940, 299), clearly identifies the Continental Divide.

appeal to viceroy and king, Escobar also recorded what the Indians told him about the geography of those lands not seen by the explorers. He learned that an estuary of the Gulf of California extended north and northeast and this suggested a possible communication with the Atlantic. Furthermore, all along the Colorado River from mouth to source, his informants said, there were Indian settlements; those near the headstreams lived on bountiful harvests, including deer and buffalo.

These resources, the abundance of good grass, and the apparent open country, would facilitate exploration, the friar wrote. The verification of these reports of riches, of the wondrous people, and of communication between the seas would be an easy matter. Were the king so inclined, "with the favor of heaven the truth about this whole matter could be established with less than one hundred men. . . ."

On the trip to the Colorado River Oñate had discovered much land new to Spain, and he had opened a new route to the sea, but he had located no golden cities, no mines, no strait. He had only heard about these things. Oñate sent Father Escobar to the viceroy to argue the case for further exploration. In the pages of his diary, Escobar filled the wilderness north and west of New Mexico with wonders and marvels that would have been irresistible at an earlier day.[8]

It was too late. The government at Mexico City had ordered curtailment of further exploration in New Mexico beyond that required by missionaries in the prosecution of their holy labors. Juan de Oñate had lost the gamble and would soon leave New Mexico.

Returning from the lower Colorado River, Oñate retraced his route through the Zuni villages. Thirty-six miles beyond them, on the western slope not far from the Continental Divide, the party camped at the foot of the massive two-hundred-foot-high headland of rock since known as El Morro. Here at the base of the rock on the east side was a natural tank of permanent water. While the Spaniards were resting, someone chiseled an inscription on the sheer wall near the tank which reads in translation: "Passed by here the Adelantado Don Juan de Oñate, from the discovery of the South Sea, the 16th of April of 1605."

---

[8] Escobar's important diary of the Oñate journey to the Pacific, 1604–1605, and other relevant documents are found in Hammond and Rey, eds. and trans. (1953). The diary was significantly annotated in 1626 by Father Gerónimo de Zárate Salmerón, and this version was published by Bolton (1916). A recent English version of Zárate Salmerón's *Relaciones* is one translated and edited by Milich (1966). Bandelier's documentary history (1892b) is indispensable for the details of Zuni history up to 1700, as is Hodge's (1937) study on Hawikuh.

This was the first of many names and legends carved on Inscription Rock while it was a part of the Spanish dominion. With Oñate's eastern journey the Spanish quest for phantom cities and fabulous places came to an end in the Southwest. The search for practical routes between New Mexico and the Pacific was not revived for over a hundred years, and most of those who passed by the great rock during that time were bent on religious or military missions to the Hopi and Zuni Indians.[9]

[9] Bandelier (1892a, 330–32) indicates that in the 1880s certain dates earlier than 1605, including one written by Chamuscado, were reported to be visible on El Morro. See Slater (1961) for a recent, detailed study of the El Morro inscriptions and their historical connections.

Chapter 4

The Great Rebellion

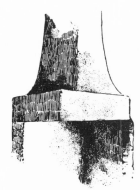

A square chimney hood

After Oñate left, New Mexico was maintained primarily as a missionary province assigned to the Order of Friars Minor — the Franciscans. In 1609 the crown assumed direct control of the government and the next year the capital was moved from San Gabriel to Santa Fe. Beyond the environs of the narrow valley of the Rio Grande where most of the colonists and the Pueblos lived, the Spanish hold was nominal, even precarious, through the remaining two hundred years of the colonial period. Thus the Western Pueblos, particularly the Hopis and Zunis, who lived, as it were, on the frontier of a frontier, escaped the full impact of Spanish power.

At times the friars in New Mexico tried to whip up stronger support for the province by reviving some of the fanciful tales of wonderful things told by the Indians of the lands beyond the horizon. To the north and west was Lake Copala, ancient home of the Aztecs, and the Island of Gold and Silver, wrote Friar Gerónimo Zárate Salmerón, who expanded on the stories reported earlier by Espejo and Escobar. He attempted also to revive interest in the transcontinental strait. In not furthering exploration of this land, the friar said, "his majesty loses a great world." [1]

---

[1] For the *Relaciones* of Zárate Salmerón, who wrote of events in New Mexico from 1538 to 1626, see the Milich (1966) translation. Much of Zárate's material was reworked and included by Benavides in his revised memorial of 1634 (Hodge, Hammond, and Rey, eds. and trans., 1945) summarizing conditions in New Mexico with particular reference to the religious establishment. A 1630 Benavides memorial has also been published in England (Ayer, trans., Hodge and Lummis, eds., 1916). The notes in both editions, mainly by Hodge, are particularly full. However, scholars will find the more recent edition of the 1630 memorial by Forrestal, trans., and Lynch, ed. (1954) to be the more useful of the two editions. The provincial designation of the Franciscan organization in New Mexico was "Custodia de la Conversión de San Pablo"; see Chávez (1957) for a catalog of the extant archives.

The king had been promised "new worlds" in New Mexico before and was probably little interested, but he did respond to Zárate Salmerón's plea for more missionaries, enough to establish stations in the more remote pueblos. Accordingly, in June 1629 a large party consisting of provincial governor Francisco Manuel de Silva Nieto and the father custodian of the New Mexican missions, Estevan de Perea, together with other members of the Franciscan establishment and thirty well-armed soldiers, set out from Santa Fe headed for Acoma, Zuni, and the Hopi pueblos.

Upon arriving at Zuni the father custodian recorded his pleasure that the Indians received the party with "festive applause," a thing unheard of elsewhere in New Mexico. The governor issued an immediate order restraining the soldiers from making any transgressions, "it being settled that with suavity and mildness an obstinate spirit can better be reclaimed than with violence and rigor."

It was summer and Perea wrote that the Zuni country was "placid and fertile, abundant in waters, agreeable with green fields." He remarked on the "civilized government" of the Indians and on their "streets and continuous houses like those of Spain." He made particular note of the rattlesnake pens. From the snakes the Indians obtained venom to poison arrows; wounds from these were "irremediable," the Zunis said.

Having come to propagate his own faith, the father custodian took note of some of the Indians' religious ways, which he described as "superstitious idolatry." In the kivas — "their temples" — they had "idols of stone and wood, much painted," and access to these chambers — limited to the Indian priests — was gained through doors in the roofs. Convinced that Zuni would be a fruitful vineyard in which to labor, the fathers "bought" a house in Hawikuh, which they called "Zibola," the largest of the pueblos and "head town" of the others. Promptly the first mass was celebrated, a cross was erected, "possession" was taken in the name of the pope in Rome and of the king in Spain, and amid "clamorous rejoicing" the soldiers fired a salvo from their harquebuses.

The date was near the end of July 1629. For the crusading Spaniards it was an auspicious beginning. Three friars and three soldiers were left at Zuni to implement the mission, and the first conversions were reported in August. But in less than three years the Franciscans had gathered their first martyrs in Cíbola.[2]

---

[2] From contemporary documents Hodge (1937, 80–93) has assembled the essential record of the beginnings of the Zuni Mission. He quotes extensively from Estevan de Perea's *Relación*, originally published in two parts in 1632 and 1633. Both parts have been translated

From time to time, since Coronado's day, the Zuni Indians had had to suffer the aliens in their midst. After the first confrontation with the Spaniards at Hawikuh in July 1540, they had received the visitors on friendly terms, sprinkling them with corn meal and providing them with food and housing. Coronado had lived at Hawikuh for four months and had comported himself with tact and diplomacy, and later arrivals did not stay long enough to wear out their welcome.

The arrival in 1629 of missionaries whose purpose it was to substitute alien dogma for Zuni belief was to strain the hospitable nature of the hosts and to invite trouble. That the Indians felt no profound sense of allegiance to the king and pope was probably apparent to the friars as they set about the task of making conversions. Indeed some of the "obstinate spirits" took such a threatening stance that a few days after his departure Governor Silva Nieto was called back to display the Spanish military strength.

That seemed to have quieted the rumblings for a time. The friars proceeded to catechize interested audiences as they supervised construction of a church–monastery, La Purísima Concepción, at Hawikuh and another, probably at Halona, named Nuestra Señora de Guadalupe. But the truce was temporary. The Spanish documents refer condescendingly to the "primitive flowers" waiting to be gathered into the new church but there is also a note of concern about the "great resistance the sorcerers" made to the preachments of the Catholics. Undoubtedly the friars antagonized the native priests.

On Sunday, February 22, 1632, Fray Francisco Letrado, recently assigned to Hawikuh, found that the Indians were slow to come in for mass. Zealous, and probably of a fiery nature, he went out to prod them. When he chided some "idolaters," the Indians killed him with a volley of arrows. His scalp was ripped off and later exhibited in ceremonial dances at Hawikuh. The exact cause of the murder is not known. The possibility exists that Sunday mass may have coincided with a Zuni ceremonial. Indeed, it is possible that Estevan the Moor, who had accompanied Friar Marcos and preceded him to Cíbola, may have been killed for similar reasons.

---

and copiously annotated by Bloom (1933). Using contemporary documents, Scholes (1932) has reconstructed the ecclesiastical history of New Mexico to 1630. Hodge (1924) has written an article on the snake pens at Hawikuh.

Hodge (1937, 90–91) is convinced that the first mission at Zuni was founded in 1629 at Hawikuh, and that the second (sometimes called Nuestra Señora de Candelaria or La Limpia Concepción) was begun at Halona about the same time. Kubler (1940, 95–97) in his detailed study of the religious architecture of New Mexico reviews the history of the Zuni missions; at times he is at odds with Hodge.

Five days after the death of Letrado, Father Martin de Arvide, who had just passed through Hawikuh en route to a tribe to the west, was overtaken and killed by the Zunis. His scalp was taken also. The Pueblos, like many other American Indians, lifted scalps. To the Zunis the scalps were not only trophies commemorating victory over the enemy but were also objects important in a number of ceremonies.

Fearful of punishment, possibly recalling the brutal sentence dealt the Acomas by Oñate, the Zunis left their homes and towns and fled to the top of Towayalane, the great sacred mesa, which had served them as a refuge from the great world flood in mythological times. From Santa Fe a small party of soldiers and missionaries was sent to avenge the deaths. The nature of the punishment, if any, is not revealed in the documents. Military action by a small force against the Indians on Towayalane would have been a formidable and foolish undertaking. The missionaries, however, were admitted to the mesa top and they exacted promises of good behavior from the Zunis. The Indians, on the other hand, were not ready to be received by the Spaniards. They took their time about leaving the great mesa. Not until 1635 did they begin to resettle the pueblos in the valley below.[3]

The Zunis were fortunate in being located on the western frontier of New Mexico. Spanish power was seldom strong enough to make itself felt very far

---

[3] The first friars stationed at Zuni were Roque de Figueredo, Agustin de Cuellar, and Francisco de la Madre de Dios. The last disappeared from Zuni history before the murders occurred; Figueredo and Cuellar were spared. Letrado was a new arrival and Arvide was a stranger passing through. Bandelier (1892b, 96–99) and Hodge (1937, 91–93) refer to the details of the murders. Bandelier (1892b, 7–16) examines the evidence in the killing of Estevan for possible motives and concludes that in some way through "boldness" he had irritated and displeased the Zunis. See also Bandelier (1890b, 151–63) and Hodge (1937, 19–26). Cushing (1896, 328) wrote of the murder of the two friars and the significance to the Zunis of the scalp-taking. See also M. C. Stevenson (1904, 576–607) and Parsons (1924). Hewett and Fisher (1943) list the Franciscan missionaries who labored in New Mexico. Forrest (1929) has a chapter on the missions of Cíbola.

Bandelier (1892a, 134–35) asserts that the Zunis fled to Towayalane in 1540 to escape Coronado's soldiers, but this rests on a vague sentence in the "Traslado de las Nuevas." See Hammond and Rey, eds. and trans. (1940, 181). See Bandelier (1892b, 99) on the flight to the mountain in 1632. The details of many events in the early history of Zuni are not to be found in the documents. It is not clear, for example, that in 1632 all of the Zunis took refuge on Towayalane. Hodge (1937, 92, 95) suggests that the Indians did not escape severe punishment; he reproduces an inscription on El Morro which indicates that a party sent to avenge Letrado's death passed that way March 23, 1632.

The inscriptions on El Morro constitute a documentary source of importance in the history of the Zuni Pueblo. Those inscribed during the period 1629–1632, including the Silva Nieto inscriptions, are of particular interest. See Hodge (1937, n. 188), Slater (1961), and Barth (1933).

beyond the Rio Grande. And even there in the seventeenth century from time to time conflicts between officials of state and church diminished Spanish effectuality and weakened the authority of the clergy over the Pueblos. In New Mexico, as elsewhere, civil authorities were expected to assist and cooperate with the missionaries in their labors. Since New Mexico was remote, far from the centers of European civilization, and otherwise unattractive as an area for settlement, men of stature and integrity were probably in the minority in government and the military service, as well as among the ranks of the colonists. The friars frequently found themselves at odds with a grasping laity over clerical privileges and jurisdiction of lands and settled Indians.

The Pueblos, of course, never fully embraced the Spanish system. As the seventeenth century wore on, they chafed and protested over exploitation by the colonists, over forced labor and tribute, and the tyrannical Spanish rule. They grew ever more hostile to those missionaries who aggressively and punitively attempted to stamp out their religious customs and beliefs, particularly those customs which the Spanish priests identified with idolatry, sorcery, and witchcraft. As the friars prohibited and punished and preached reform, they bred a comparable intolerance in the Pueblos, who began to talk of rebellion against the hated foreigners.

The more distant pueblos were largely spared the pain of these troubled times and confrontations. In this deteriorating situation officials seldom traveled far beyond Santa Fe. An exception was the colorful and notorious Diego Dionisio de Peñalosa Briceño y Verdugo, governor of New Mexico, 1661–1664. During a journey, one which may have carried him to the Zuni and Hopi pueblos, he heard some tall tales of the country north and west beyond the Pueblo frontier. Among other things, he learned of the fabulous kingdom of Gran Teguayo, located on a lake, and of the Cerro, or Sierra Azul, a mining region rich in gold and silver, and he revived the story of the Seven Cities! But before the governor could get outfitted to go to look for these places, he found himself in trouble with the New Mexico churchmen who filed charges against him before the Inquisition. Broken and degraded by that body and exiled from New Spain, Peñalosa went to England and then to France in a futile attempt to interest those powers in the wonders of the wilderness beyond the frontiers of New Mexico.[4]

---

[4] Hodge (1937) finds nothing in the documents referring to Peñalosa's visit to Zuni but he does reproduce a section of Peñalosa's map of 1665 showing "Las Siete Ciudades" (The Seven Cities) in the Hopi country (pp. 94, 125). The entire map showing Teguayo north

The viceregal government showed little interest in Peñalosa's plans. Disturbed conditions in New Mexico precluded far-flung explorations beyond existing settlements. Indeed the times were not at all propitious for the maintenance of even the present missionary frontier, let alone its extension to remoter areas.

Zuni, for example, saw but few missionaries after the affair of 1632. In the mid-1660s a single friar, Fray Juan Galdo, was stationed there, at Halona; he also ministered to the Indians at Hawikuh and at two *visitas*, or neighboring missions, probably at Matsakya and Kechipbowa. Two friars were stationed at Zuni in 1672 when trouble erupted. On October seventh Fray Pedro de Avila y Ayala was struck down in his church at Hawikuh. The following day Fray Juan Galdo found the corpse; the head had been battered and crushed with a bell — the work of Navajos or Apaches.[5]

The decline of Spanish power exposed the settlements in New Mexico and the pueblos to attack by the nomadic Apaches and Navajos. These two related Athapascan-speaking peoples, themselves intruders in the region, were probably present when the Spaniards arrived in the Southwest, but for about a hundred years thereafter they occupied only a minor place in the annals of New Mexican history. Inclined more toward nomadic and predatory than sedentary ways, the Apaches and Navajos began to pose a threat to Spanish colonists and the Indian pueblos as they acquired and bred Spanish horses in greater numbers.

Missionary efforts to convert and pacify these wild tribes failed. Encouraged by weakening Spanish power and impelled by famine following several years of drought, the nomads grew much bolder in the 1660s and 1670s. Raiding the

---

of Santa Fe, is reproduced by Wheat (1957–1963, 1: 44). S. L. Tyler (1952) traces the history of the myths of Copala and Teguayo, highlighting Peñalosa's creation of the latter. See also Gilberto Espinosa, ed. (1964), a reprint of a work on Peñalosa originally published by Shea in 1882. Hackett, ed. and trans. (1923–1937, vol. 3), has reproduced a number of primary documents relating to Peñalosa.

[5] From 1632 until the Pueblo Revolt in 1680, there are few contemporary documents touching Zuni affairs mainly because there was little Spanish contact with the Indians. During these years, however, a good many names were inscribed on El Morro, suggesting more intercourse than is apparent in the extant documents. See Slater (1961). Scholes (1929, 50, 56) reproduces two documents of the period which touch briefly on Zuni history.

Hodge (1937, 94–97), who summarizes the history of the period 1635–1672, believes that the two *visitas* were Matsakya and Kechipbowa. At the latter site, a small stone church, part of the walls of which still stand, was probably begun at a later date, but it may never have been completed.

The killing of Fray Pedro in 1672 is attributed by Hodge (1937, 99) to Apaches; Bandelier (1892b, 106–7) blames the Navajos. In the contemporary documents the term "Navajo–Apaches" is occasionally used as the name of either one or both peoples.

pueblos, they stole foodstuffs, cattle and horses and other stock, and carried off captives. The frontier Pueblos, touched but lightly by Spanish civilization, found themselves beyond the reach of effective military protection. Thus the missions at Zuni were highly vulnerable, and the priest at Hawikuh was a victim to the rising nomadic power.

Threatened by unfriendly Indians at other and more vital points, Spain was unable, with the meager military forces at hand, to avenge the attack at Zuni. Furthermore, the threat from within was rapidly becoming more serious. Oppressed, exploited, and persecuted, the Pueblos dreamed of the time when they could free themselves from the hated Spaniards and restore their world as it had been, a world in which they could live in peace among themselves, and most important, in which they could worship according to their custom.[6]

As the decade of the 1670s wore on, the time seemed right to throw off the Spanish yoke. A leader appeared — Popé of San Juan Pueblo. Plans were worked out for a general rebellion of the Pueblos, to take place in August 1680. Probably for the first time in their history all the Pueblos worked together, a sign of the depth of their feeling. The Indians, acting by prearranged signal, rose in concert and, simultaneously throughout New Mexico, attacked the Spaniards. They slayed over four hundred, but about twenty-five hundred escaped and, under the direction of Governor Antonio de Otermín, fled to El Paso.

The Zunis, who had taken part in the planning, joined in the revolt. The missionary at Halona, Juan de Bal, possibly the only Spaniard present at the time, was killed by the Indians on August tenth. New Mexico had returned to its pristine state; as Bandelier said, "The rebellion appeared to be a success, and the Pueblos exulted over it. Their 'good old times' had returned." [7]

But the good times were clouded by the fear of Spanish power. Fully expecting that the Europeans would return, the Zunis once more looked to the great mesa Towayalane — Corn Mountain — where again they took refuge. Three miles southeast of Halona, Towayalane stands in splendid isolation, a neat thousand feet above the country round and about. A mile and a half long by

---

[6] The decline of Spanish power in New Mexico and the rise of the Apaches and Navajos is thoroughly examined and documented by Forbes (1960); see also Spicer (1962, 210–61). For contemporary documents see Hackett, ed. and trans. (1923–1937), and the articles by Scholes (1936–1937, 1937–1941).

[7] The Pueblo Revolt of 1680 has been much written about. The basic documentary collection is the two-volume work by Hackett, ed., and Shelby, trans. (1942). See also Hackett, ed. (1923–1937), and Spicer (1962, 152–65).

nearly a mile wide at its greatest width, the mesa dips slightly toward the southwest and is on all sides precipitous and difficult of ascent. Near the extreme
southwestern rim, on both sides of a shallow wash, the Zunis built three or four
clusters of rock houses running up to two or three stories in height and containing
about two hundred rooms. The floor plans of many buildings are marked even
today by the remains of walls standing as high as five feet.

The nearby impregnable mesa-top location was reached by at least two hand-
and-foot trails topping out near the village; another trail, passable to horses,
reached the top on the northeast slope. The Zunis built their refuge on the low
side where nearly the whole drainage of the mesa top collected and could be
impounded in reservoirs. When it snowed they turned out and rolled up huge
snowballs. These were rolled into the reservoir areas; the gradually melting snow
supplied a considerable amount of water. But the supply from this source was not
enough; the Indians were forced to carry up not only most of their water from
springs at the base of the mesa but also the crops harvested from fields planted
along the Zuni River and its tributaries. The refugees lived on Towayalane for
twelve years.

Had the viceroy of New Spain wished to quit New Mexico altogether, the
Pueblos in 1680 certainly gave him a splendid opportunity. Instead, he ordered
the reconquest of the province, but had only limited funds provided him for the
project. Little significant progress was made until Diego de Vargas Zapata
Luján Ponce de León y Contreras, nobleman and experienced soldier, volun-
teered to reclaim New Mexico for the crown at his own expense. Among other
things, Vargas promised to search for the Sierra Azul mines, reported by Peñalosa, which were thought to be somewhere west of the Zuni and Hopi pueblos.

As governor and captain-general, Vargas in 1692 made an extensive reconnaissance of the province. He encountered little resistance, discovering that
Pueblo solidarity had been broken by factionalism and dissension. Furthermore
he found that certain of the Pueblos were willing to assist as allies and auxiliaries
in restoring Spanish rule.

With a troop of eighty-nine soldiers and thirty Indian allies Vargas in
November and early December made a quick tour of the Western Pueblos. On
Saturday, November eighth, he camped at El Morro (which Vargas in his diary
refers to by that name), and someone in the party carved an elegant inscription
in the rocks to document the visit. In translation it reads: "Here was General
Don Diego de Vargas, who conquered for our holy faith and for the royal crown,

all New Mexico, at his expense, year of 1692." Although Vargas may not have incised the legend himself, we may be certain he supervised the job, for he wanted the world to remember (and the inscription is still clear and distinct) that he paid for the reconquest himself.

Next morning after mass the campaigners moved on to "El Ojito de Zuñi" (Zuni Spring) on the Rio Pescado, and there they were met by a party of Zunis, ten or twelve on horseback and two on foot. The Indians brought gifts —mutton, watermelons, and tortillas — and there was much talk. The Spaniards would be welcome to return to Zuni, said the Indians.

The next day the Europeans moved down the Rio Pescado; after traveling eight miles they came to the mouth of the Rio Nutria and the "Gates of Zuni," or "Zuni Pass," where the two streams united to form the Zuni River. Passing through the gates the campaigners continued for five miles and camped in full view of Towayalane — the "great rock," Vargas called it — towering above the valley.

Tuesday, November 11, 1692, Vargas, at the head of two mounted and armed companies, advanced toward the northeastern base of Towayalane and the main trail leading to the mesa top. Finding the trail rocky and steep, the soldiers soon dismounted and "with considerable effort" clambered up to the top on foot, leading their mounts. The rim of the mesa was "crowned with the people of the Pueblo," watching the maneuver with high interest.

Mounting his horse, Vargas rode into the pueblo, which consisted, he said, of three dwelling complexes arranged around a plaza. There, after the exchange of warm and affectionate greetings, Vargas ordered the erection of a large cross. This being done, the governor and captain-general, through an interpreter, the "coyote Indian, Ventura," said that the king of Spain, "our lord, was master of that rock, its pueblo, and all this land and kingdom, and that they were all his vassals. . . ." Thus, Vargas wrote in his campaign journal, "I reclaimed said possession." The ceremonies were completed when the two friars granted absolution to the Indians and baptized, "of all ages and both sexes," 294 of those present.[8] Amen. The Spanish overlords had returned to Zuni.

---

[8] The documents of the Reconquest, 1692, which include the campaign journals of Vargas, have been edited by J. M. Espinosa (1940). The use of Pueblo allies and auxiliaries in the Reconquest and later wars has been developed in a scholarly study by Jones (1966).

The Vargas inscription on El Morro is dated only by the year. The Spaniards camped at Inscription Rock on November eighth and again on December first and the inscription could have been made on either date. Hodge (1937, 103) and Slater (1961, 105) reproduce

Before leaving the Zuni village on Towayalane, Vargas was escorted to a second story room where he was surprised to see two large candles burning on an altar. Some pieces of vestments had been placed to cover religious articles and books, all apparently salvaged from the missions at the time of the revolt. The Spaniards "all marveled" at this discovery, Vargas wrote, for the Zunis were the only Pueblos in all of New Mexico who for the past twelve years had continued to show any respect for Christianity.

For at least two centuries after the arrival of Vargas, the Indians preserved a tradition that may explain how it was that the sacred objects were carried to the top of Towayalane. It seems that one of the missionaries in Zuni at the time of the Pueblo Revolt escaped martyrdom by abjuring his own faith. He went with the Indians to live on the great mesa and he may have been present when Vargas and company arrived. Zuni tradition relates that the friar, affectionately known as "Juan Gray-robed-father-of-us," elected to remain with his Indian hosts rather than rejoin his countrymen. Thus, though he may have lighted the candles when Vargas approached, the friar did not disclose his presence; he died shortly thereafter.[9]

Whatever may have been the basis of the tradition about Father Juan, the fact that some of the sacred objects had been salvaged and preserved during the

---

the Vargas inscription. Vargas' detailed journal and correspondence covering the campaign at the Zuni and Hopi towns is in J. M. Espinosa, ed. and trans. (1940, 197–238, 255–77).

The Zuni village on Towayalane, occupied approximately from 1680 to 1692, consisted of several irregularly-placed housing complexes covering about ten acres. In addition to the three trails mentioned in the text, a fourth quite recent foot trail (steel ladders scale a short distance of the steepest part) was built at the extreme northeastern point of the mesa to permit the servicing of an airline beacon. The beacon is no longer in operation but the trail is frequently used today to reach the mesa top.

The ruins of the village atop Towayalane were visited, mapped, and described in 1881 by Victor Mindeleff (1891, 89–91 and pl. 60). Mindeleff from Zuni sources gives the account of the storage of water in snowballs. See also Cushing (1890, 156–57 and pl. 4), and Spier (1917a, 231). Earlier American visitors were Möllhausen (1858) and Whipple (1856).

[9] The story of "Juan Gray-robed-father-of-us" rests on Zuni tradition. Davis (1938, 286), in a work first published in 1857, reported a version of the story; others are recorded by Bourke (see Bloom, ed., 1933–1938, 11: 202), Cushing (1896, 330–31), M. C. Stevenson (1904, 286–89), and Boas (1922, 97–98). Zuni tradition includes the suggestion that the friar by means of a message written on skin opened the way for Vargas to climb Towayalane unopposed. Vargas, however, does not mention this incident. Apparently, he did not suspect the presence among the Zunis of Father "Juan." See Vargas' journal, J. M. Espinosa, ed. and trans. (1940, 198–204), and Leonard, ed. and trans. (1932) of Carlos de Sigüenza y Góngora's *Mercurio Volante*.

years of the insurrection indicated an acceptance of the Catholics not found elsewhere. Furthermore, the Zunis open-mindedly, and in a friendly manner, welcomed Vargas and his company to their place of refuge on Towayalane where nearly three hundred of their number submitted to baptism. In this seemingly strange about-face, the Zunis quite possibly acted, not out of love for the foreigners, but out of need for a powerful ally.

Chapter 5

Pueblo Diplomats

A Zuni roof hole with cover

Lasting changes in the life of the Indians followed the coming of the white man. None of those in New Mexico escaped the touch of Spain though the measure of change varied from tribe to tribe. The Zunis took up some new ways: Spanish influence modified their religious ceremonies and political organization; the Indians accepted technological innovations and adopted plants and animals new to them. Among the European imports, only the horse radically changed the Zunis' relations with their Indian neighbors.[1]

The Zunis, like the other Pueblos, were somewhat slow to take to the horse. An agricultural people, they lived close to their fields, and their compact, multi-storied villages were an adequate defense against an unmounted enemy. The Spanish overlords at first denied the Indians the use of horses, but even after the Pueblo Revolt, when such restrictions vanished, the Zunis elected to remain pedestrians.

Not so the hunters and gatherers, the wilder and less domesticated Apaches and Navajos, who reckoned that on horseback a better life would be theirs. When the Spaniards returned after the Great Rebellion they found the heartland of New Mexico menaced by these peoples as well as by the Utes and Comanches. The Apaches and Navajos had transformed themselves from poverty-stricken wanderers, often living close to and on peaceful terms with the Pueblos, to equestrians reckoning their wealth in extensive herds and flocks. They had become independent, free to roam from place to place. The herds of horses gave them mobility; the flocks of sheep, clothing and food. Hunting was easier on horseback. If they stopped long enough in one place, they might grow a few

---

[1] On the cultural changes wrought by Spain consult Dozier (1970, 63–71), and Leighton and Adair (1966, 20–21).

crops, but a raid on the Spanish settlements or on a neighboring pueblo was an easier and far more exciting way of stocking the larder.

Their way of life revolutionized, the Apaches and Navajos (and the Utes and Comanches) staked out and secured to themselves vast areas where they roamed at will for about two hundred years. West from the Continental Divide the Navajos moved onto the lands between the San Juan River and the heads of the Little Colorado, centering their power and influence in Canyon de Chelly on the eastern slope of the Chuska Mountains. The western bands of the Apaches ranged over the country south of the Navajos between the Rio Grande and the heads of the Gila River.[2]

The Zuni Indians found themselves in the path of these expanding peoples, who posed a greater threat to their cultural identity — always a matter of great concern to them — than the power of Spain. Even before the Pueblo Revolt the nomads had threatened; in 1672 at Hawikuh they had killed Fray Pedro de Avila y Ayala. At Zuni twenty years later Diego de Vargas encountered Apaches in some force. One stormy night he lost sixteen head of cattle to some "crafty and hostile" Apaches of the "Faraon" band, but he also met some "Salinero" Apaches who professed friendship for the Spaniards.

There is reason to believe that the Zunis after the Pueblo Revolt continued to live on Corn Mountain not so much from fear of Spanish reprisal, as for defense against Apache marauders. In fact, Vargas wrote the viceroy that the Zunis had abandoned their several villages and fled to the rock in response to repeated raids by the Apaches.[3] Whatever the truth of the matter, the Spaniards returning to Zuni in particular, and to the Pueblo country in general, were welcomed — for they offered the only possible counterbalance to the rising power of the nomads.

------

[2] The revolutionary changes in aboriginal life following the Pueblo Revolt have been well documented. Forbes (1960) makes the point that before the Pueblo Revolt relations between the Apaches and Navajos and the Pueblos were essentially peaceful; the three shared a hostility toward the Spaniards which broke into intermittent warfare after the rebellion. Spicer's work (1962) is a masterly summary of Indian–white relations in the Southwest, 1533–1960. On the Navajos see Underhill (1956, chap. 6) and Hester (1962). In a succinct essay Schroeder (1968) examines Indian population shifts in the Southwest, 1540–1820. Worcester (1947) documents the rise of Navajo power, 1600–1800.

[3] Vargas lost his cattle on November 11, 1692, the day he ascended Corn Mountain; on the thirteenth some eight or ten Salineros came into camp for a talk. See J. M. Espinosa, ed. and trans. (1940, 199–200, 205–6). Vargas' letter to Viceroy Conde de Galve is in J. M. Espinosa, ed. and trans. (1940, 266).

After Vargas reclaimed the territory, however, Spanish power, as before, was never strong enough to have much impact in the country of the Western Pueblos. In the face of constant Apache danger and in the absence of any protective military force, the Zunis were slow to leave their refuge on Towayalane. Furthermore, they involved themselves in a second uprising of the Pueblos in 1696 and they probably feared reprisal. The record is not very clear, but it appears that, after Vargas, the Zuni Indians were not visited by any Spanish parties until mid-1699, when New Mexico's Governor Pedro Rodríquez Cubero made a tour of some of the Western Pueblos.

Cubero found the Indians — still living on Corn Mountain. When assurances were given, the Zunis renewed their allegiance to the Spanish crown and, probably responding to the persuasion of zealous Father Juan de Garaycoechea, agreed to move from the mesa and return to their homes in the valley of the Zuni River. To achieve this end the Spaniards must have offered some promise of protection against the hostiles. Since defense of all the villages was impossible, the Zunis elected to resettle one village — Halona — and not reoccupy the others. Located on both banks of the shallow Zuni River, Halona was a good location, though one not easily defended. There was spring water and ample land suitable for dry farming nearby, enough to supply food for all the people. And it was the center of the world — Itiwana, the Middle Place — where in ancient times the ancestral Zunis had built the first pueblo.

In 1700, a troop of eleven soldiers was sent from Santa Fe to guard the village against hostile attack; accompanying them were three Spanish civilian settlers described in the documents as "exiles." Father Juan de Garaycoechea, named resident missionary, was already on the ground and planning the restoration of the Mission of Nuestra Señora de Guadalupe.[4] Thus it was that the six or seven "Cities of Cíbola" were reduced to one, which was to become the Zuni of today, the largest of all the pueblos.

---

[4] Bancroft (1889, 221), Jones (1966, 63–64), Adams and Chávez, eds. and trans. (1956, 196–98, n. 2), J. M. Espinosa (1942, 347–52), Bandelier (1892a, 371, n.1). The authorities differ on the dates (1699 vs. 1700) of the reestablishment of Halona (or Alona, as it frequently appears in the Spanish documents). Bandelier cites the manuscript *Libro de Entierros de la Mission de Nuestra Señora de Guadalupe de Zuñi* which begins in 1699 with entries in the hand of Father Garaycoechea (also spelled Garaicoechea in the documents). Chávez (1957, 21) gives a baptismal record kept by the priest at Zuni, 1699–1700. The fact seems to be that the Franciscan was present in 1699; probably the soldiers and three civilians did not arrive until 1700.

We have few details concerning the rebuilding of ancient Halona. To insure the best defense, the higher ground on the north side of the river was chosen for the site, but there was little building stone in the immediate vicinity. That part of Halona south of the river and Matsakya, one of the larger cities of Cíbola and less than two miles away to the east, may have been razed to supply the stone which Zuni builders preferred to other materials. Much of the new construction went up around the mission located on the site of the present church.[5]

Father Garaycoechea made some conversions and seemed to get on well with the Zunis, but things went poorly between the Indians and the resident troops and settlers. The soldiers were haughty and harsh, peremptory with converts and licentious in their conduct toward Indian women. The settlers were no better.

The anguish of the Zunis was shared by large numbers of other Pueblos. Flight and migrations had followed the cataclysmic revolt in 1680 as the rebels sought more defensible living places or, as refugees, moved in with other Pueblos. For those concerned with preserving the old ways, the conditions of life worsened after the Spanish reconquest of New Mexico. The splendid unity which had brought victory to the Pueblos in the Great Rebellion was born of their common hatred of Spain, but when the enemy returned to New Mexico, Pueblo solidarity fell apart. Differences over the degree of acceptance of Spanish authority caused upheaval, conflict, and genocide. Far from the capital at Santa Fe, the Western Pueblos had greater freedom to choose their own policies toward Spanish rule. Their decisions were tempered by the rising power of the Apaches, Navajos, and other nomadic peoples.

The Hopis, living in a cluster of villages — the Province of Tusayán — a hundred miles west-northwest of Zuni, had participated in the revolt and had taken measures to defend themselves and prevent the return of the overlords. Those Hopis not already living on the mesa tops had moved their villages to more easily defensible locations along the rims. Furthermore, the Hopis had offered asylum to large numbers of refugees from the Rio Grande pueblos and had forged an alliance with the newcomers powerful enough to rebuff Spanish

---

[5] The present church, rebuilt and beautifully restored in 1969, is located on the site of the mission which, Kubler (1940, 95–96) believes, dates back to 1667. However, see n. 100 by Hodge in Hodge, Hammond, and Rey, eds. and trans. (1945, 291). On the location of ancient Halona with reference to Zuni as it was in 1881 see V. Mindeleff (1891, 88–89, 97–99). Sometimes the ancient city of the Zunis is called Halona Itiwana as in Cushing (1896, 332).

attempts to reestablish colonial rule in Tusayán. The Hopi hero, the organizer and genius behind this determined resistance, was Francisco de Espeleta.

Naturally, not all Hopis were of the same mind on these questions. There was one faction composed of Christianized Indians, joined by those who felt that restoration of the Catholic missions would prevent warfare, who even invited the missionaries to return to Hopiland. Father Juan de Garaycoechea learned of this not long after persuading the Zuni Indians to leave Corn Mountain. Full of apostolic zeal, he and Father Antonio Miranda of Laguna Pueblo in 1700 journeyed to Tusayán.

At the village of Awatovi they were well received, but the situation soon became tense when many hostile Hopis arrived from the other villages to harry and threaten them. Nevertheless the missionaries made some conversions and then departed, planning to return and set up a mission. Once they had gone, Francisco de Espeleta with a force of militant, anti-Spanish Hopis, attacked Awatovi. The village was destroyed, the men who resisted were killed, and the women and children were distributed to the other villages. It would appear that Awatovi had been the center of the Hopi pro-Spanish faction. In this bloody massacre, this faction must nearly have been destroyed. It was a harsh measure, but the freedom-loving Hopis carried their cause. Spanish rule was never restored and no Christian missionaries ventured to take up residence in Tusayán for over a hundred and fifty years.[6]

The Zuni Indians also were divided over the course to follow in their relations with Spain but they showed far less xenophobia. The pro-Christian faction among them seems to have been stronger than it was among the Hopis. In 1699 the Zunis had moved down from Towayalane to accept the protection of Spanish sovereignty. But numbers of Zunis were hostile to the Spanish presence; some moved to Tusayán and the Hopis themselves tried to incite the Zunis to rebellion. It is more than likely that the current of revolt was running strong when on Sunday, March 3, 1703, the Indians attacked and killed the three settlers while they were in church; the troops, absent from the pueblo at the time, escaped. Father Garaycoechea was spared. Fearing reprisals, once more — and for the

---

[6] Gleaned from the documents, the essential facts of Spain's relations with the Hopis, and particularly with the residents of Awatovi, have been assembled by Brew, in Montgomery, Smith, and Brew (1949, 1–43). But see also Dozier (1954), Spicer (1962, 190–6), Euler and Dobyns (1971, 33–53), and Hackett, ed. and trans. (1923–1937, 3: 385–87). The threat of competition with the Jesuits in missionary work among the Hopis occasioned an intensification of Franciscan activity in the 1740s.

last time — the Zunis fled to Towayalane. What was the Spanish reaction to the killings? The priest and soldiers were withdrawn and Zuni was abandoned to the Indians for two years.[7]

In 1705, Father Garaycoechea returned, and again the Zunis were induced to leave Corn Mountain, return to Halona, and accept military protection. This acquiescence enraged the militant Hopis who saw their position threatened by the Spanish post at Zuni. There followed some years of hostility and intermittent minor guerilla warfare between the Hopis and Zunis. At times the latter were assisted by feeble Spanish forces, but no major encounter marred the relations of the two Pueblos.

As the eighteenth century wore on, the differences between the Pueblos over the acceptance of Spanish rule subsided in the face of the growing power of the Apaches, Navajos, Utes, and Comanches. In fact, from the time of the Reconquest by Vargas and on through the eighteenth century, the several Pueblos, including the Zunis (but not the Hopis), on occasion underwent a "diplomatic revolution" and joined Spain as military auxiliaries in defense of the realm.[8]

Owing to their cooperative attitude and their location on the western frontier of New Mexico, the Zunis were affected by some of the critical imperial problems facing Spain during the last fifty years of her rule in North America. After 1763, when the Seven Years' War ended, defense was the most serious matter. Spain (who had lost heavily) found herself threatened by England (who had triumphed in the war), both in the Mississippi Valley and on the Pacific coast. In response the Spanish government sent to America a number of able administrators who expanded, reorganized, and consolidated the frontier salients of the empire between the Mississippi and the Pacific.

---

[7] Robinson, trans., and Hodge, ed. (1944, 110–16), reproduce reports by Fathers Garaycoechea and Miranda, 1702–1703. See also Bandelier (1889, 168–70), and J. M. Espinosa (1942, 347–52).

[8] Inasmuch as the Zunis were in general peaceably inclined toward Spain in the eighteenth century, there is less primary documentation about them than about the defiant Hopis. Hackett, ed. and trans. (1923–1937, 3: 366–509), reproduces a number of pertinent documents. Bandelier (1889, 173–74) writes of guerilla attacks by the Hopis on the Zunis and lists casualties. New Mexico's Governor Félix Martinez in 1716 led an elaborate expedition from Zuni against the Hopis but it was a flat failure. Bandelier (1889, 177–80). Bancroft (1889, chaps. 11–12) has many details. Escalante, writing in 1776, states that the Zuni–Hopi war ended in 1717–1718; see A. B. Thomas, ed. and trans. (1932, 163). See Dozier (1970, 71–88) for a scholarly synthesis. M. C. Stevenson (1904, 283–96) contains a chronology of Zuni history prepared by F. W. Hodge. Jones (1966) is a scholarly account of the Pueblo auxiliaries.

Every Spanish frontiersman knew that the unassimilated Indians of the northern frontier were a more constant and serious danger than all the posturings and policies of Spain's European neighbors. The Marqués de Rubí saw this clearly in 1766–1768 when he made a general inspection of the northern frontier between the Gulf of California and the Gulf of Mexico, but in response to Rubí's recommendations the central government did little more than relocate a few presidios. The extreme frontier — Sonora, Arizona, New Mexico, and Texas — was soon seriously threatened by the hostile tribes.

In 1776 Spain finally took decisive action in the interior. The king joined the northern frontier provinces together to form a new political jurisdiction, called appropriately enough the *Provincias Internas*, or Internal Provinces, which was to be ruled by a commandant general and be virtually independent of the viceroy of New Spain.[9]

Teodoro de Croix held the post from 1776 to 1783; he too clearly identified the Indian raiders as Spain's major enemy across a very weakly held frontier spanning the continent from the mouth of the Colorado to the mouth of the Rio Grande. Guided by "continental" vision, Croix stabilized the frontier defenses from Arizona to Texas, launched frontal attacks on the Apaches, and worked out alliances with other tribes. His successor, Jacobo Ugarte, holding office until 1791, followed a similar policy.

In New Mexico, Croix's policies, and Ugarte's, were elaborated and executed by Juan Bautista de Anza, who served as governor, 1777–1787. In a number of campaigns and diplomatic maneuvers, Anza managed to bring the Utes, Comanches, and Navajos as allies into the Spanish camp. The allies, together with the Pueblos, turned their combined power in a general movement against the Apache bands who were forced, one by one, to submit to the superior power. By the time Anza left his post a general calm prevailed. Spanish New Mexico — the bulwark of Spain's defenses in the interior of New Spain — together with the

---

[9] The deterioration of Spain's northern frontier, the formation of the *Commandancia-General de las Provincias Internas*, and the founding of Alta California, have received much scholarly attention. Basic books are Priestley (1916), Chapman (1916), Bolton (1939), Bobb (1962), Kinnaird, ed. and trans. (1958), A. B. Thomas, ed. and trans. (1941), and Moorhead (1968). Lafora's account (Kinnaird, ed. and trans., 1958) of the Rubi inspection is a detailed description of the northern frontier, but the emphasis is on the military frontier below the Rio Grande; Lafora's map of 1771 includes all the northern provinces from Sonora to Texas. The important *Reglamento* of 1772 setting the rules and regulations for the government of the northern frontier has been Englished by Galvin, ed., and Smithers, trans. (1963).

Pueblo Indians, may well have been saved by Anza's policies from total destruction.[10]

A glance at the map of eighteenth-century New Mexico must have brought small comfort to those who worried about frontier defenses. There it was, a narrow peninsula of settlement connected with the Mexican heartland five hundred miles away by a few villages scattered along the Rio Grande and in the desert of Chihuahua. East, across the Pecos, the nearest settlements were in Texas and Louisiana. West, across the Continental Divide and beyond the Zuni and Hopi villages, the nearest settlements of Spanish origin were on the coast of California. Following the occupation of California the matter of connecting this salient of the empire with New Mexico occurred to a few minds as a defensive possibility.

Since 1605, the year Juan de Oñate completed his traverse from Zuni to the mouth of the Colorado River, the Spanish government had devoted little attention to the vast triangle of country between the Western Pueblos and the Pacific coast. Espejo, Oñate, and Peñalosa had filled the region with those imaginary wonders, Copala, Teguayo, and Sierra Azul. But the age of El Dorado had passed and no capital was found to track down these fanciful chimeras. During the Reconquest, Diego de Vargas had looked for the Sierra Azul, one of Peñalosa's visions. From both the Zunis and Hopis Vargas had solicited information about the mine; he learned that it was too distant for his spent command to attempt discovery. But from a Zuni Indian he had obtained a sample of the ore — bright red — and sent it off to the viceroy for assay. That official had not followed through.[11]

During the first half of the eighteenth century the friars often sought to win more viceregal support for their work in the Western Pueblos by reawakening

---

[10] A. B. Thomas, ed. and trans. (1932), Moorhead (1968), Bancroft (1889, chap. 12). For a discussion of Spain's persistent problems with the Apaches on both sides of the Rio Grande in the last half of the eighteenth century, see Moorhead (1968). The documentary history of Spain's frontier defenses and Indian affairs in New Mexico through much of the eighteenth century has been published by A. B. Thomas in several books (1932, 1935, 1941).

[11] The Sierra Azul becomes "Cerro Colorado" in Vargas' diary and correspondence; see J. M. Espinosa, ed. and trans. (1940, introduction and 224–26, 272–74). The sample, vermilion in color, of the substance with which the Indians "paint themselves" came from the land of the "Conina," who were Havasupais living in the Grand Canyon. The Havasupais have long exported red paint, or ochre, to other tribes; both the Hopi and Zuni villages came within their trading area. See Bancroft (1889) for a number of references to Sierra Azul.

interest in the Sierra Azul, Teguayo, and other wonderful places. In 1744, Fray Carlos Delgado reported that the Sierra Azul, four days travel west of Tusayán, was blue in color but marked by "green, red, yellow, and purple veins." He wrote that this mineral region was thought to be "the richest in all New Spain." Of Teguayo, Delgado wrote that, according to the Navajo informants, one of its cities was so large that one could not "walk around it in eight days." But, again, the viceroy was not tempted.[12]

After about mid-century the situation changed. Defensive strategy, not quixotic dreaming, clearly indicated the need for communication between the Zuni–Hopi outposts in New Mexico and the California coast. Officials in Mexico City were quite aware that the California settlements were as far from a supply base as any in North America. Monterey, California's capital, and Santa Fe were on nearly the same latitude. Why not open communication between the two provinces and thus strengthen both salients of the frontier? In mid-1775 the question was sent to the governor of New Mexico who forwarded it to the priest at Zuni for reply. Indeed, the viceroy had already instructed the friars of Sonora and New Mexico to be on the lookout for possible interprovincial routes during the course of their evangelical travels.

Father Francisco Vélez de Escalante had been resident missionary at Zuni since early in 1775, and when the governor's letter arrived he already knew something of the lands to the west. He had learned that the Zunis some years before had participated in a general campaign against the Apaches which had taken them to the valley of the Gila River; later, a hundred Zuni Indians and a party of three Spaniards attacked a village of Gila Apaches in the same region. Eliminate the "hostiles," Escalante reported, and the road between New Mexico and Sonora, paralleling the Coronado trail, would be "passable without risk." [13]

---

[12] Included in a declaration made by Fray Miguel de Menchero; see Hackett, ed. and trans. (1923–1937, 3: 395–413). In some additional correspondence (*ibid.*, pp. 391–95, 415–16) Delgado indicated that he planned to visit Teguayo in the spring of 1745; he made it clear that the Franciscans of course were not interested in riches but only in the saving of souls! He ascribes somewhat different motives to the Jesuits who at the time were planning to enter the Hopi area. See also Bancroft (1889, 246). Bishop Tamarón in 1760 mentioned the Sierra Azul, twelve days travel from the Hopi villages. Nearby was a "great town of bearded men and costly buildings"; see Adams, ed. (1954, 74).

[13] Letter by Escalante to Governor Pedro Fermín de Mendinueta, October 28, 1775; see A. B. Thomas, ed. and trans. (1932, 150–58). Bishop Tamarón mentions a campaign of 1747 against the Western Apaches involving seven hundred mounted men; the campaigners visited Zuni on the return. Adams, ed. (1954, 89). The bishop had some cogent observations on New Mexico's defenses.

Late in June Escalante traveled to the Hopi villages to find out what he could about opening a trail from Tusayán across country to California. His hosts were pessimistic — the way west would be long, dry, rough, and difficult. The Indians did not mislead the priest. (Their information was nicely corroborated one year later by Father Francisco Garcés, another Franciscan, who worked his way eastward from the coast to the Hopi village of Oraibi.) This and other considerations led Escalante to recommend that a more northerly route to California be sought through the land of the Utes. He was, he reported, ready to go on such a quest.[14]

Escalante's offer was accepted. In June 1776 he was recalled from Zuni by Father Francisco Atanasio Domínguez who was then making an official inspection of New Mexico for the Franciscan order. The two men set out with a small party to find a route to Monterey somewhere in latitudes north of Santa Fe. They failed in their basic objective but, making a most remarkable five-month journey, they traveled in country — most of it new to the white man — through western Colorado, central Utah, and northern Arizona. Late in November, cold and bone-tired, they arrived at the friendly Zuni Pueblo where they spent sixteen days recuperating before going on to Santa Fe.

During their stay at Zuni, Domínguez made his inspection of the church and pueblo, and wrote a detailed description of both. The mission church, "Nuestra Señora de Guadalupe," its "walls nearly a *vara* thick," by 1776 stood in the middle of the pueblo surrounded on all sides by "many tenements" (350 houses were counted by Father Morfi in 1779) and small plazas. The Zunis, Domínguez reported, numbered 1,617 persons (396 families) and were of a "very docile and gentle disposition." [15]

---

[14] Letters of Escalante August 18, October 28, 1775; May 16, 21, July 29, 1776. Adams and Chávez, eds. and trans. (1956, 302–8), A. B. Thomas, ed. and trans. (1932, 150–66). Escalante's Hopi diary of 1775 has been published by Adams, ed. (1963). The truly remarkable travels of Father Francisco Tomás Hermengildo Garcés, O.F.M., 1775–1776, are described in his detailed diary, translated and edited by Coues (1900). Garcés opened a route across the Mojave Desert to California and traversed the southern San Joaquin Valley before returning across the Mojave to the vicinity of Needles. Then by way of Havasupai Canyon and the South Rim of Grand Canyon he reached Oraibi on July 2, 1776. The Hopis, as might be expected, were cool and unfriendly, and he turned back rather than continue to Zuni as planned.

[15] The basic document of the Domínguez–Escalante expedition is Escalante's diary edited by Bolton (1950). The findings of Domínguez' visitation, which includes descriptions of all the New Mexico pueblos, have been published by Adams and Chávez, eds. and trans. (1956). Father Juan Agustín de Morfi (Thomas, ed. and trans., 1932, 106) gives eighteenth-

Gentle was a better word than docile. For a long time the Zunis had accommodated a few foreigners in their midst, but it is questionable whether the outsiders were influential enough to lead these resilient Indians far along paths they did not want to travel. And from 1776 that influence, whatever it may have amounted to, waned rapidly as Spain's empire in America declined. The fateful year 1776 saw the birth of a new nation on the Atlantic seaboard. Spain, caught up indirectly in the American Revolution, could scarcely spend much time or treasure on faraway New Mexico. Through clever strategy and diplomacy, Governor Anza had saved the province from ruin, and the general peace he achieved with the tribes continued through the first decade of the next century.

But this peace was sustained in large part by Spain's Indian allies and auxiliaries. Thus in 1804–1805, when the Navajos rebelled against Spanish authority and holed up in the nearly impregnable Canyon de Chelly, the Zunis, who had long suffered the raids of the Navajos, were willing to assist in an assault on the canyon stronghold of the rebels. In January 1805 well over a hundred Navajos were killed at Canyon del Muerto in a place since known as Massacre Cave. On the Spanish side sixty-four were wounded; the only death was that of a Zuni chief. After this and some other engagements, peace was restored with the Navajos — at least for a time.[16]

By 1810, Spain's own empire had begun to fall apart in revolution; her richest possession, the Viceroyalty of New Spain, emerged in 1821 as independent Mexico. The war for Mexican independence was largely confined to central Mexico and touched the northern frontier provinces but lightly. On January 6, 1822, at Santa Fe, "at the very extremity of North America," Mexico's independence from Spain was formally celebrated with salutes, dances, *paseos*, and speeches liberally laced with words like "independence" and "freedom" which called forth *vivas* and shouts from the crowds.[17] It is not apparent that New

century population statistics as follows: in 1707 there were 1500 souls in Zuni; in 1744, 150 families; in 1765, 181 families or 664 souls; in 1779, 365 families or 1199 souls lived in 350 adobe houses. Bancroft (1889, 279) gives the population of Zuni in 1799 as 2716 Indians and 7 Spaniards. At that date Zuni, by a margin of over a thousand persons, was still the largest pueblo in New Mexico.

[16] Twitchell (1911–1915, 1: 457–58); Bancroft (1889, 285); Jones (1966, 182–88), Carroll and Haggard, eds. and trans. (1942, 132–33). For a Navajo chronology, see Hester (1962, 21–23). Zuni relations with the Navajos from 1641 to 1865 have been documented: U.S. Indian Claims Commission, *The Navajo Tribe of Indians* (n.d., 5: 1192–215). The authors of the brief argue that despite occasional hostilities during the period 1804–1805, the two peoples coexisted on generally peaceful terms.

[17] Bancroft (1889), 308–9.

Mexico's Pueblo Indians were invited to the party, though most of them would have enjoyed celebrating the end of Spanish rule. Since the coming of Coronado, save for a few significant intervals, they had borne the foreign yoke for 282 years!

After their encounter with Coronado at Hawikuh back in 1540, the Zuni Indians had followed a prudent and diplomatic course in their dealings with the foreign invaders. Living on the periphery of Spanish New Mexico, they generally avoided direct confrontations with their would-be conquerors. When it suited their purposes, the Zunis pledged allegiance to the Spanish crown and adopted those features of Spanish culture which appealed to them. With great vitality they had coped successfully with all who threatened them, and they had avoided civil war. Clearly, they were well prepared to survive the vicissitudes that were to be visited upon them during the next 150 years.

Chapter 6

The Americans Welcomed

Crosspiece of a Zuni ladder

If the Zuni Indians displayed regret when Spanish rule ended, it is not a matter of record. They, like the other Pueblos, had never fitted comfortably into the civil and ecclesiastical structure of the Spanish colonial system, and they were undoubtedly relieved when the Franciscan missionaries and the local political officials departed with the emergence of a sovereign Mexico. But whatever the Zunis may have thought of Spain, the Spaniards left an indelible mark on the pueblo.

The one local symbol of Spanish political authority had been the *alcalde mayor* appointed by the governor to serve the king and to look after the interests of the people resident in the local jurisdiction, or *alcaldía*. One such was the Alcaldía de Zuni, which in the late 1770s was bounded on the east by the "Sierra de Zuni" and the "Alcaldía de Laguna," and on the north by the frontier of the Navajo country. The *alcalde mayor* lived in Zuni, the only settlement in his jurisdiction. The names of a few of these officers have been preserved, but virtually no details of their rule have come to light. The king's rule at Zuni, on the frontier of the "very extremity of North America," we may conclude, was weak and ineffective.[1]

---

[1] Few matters touching the history of the Zuni people during the long Spanish colonial period are adequately documented. Thus in the records touching on affairs in the pueblo the *alcaldes mayores* are but shadowy figures appearing by name only here and there. One, José Lopez, held the office in 1700 (Bandelier, 1889, 164); Chávez (1957, 240) cites one in 1706 killed by Apaches; another in 1750 testified on the Apache danger (Hackett, ed. and trans., 1923–1937, 3: 436–37). Juan Pedro de Cisneros, *alcalde mayor* of Zuni, accompanied Domínguez and Escalante on their exploratory expedition in 1776; see Bolton, ed. and trans. (1950), and Adams and Chávez, eds. and trans. (1956, 286, 305). In a much-needed study on Spanish government in New Mexico, Simmons (1968, chap. 9) has examined the functions of the *alcaldes mayores* and other officials, as well as the general effects of

The impact of the missionaries was greater. When the Franciscans withdrew from Zuni and the church of Nuestra Señora de Guadalupe was abandoned, the Indians were left free to follow their own religious customs without any external restraints or interference. Although the pueblo thereafter was visited occasionally by a priest, the mission at Zuni was not reestablished for another hundred years. In that period the deeper values of the Catholic faith, insofar as they had taken root at all, were largely forgotten.[2] But the Zunis did not easily forget the crusade of the Spanish missionaries against their religion; for decades they distrusted anyone of Spanish ancestry. As late as the 1880s, and occasionally even later, Spanish-speaking Catholic visitors were prevented from viewing sacred ceremonials and dances.[3]

Yet the Zunis, a profoundly religious people, clung to certain features of the alien faith; if anything, the Spanish presence had enriched the ceremonial and religious life of the Indians. The mission church in their midst was cared for by

---

the reorganization of the viceregal frontier after 1776. Jenkins (1961, 53) writes that the office of "*alcalde mayor* was probably the weakest link in the Spanish government of New Mexico." The relationship between Spanish institutions and the emergence of Zuni civil government has been examined by Smith and Roberts (1954).

The boundaries of the *Alcaldía* of Zuni are precisely given on maps drawn by Bernardo de Miera, who lived at the pueblo for a time; see Adams and Chávez, eds. and trans. (1956, 2–3), and A. B. Thomas, ed. and trans. (1932, 87). The northern boundary, coterminous with the "Fronteras de la Provincia de Navajó," was set at about 35°30′ and the southern boundary at about 34°45′ north latitude; the western boundary is set at about 109°15′ west longitude.

[2] A history of the Franciscans in colonial New Mexico from the time of the Pueblo Revolt is needed. The order itself suffered several vicissitudes, as witness that period in the eighteenth century when the secular arm of the church — in this case the Bishop of Durango — asserted control over the Franciscan establishment of New Mexico. Visits by the bishops between 1730 and 1760 produced some noteworthy documents, that in 1760 by Bishop Tamarón among them. Bishop Martín de Elizacoechea came to New Mexico in 1737 and apparently was the only Durango prelate to visit the Zuni people. But little is known of this visitation. See Adams, ed. (1954, 1–33). Elizacoechea's name and the date 1737 appear as one of the inscriptions on El Morro. Slater (1961, 20, 113–14).

Bandelier (1889, 184) indicates that before the opening of the Mexican war of independence Zuni was without a resident missionary; priests from Acoma, Laguna, and Isleta administered to the pueblo on occasional visits. It is not clear that the Franciscans abandoned Zuni altogether in 1821; visitation by the regulars probably continued until they were replaced by the secular priests in the mid-1820's; see Bandelier (1889, 192–93). Smith (1970) and Spicer (1962, 198), however, say that abandonment was complete in 1821. Salpointe (1898) sketches the history of the church in New Mexico during the Mexican period.

[3] Cushing (1920, 535) makes a point of Zuni hostility toward the Mexican-Americans; see also Vogt and Albert, eds. (1966, 53–54).

them long after all priestly visits had ceased, and they even decorated the walls with their own religious symbols. The consecrated cemetery adjoining the church continued (and continues) to be their preferred burial place. Furthermore, the Indians preserved some of the Catholic sacred objects, the most significant of which was a small foot-high, enamel-coated wooden statue representing the Christ child.

This statue may well date back to the earliest Franciscan establishment at Zuni. In his inventory of mission property compiled in 1776, Father Atanasio Domínguez noted the presence of a "very old lacquer Child Jesus, vested as a priest, the clothing also old." In any case the Zunis had acquired a foot-high statue — the "Santu" — of the Christ child, one which today is venerated by them and also by regional Catholic Spanish-Americans who call it the "Santo Niño" and make it the object of pilgrimages. The Zunis have clothed the figure in a rich fabric of legend woven of Catholic and Indian threads, but, as with the church and cemetery, they have adopted the "Santu," or "Santo," and, unrestrained by considerations of historical origin, have made it essentially their own.[4]

---

[4] Matilda Coxe Stevenson (1904, 15), who first saw the church in 1879, is authority for the statement that the Zunis were "allowed" to decorate its walls with their own religious symbols. Oral tradition which supports the existence of such symbols — usually described as representations of the Shalako gods — persists today in the pueblo; see Cushing (1896, 332–41). That the "Santu," or "Santo Niño," is the statue described by Domínguez is suggested by Adams and Chávez, eds. and trans. (1956, 198). There is some indication that the statue was an object of veneration for the Zunis as early as the Pueblo Revolt; see Boas (1922, 97–98). Kirk (1940), Kelsey (1958), and particularly Parsons (1918b) point up the significance of the "Santo Niño" in contemporary Zuni life. See also Fergusson (1931) and Dickey (1970). The Duke Indian Oral History Collection at the University of Utah contains several accounts by Zunis (stories 226, 301) of the origin legends of the "Santo" who in Zuni legend is usually given the female sex. See Vogt and Albert, eds. (1966, 66, 323–24) for a Zuni origin myth. Kroeber (1917, 204) points up the "unhistorical" attitude of the Zunis and their "conservation of the present"; adaptations, therefore, easily become "integrally and inherently Zuni." This may account for the willingness of the Zunis to save the Catholic sacred objects in the Great Rebellion of 1680, objects which Vargas in 1692 found carefully stored on Corn Mountain. See Vogt and Albert, eds. (1966). Bandelier (1889, 185–92), whose Catholic bias frequently surfaces, refers to the church objects held by the Zunis as being "superstitiously preserved."
The Church at Zuni, recently restored, lacks the adjoining sacristy, baptistry, and convent found in the original complex. See Adams and Chávez, eds. and trans. (1956, 195–202) and Smith (1970, 12–18). Laton, ed. (1971), is a brief history containing an account of the restoration. As this book was written the north and south walls of the nave of the restored church were being decorated by the Zuni artist Alex Seowtewa with magnificent life-size figures of Zuni dancers. According to the publication issued by St. Anthony's Mission, this adornment signifies "the unity of the people and the old missions"; see Laton, ed. (1971).

In other ways the Spanish presence extended the dimensions of Zuni life. Before the "conquest" the Indians of Cíbola lived in six major villages, each more or less a separate entity. Conditions following the "Reconquest," namely the rise of hostile neighbors, forced consolidation upon the people, who found unity, cohesion, and cooperation easy and natural. In contrast to the Hopis, who, during the same period, exhibited genocidal and divisive tendencies, the Zunis formed one large pueblo at Halona, or Zuni, and their social order and tribal organization thereby became stronger. Their folklore was enriched by adaptations from Spanish sources. Even European views on sorcery and witchcraft were taken over by the Zunis and used by them to strengthen the social ideal of group rather than individual action; those accused of sorcery were usually people who had defied tradition and thus were threatening the sober, orderly processes of pueblo life.[5]

In material matters also, Spain left a permanent mark. The Indian economy was transformed, enlarged, and diversified through the introduction of new plants and animals and technological processes. The Zunis took to growing wheat, oats, chiles, onions, watermelons, and peaches. They raised sheep, goats, burros, cattle, and horses. Horses were widely used outside the village and far-reaching changes came with the introduction of sheep. Sheep served many purposes. They lent variety to the menu, supplied a valued textile, provided a trade item — and offered attractive booty to predatory neighbors! In 1760 Bishop Tamarón noted that the Zunis had "large flocks" and in 1779 Father Morfí, with confident exactness, reported that they then were ranging 15,736 head of these animals.[6]

A number of new materials — metals, textiles, and leather — and the tools for working them — axes, knives, and needles — as well as the crafts and tech-

---

[5] Parsons (1918a, 1918b), Boas (1922), and Boas and Parsons (1920) contain Zuni folk tales derived in part from Spanish sources.

The place of witchcraft, or sorcery, in Zuni culture has been described by M. C. Stevenson (1904, 392–406), among others. See Benedict (1969) for a sampling of Zuni folklore. Accusation and punishment for sorcery and witchcraft as a means of social control has been examined by Parsons (1916), Adair (1948, chap. 2), and Goldman (1937), who avers that the *practice* of the black arts and magical techniques does not exist. Parsons (1927) believes that Zuni witchcraft customs were affected by Spanish belief.

[6] For the place of native and foreign grains in the life of the Zunis see Cushing (1920). Bishop Tamarón's and Father Morfi's reports have been edited by Adams (1954, 68) and A. B. Thomas, ed. and trans. (1932, 106), respectively. Domínguez in 1776 (Adams and Chávez, eds. and trans., 1956, 195–202) mentions the farmlands on all sides of the pueblo but says nothing about sheep.

niques for fabricating products, and the corresponding manual arts, gradually crept into Pueblo life and accordingly changed it. After the Great Rebellion, the overall industrial growth of the Pueblos gained momentum.

Traditionally conservative in dealing with matters foreign to them, the Zunis were perhaps slower to accept new ways than the Pueblos of the Rio Grande.[7]

Spain may have opened new doors to the world for the Zuni people, but in the Zuni social makeup there was very little innate sympathy for the alien Europeans themselves. During the entire colonial period only a few Spaniards had entered into the life of the pueblo. In 1799, seven were living among 2716 Zunis. Statistics are lacking, but it is reasonable to assume that the mixed or *mestizo* population resulting from unions between the two peoples must have been small. In any event, we may venture the opinion that it would not have been long before the mixed bloods would have emerged as fully acculturated Zunis.[8]

The Spanish *entradas* from Coronado to Anza had disturbed the equilibrium of the tribes, throwing them either into alliance or into conflict with one another. One result was a certain amount of fraternization and intermarriage between Indians of diverse origin and culture. Zuni received very small quotas of immigrants from neighboring tribes, most of them after the Great Rebellion when the Navajos and Apaches pressed hard on the Pueblo. Possibly more alien Indians than Spaniards moved in with the Zunis but the number was probably very small. And, like the Mexican Indians left at Cíbola by Coronado, they must soon have lost their identity in the Zuni melting pot.[9]

---

[7] Dozier (1970, 65–71) comments on the many material and non-material introductions from Spain and the changes which these made in the Pueblo world. Cushing (1896, 339–41) pointed out that material additions introduced by Spain did not greatly change the lifeway of the Zunis. Cushing's article (1894) on primitive copper working is illustrated with some references to the Zuni Indians.

[8] Statistics for Zuni during the Spanish period are scarce and of questionable reliability. Bancroft (1889, 279–82), from various sources, has assembled population and other statistics for Zuni and the other pueblos. Bloom (1913–1915, vol. 2) cites a report dated December 31, 1821, compiled by the Franciscan Custodian of New Mexico, listing 1597 residents in Zuni — 803 women and 794 men. No minister was then living in the pueblo, nor Spaniards, nor "people of other classes." Ward (1868, 213), after consulting "Spanish authorities," tabulates Zuni's population as follows: 1935 in 1790, 1557 in 1808, 1598 in 1809. Using statistics compiled by the American government, he finds the population to be 1500 in 1850, 1300 in 1830, and (his own estimate) 1200 in 1864.

[9] Adequate reference for Indian immigration to Zuni would make a very short note. There is only incidental reference to Navajos (less to Apaches) in the literature of the colonial period. With respect to the Navajos a good sampling of specific references will be

During the period of Mexico's rule over the area, 1821–1846, few changes occurred in the Zuni pattern of life. Spanish civil and ecclesiastical authority, already diminishing before the Mexicans won their independence, practically disappeared. The elaborate system of alliances with the tribes and the frontier defenses so laboriously erected by Spain during the 1770s broke down under the Mexican regime. Apache bands bent on looting, raiding, and slave trading turned south into Chihuahua and Sonora, while an open raiding war developed between the Navajos and the Mexican settlements along the Rio Grande.

The Zunis, in a troubled, dangerous time, played an astute diplomatic game and managed to maintain something of a neutral position between the warring parties, though they hit back when attacked by marauding neighbors. Given their isolated position and the hostile stance of the Apaches and Navajos, it is remarkable that the Zunis (and the other western Pueblos) survived these perilous times. But, fortunately, their Indian enemies never attempted conquest. Why destroy a people who could be counted upon as a ready source for sheep and other livestock, fruit and corn, and even slaves?[10]

During the 1820s a people new to the Zunis appeared in the pueblo: Americans. The forerunners were fur men, on their way from Taos and Santa Fe to trap the Gila River and the valley of the lower Colorado. In the few short years since 1776, the United States had grown as rapidly in the east as Spain had declined in the west. Westering Americans crossed the Appalachians and then crossed the Mississippi into the lands of the Louisiana Purchase. When Mexico

---

found in U.S. Indian Claims Commission, *The Navajo Tribe of Indians* (n.d., 1192–215). Bandelier (1889, 168–70) found some indication that, during the time of troubles between the Zunis and Hopis after 1700, there was a substantial *emigration* to the Hopi towns. In 1780 Anza found the Zuni Pueblo seriously reduced in numbers owing to a bad drought of two years. A large number of the Zunis, he reported, were living in "our interior pueblos"; see A. B. Thomas, ed. and trans. (1932, 230). Brugge (1969) has pointed out that alliances and alignments between the Zunis and other Indians were sometimes the product of intra-tribal factionalism.

[10] Specific references to Zuni–Navajo–Apache–Mexican conflicts and alliances are given in U.S. Indian Claims Commission, *The Navajo Tribe of Indians* (n.d., 1195–99). M. C. Stevenson (1904, 61) cites an incident in which the Zunis clubbed to death a number of Navajos in retaliation for previous brutalities. See Underhill (1956, chaps. 6–7).

In the Duke Indian Oral History collection at the University of Utah there are a number of stories recounted by the Zunis of raids and kidnappings by both Apaches and Navajos. The extent of Apache–Zuni contact is indicated by Goodwin (1969, 76–108), who also used oral sources. Much of the Indian–white warfare during the Mexican period involved the capture of slaves. The Navajos were the heaviest sufferers. See Bailey (1966) and Brugge (1968), as well as stories by the Zunis themselves in Quam, trans. (1972).

emerged from the ruins of the Spanish empire and all barriers to trade were dropped, the Americans were ready to grasp their opportunity. Even as Mexico achieved independence the first traders reached Santa Fe.

The trappers followed the traders. Fanning out from the Mexican towns along the Rio Grande they found good beaver to the north and west, in the central Rockies, and southwest along the Gila. Some of the mountain men en route to the Gila stopped off at the Zuni Pueblo. Here they found a friendly people, readily available supplies, and Indians who usually knew the whereabouts of unfriendly tribes in the country ahead. Then, returning from the lower Colorado or from several points in California, the trappers usually struck out for the friendly pueblo on the Zuni River. For one thing, after weeks of hardship and scanty rations in the wilderness, it was good to think of sitting down to mutton stew, beans, chiles, corn, and home-baked bread, comfortably served indoors on a hard, dry floor.

During the great years of the trade, numbers of fur men enjoyed Zuni hospitality. Mexican authorities reported that an early party of twelve Americans reached the pueblo in October 1826. During the next five or six years such worthies as Richard Campbell, William Workman, George Yount, Ewing Young, and Kit Carson passed through the pueblo.[11]

The trappers were transients, restless men of action. Few of those who stopped off at Zuni wrote anything at all about their hosts; probably most of them were illiterate. George C. Yount, who told his story to a friend years later, is one of the few who have left us any details. Yount's party after many hardships traveling eastward from California reached the "Nation of the Sunies," more dead than alive. "These kind and humane people," Yount remembered, took pity on the famished trappers and served them a small but nourishing meal. Some of the men ignored Chief "Philepa's" advice to eat slowly and four of them were dead within twenty-four hours. Yount was more prudent and he dreamed all that night of "feasting and felicity."

George C. Yount never forgot the "Sunies" and it was with regret that he predicted their demise. This "very good people," he told his biographer, had been "corrupted by the Spaniards" and later by "American adventurers," and

---

[11] Weber's work (1971), summarizing the fur trade of the Southwest, fills in a number of gaps left by Cleland (1952). Kit Carson, one of Ewing Young's party of forty American, Canadian, and French trappers, visited Zuni in August or September 1829. See his autobiography edited by Quaife (1966, 9).

this could only lead to "utter annihilation," a fate they would share with other American Indians.

When it came to the Zunis, Yount was overly pessimistic. He probably didn't realize when he dictated his memoirs in 1855 that the Pueblos had known and lived near the "corrupting" Spaniards for over three hundred years and still had managed to preserve their cultural identity and even to have gained something from the aliens. Perhaps thinking of the "American adventurers," Yount mentioned seeing some persons in the pueblo of "sandy complexion." This may be the first record of the Zuni albinos—not of the offspring of mixed marriages![12]

In their wanderings southwest and west of Zuni, the American trappers opened some practical routes leading from the Rio Grande to the Rio Colorado and on to southern California, but the hostile Navajos and Apaches made travel dangerous in that region. As a consequence, New Mexican traders in the 1830s, finding a good market for woolen goods in California, opened a caravan route northwest from Santa Fe through the Utah wilderness to the Great Basin and thence southwest across the Mojave Desert to Los Angeles. Known later as the "Old Spanish Trail," the route was a long twelve hundred miles, but it was fairly safe, though difficult, to travel. Until 1848 it was the main thoroughfare between Santa Fe and Los Angeles.[13]

By the early 1830s the fur trade along the Gila was all but finished, and after the opening of the Old Spanish Trail few travelers from New Mexico chose to take the southern route to California. To the Zunis this meant that after Ewing Young's large party left the pueblo in 1839, the trickle of visitors dried up, and for nearly twenty years the peace of the village was seldom broken by the coming of outsiders.

The Zuni Indians were touched but lightly by war between Mexico and the United States. The American invading forces, commanded by Col. Stephen W. Kearney, occupied New Mexico without resistance, but they quickly found themselves facing the same defensive problems that had plagued the Mexican governors. For the most part, the Rio Grande Pueblos welcomed the new foreigners,

---

[12] George C. Yount's narrative was edited by Camp (1966). Albinos, noted by a number of visitors since Yount's day, are still to be seen in Zuni. As do a number of other references cited elsewhere in this work, the writer of "A Visit to Zuni" (1864) comments at length on them. Beale (1858, 38) mentions albinos with "blue eyes."

[13] The opening of the Old Spanish Trail, which deflected overland travel from following a more direct route between Mexican New Mexico and Mexican California, has been told by the Hafens (1954).

but the outlying tribes were less hospitable, especially the Navajos, who responded with raids when the Americans invited them to treat and make peace.[14]

Determined to force the issue, Kearney sent Alexander W. Doniphan with a large troop to meet the Navajos in their own country. Doniphan headed west from Albuquerque while a detachment under Maj. William Gilpin swung north to the San Juan River. They planned a rendezvous at Ojo del Oso, or Bear Spring (where Fort Wingate was later built), a watering place on the northern slopes of the Zuni Mountains well known to Navajos, Zunis, and Mexicans, if not to the Americans. Indians met en route were invited to a general council at the spring.

The Navajos were interested in meeting these new aliens who had so easily defeated the common enemy, the Mexicans. Some five hundred mounted Navajos, including most of the chiefs and headmen, showed up at the council, outnumbering Doniphan's command of 330 officers and men. Speech-making and oratory followed for a day. The Navajos, professing some admiration for the Americans, were puzzled that the newcomers should interfere with *their* war against the Mexicans. Doniphan told them that the United States claimed New Mexico by right of conquest and he expected peace among all parties to settle upon the province, a peace to be enforced if necessary. On Sunday, November 22, 1846, a treaty of "lasting peace and amity" between the Navajos and the "American people" (this term included the Mexican and Pueblo population of New Mexico) was signed by fourteen Navajo chiefs and three of the American officers present. Undoubtedly the Indians were more impressed by the troop strength than the diplomacy, and they signed as a matter of expediency.

Knowing that the Zunis had long been harassed by the encroachment of the Navajos, Doniphan with Gilpin's detachment, accompanied by three Navajo chiefs, now traveled to Zuni to attempt to work out a peace between the two enemies. Although they probably resented such meddling, the Zunis assumed a friendly attitude and received the Americans into the pueblo, but they were ready to kill the Navajos when they saw them. While the bluecoats watched, the

---

[14] The history of the American war with Mexico and the conquest of New Mexico is to be found in many books about the West, the Southwest, and each of the several states. H. H. Bancroft's histories (used by so many, cited by so few) of Texas, California, Arizona, and New Mexico are always useful (I have used and cited only his *History of Arizona and New Mexico*, 1889). Hollon (1961), Lamar (1966), and Perrigo (1971) set the matter in regional perspective. Twitchell (1911–1915, vol. 2) and Keleher (1952) provide an abundance of local detail.

enemies made fiery speeches and tongue-lashed each other. Some two hundred angry Zunis listened while the Navajos acknowledged they had suffered many casualties in their guerilla "war." But they went on to boast that they had "out-stolen" the Zunis; they accused the Zunis of killing women and children while the Navajos merely enslaved their captives. These bravados must have enraged the Zunis but Doniphan managed somehow to bring the parties together on November twenty-sixth when (as Doniphan's biographer has it) "after much debate" they "consummated a treaty of peace and amity."[15]

The Americans were much impressed with the Zunis. Lt. John T. Hughes, chronicler of Doniphan's expedition, noted that the Zunis were well known for their "intelligence and ingenuity in the manufacture of cotton and woolen fabrics." And he added that they "had long been celebrated for their honesty and hospitality." Indeed the Indians, despite the strained circumstances of the occasion, supplied the soldiers with provisions and with "various fruits in which the country abounds."

A detachment of sixty soldiers visiting Zuni almost a month earlier had been treated equally well. Hungry and cold, the men were housed and given dinner in the homes of several different families. Marcellus Edwards with a "good, keen appetite" enjoyed a meal of mutton stew with vegetables and wafer bread. "It was the best dinner I had ever sat down to," he wrote in his diary. Moreover, as the soldiers walked about town and visited other homes they were offered more food; to refuse was to risk insult. And the Zunis gave the troops enough provisions to carry them back to the base camp. Private Edwards warmed to his hosts. "They have the reputation of being the most hospitable people in the world, which I believe they merit in every respect," he wrote. And not a single article had been stolen from the soldiers. Where else, Edwards asked, "can such a mass of honest people be found?"

---

[15] Doniphan's part in the Mexican War, including details of treaty-making with the Navajos and Zunis, was published by eye-witness Hughes (1848). The Hughes account with some additional material was reprinted by Connelley (1907). Interpreters of the treaty-making with the Navajos are Coolidge and Coolidge (1930), Underhill (1956, chap. 8), and McNitt, ed. (1964, xxiv–xxix). Hughes (1848, 192–97) gives us interesting details of the treaty-making at Zuni; particulars of the treaty itself are not disclosed. In the Hodge–Cushing papers there is a copy of a treaty of amity of July 1, 1848, signed by the governor of Zuni and by W. P. Bogutin for the U.S. Army, in which the Indians are to be protected in their rights of "private property and religion." Both parties agreed "to be and remain good friends forever."

To the soldiers of Kearney's "Army of the West" (most of whom were from frontier Missouri), the pueblo itself was an amazing sight. Edwards commented on the layout of the town: "Divided into four parts by two streets that cross each other at right angles in the center, or public square"; he found that each quarter was "a perfect block of buildings," some houses being five stories high; the rooms, he observed, were small "but very neat and clean and whitewashed."

"Zuni," wrote John Hughes, was "one of the most extraordinary cities in the world." It was, he said, "a city built after the manner of the ancient Aztecs" and "perhaps the only one now known resembling those of the ancient Mexicans." [16] Romantic notions about the migrations of the Aztecs stirred the imaginations of many Americans of that day. In 1843 William H. Prescott had brought out his popular *History of the Conquest of Mexico*, the first part of which contained a lengthy description of the opulent civilization of the Aztecs. In an appendix he discussed the evidence of their origins. Aztec tradition, Prescott reminded his readers, pointed to an original home somewhere north of Mexico City, in the heart of the continent; it was the same tradition that had quickened the imaginations of Fray Marcos and Coronado.

Prescott noted that the "antiquaries have industriously sought" some traces of the Aztec migrations and he indicated that ruins along the Gila River, discovered by the Spaniards in the eighteenth century, were "quite worthy of the Aztecs in their style of architecture." This suggestion had been made more than thirty years earlier by the renowned German scientist Alexander von Humboldt. Writing in his *New Spain* (1811) about the pueblos of New Mexico, Humboldt said that "Everything in these countries appears to announce traces of the cultivation of the ancient Mexicans." Then he went on to say that, according to "Indian traditions," the first stopping place of the migratory Aztecs was located on the San Juan River, north of the Hopi villages, and he fixed the spot on the

---

[16] On October 30–31, 1846, a detachment of some sixty troops, chasing Navajo horse thieves, visited the Zuni Pueblo. The main command, stationed near Cubero, later joined Doniphan and went on with him to conclude the treaties with the Navajos and Zunis. Pvt. Marcellus Ball Edwards, whose journal is cited here, visited Zuni in October but did not accompany Doniphan's main command when the treaties were made. See Bieber, ed. (1936, 20–44, 189–208). Edwards has some interesting details concerning the town criers, breadmaking, and the ruins at Pescado. See Hughes (1848, 194–95) for his views concerning the Aztecs. Jacob Robinson said (Cannon, ed., 1932, 42) that one of the party of sixty stayed behind at Zuni because of illness and was treated very well.

map accompanying his book. Since his map was copied by a number of American cartographers, among them Henry Tanner, the Aztec myth was widely
circulated.[17]

The Aztec "tradition" in the Southwest was strengthened by Josiah Gregg
in his *Commerce of the Prairies*, the classic account of the Santa Fe trade published in 1844. Although his main theme was the overland trade between the
United States and Mexico, Gregg packed into his book a great deal of material
on animal life, weather, and the dress and customs of the Mexican-Americans,
as well as two chapters on the Indians of New Mexico. Most of the Pueblos,
Gregg asserted, "call themselves the descendants of Montezuma," which was
certainly stretching the truth. *The Commerce of the Prairies*, like Prescott's
Conquest of Mexico, was a best seller.[18]

Many Americans who followed news of the course of the war with Mexico
were intrigued by the reports of strange sights seen by the soldiers in the field.
Accounts of the ruins of communities of prehistoric peoples, of rock and adobe
walls still standing, of artifacts and petroglyphs, were of particular interest, and
many found an analogy between the walls and halls of Montezuma's Tenochti-
tlán and those of the abandoned historic and prehistoric towns of the Southwest.
What of the possibility of finding some of the living descendants of Montezuma's
people?

Lieutenant Hughes of Doniphan's expedition thought the Zunis might
qualify: "The discovery of this city of the Zunians will afford the most curious

---

[17] William H. Prescott's *History of the Conquest of Mexico*, first published in 1843,
enjoyed a wide sale and passed through several editions. I have consulted an edition of 1892.
Prescott's essay on the origin of Mexican civilization forms an appendix to the *History*;
see p. 590 for his reference to the ruins on the Gila.

Humboldt's great work on New Spain (1811) did much to make known the extent of
Spanish discoveries in North America, the reports of many of which had remained in manu-
script form in the archives. Humboldt, as a scientist, was permitted use of the archives in
Mexico. His reference to the migratory Aztecs appears in vol. 2, p. 315; on the accompanying
map Humboldt locates (caption in French) the "first stopping place of the Aztecs after their
departure from Aztlán in 1160." On the "Map of North America" published in his *New
American Atlas* (1823), the influential H. S. Tanner placed the "former residence of the
Aztecs" precisely where Humboldt had located it. In my *Standing Up Country*, chap. 3,
I have touched on the importance of Humboldt's work on the history of the exploration of
the Colorado Plateau.

[18] Gregg's *Commerce of the Prairies*, first published in 1844, passed through several
editions; I have used the most recent one, edited by Moorhead (1954); chap. 14 contains
Gregg's discussion of the Pueblos and his statement, based mainly on assumption, that these
town dwellers were related to the Aztecs.

speculations among those who have so long searched in vain for a city of Indians, who possessed the manners and habits of the Aztecs." At least, he added, there was "no doubt" that the life of the Zunis in 1846 was just like that of the Aztecs when Cortés arrived in Mexico. Major Gilpin, who was with Doniphan at Zuni, was convinced that his hosts were "one of the last specks of the antique Aztec race." This idea endured. Even as late as 1870 William Bell was willing to assert that the Zuni Pueblo at one time was the capital of the Aztec kingdom of Cevola (Cíbola)! During the centuries since Coronado's time the synonymy of Cíbola and Zuni appears to have been lost. Thus some American army officers in New Mexico actually sought the Seven Cities of Cíbola apparently without associating them with the Zunis who had abandoned all but one of their towns following the Pueblo Revolt.[19]

The finding of several albinos among the Zunis led some observers to see in this phenomenon reason to believe that Europeans before Columbus had not only reached the coasts of America but had traveled to the interior to settle

---

[19] Hughes (1848, 196). The quotation from Gilpin is from a speech given in 1847, as he recorded it in Connelley, ed. (1907, 594). Bell (1870, pt. 2, chap. 5, pp. 224–26) imagined that the Aztecs moved north from Mexico to build the pueblos of the Southwest. The Pueblos, he writes, "were the skirmish line of the Aztec race." These people, "having established the kingdom of Cevola, of which Zuñi was the capital, and several other clusters of towns . . . ," pushed on northward. Some of this material may have come from Abert's (1848) report. While Doniphan was in the Navajo and Zuni country, Lt. J. W. Abert was exploring some of the ruined and modern pueblos on both sides of the Rio Grande. Abert first checked into the Spanish authorities — Solís, Venegas, and Clavigero — and then concluded, after exploring the region, that the pueblos of Acoma and Laguna, together with some of the nearby villages, must have been the kingdom of "Cibolo." See Abert (1848, 489–92), who finds in architecture alone strong "proof of the common origin of the New Mexicans and Aztecs." Squier (1848) wrote a learned article placing the reports of the American Army officers in the perspective of history. He reminded his readers that the ruins of the Southwest had been seen first by Europeans fifteen years after the fall of Mexico. Whipple on his railroad survey in 1853 (Foreman, ed., 1941, 149) correctly identified Coronado's Cíbola with Zuni. The matter was quieted and pretty well stabilized by Simpson (1872). Goetzmann (1959, chap. 4) reviews the exploration of the army's topographical engineers during the Mexican War.

Although Susan Wallace in her fanciful book (1888, 133) claimed that the Zunis ("the sons of Montezuma, as they love to call themselves") until recently had kept the "Montezuma fire" burning on Corn Mountain, it would appear that by 1890 most observers of the Pueblos were willing to let the Aztec business die. Special agents of the U.S. Census Office working that year in Arizona and New Mexico were instructed to look out for any living traces of the "Montezuma Legend." They reported that "neither sacred fires nor Montezuma hunters or watchers" were found at Zuni or any of the other pueblos; see U.S. Census Office (1894, 164). It would be interesting to know if the three Nahuatl-speaking Aztecs left at Zuni by Coronado contributed anything toward the creation of the Aztec legend in Zuni or the Southwest.

among the Pueblos. Both Hughes and Gilpin of Doniphan's command commented on the albinos. Hughes thought it was they who had given rise to the story that somewhere in the Rocky Mountains there lived a "tribe of white aborigines."

And it was not long after the United States acquired New Mexico before the Zunis were identified with the Welsh-speaking "Indians." One of the more persistent and popular myths of pre-Columbian discovery tells how in the twelfth century a colony was planted in America by Prince Madoc of Wales. The colony was never found by later arrivals from Europe but the colonists' descendants, usually identified as Indians with Welsh accents, popped up in a number of places as the Americans moved westward into the continent.[20]

The Americans, apparently, were quite as capable as the Spaniards of dreaming about fabulous places in the West. National attention was focused on the Zunis — whose ancestors had lived in Coronado's Seven Cities of Cíbola! — thanks to the reports of the first army officers who visited the pueblo early in the Mexican war. During the next thirty years or so many westering Americans stopped off at Zuni for rest and refreshment before setting off into the wilderness ahead, to see for themselves the village and its people. They found that the Zunis were no less hospitable and friendly than they had been to most Spanish visitors but that they spoke neither Nahuatl, the language of the Aztecs, nor Welsh.[21]

---

[20] Hughes (1848, 195) refers to "some thirty albinos" resident in Zuni. Gilpin (Connelley, ed., 1907, 594) speaks of the Zunis: "This people, many of them albinos. . . ." Ten Broeck (1854, 80–81) visited the Zunis in 1851 or 1852 and reported that they are "supposed by some" to be descended from the Welsh colony founded by Prince Madoc. This indeed, as Morison (1971, 84) states, is one of the most persistent stories of pre-Columbian travel to America. "Welsh Indians" have been located here and there in North America at different times since the 1580s. There is abundant literature on the subject. See Morison's bibliography, pp. 106–10.

[21] In the Hodge–Cushing papers in the Southwest Museum there are numerous testimonials to Zuni hospitality and friendship for the United States. These date from 1859 to 1891 and include such names as E. F. Beale, William Redwood Price, W. F. M. Arny, George M. Wheeler, W. T. Sherman, Frank H. Cushing, and John C. Bourke.

Zuni River and silhouette of Towayalane.
Photographed in 1911 by Jesse L. Nusbaum.

The Zuni sky. Summer rain over the
distant pueblo (left) and Towayalane.

C. Gregory Crampton

A summer farmhouse at the eastern base
of Towayalane.

C. Gregory Crampton

Pueblo center of modern Zuni.

C. Gregory Crampton

A corner of an excavated room at the Village
of the Great Kivas.

C. Gregory Crampton

C. Gregory Crampton

A modern Zuni woman in traditional dress.

The Zuni salt lake. The Spaniards who visited
the site in 1598 were much impressed with the excellent
quality of the salt. They reported the lake
a "marvelous thing."

C. Gregory Crampton

The land of Cíbola as the Spaniards first saw it.
Looking from the site of Kechipbowa toward the site
of Hawikuh in the distance.

C. Gregory Crampton

Once, according to legend, the Zunis were forced by
a great flood to seek refuge on Towayalane. As the waters
rose to the very rim of the mesa, the people were saved by the
courage of two children who walked into the menacing sea.
The waters then began to recede and the sacrificial
victims appeared in the form of two stone monoliths visible
on the western side of Towayalane.

C. Gregory Crampton

C. Gregory Crampton

El Morro. From Oñate's day on, travelers
heading west toward Zuni and points beyond
stopped near the great Inscription Rock for water
and rest. Many recorded their names in stone.

Diego de Vargas recorded on El Morro his reconquest of New Mexico
in 1692. Photographer unknown.

This legend reveals that Martin de Elizacoechea (spelled "Elizacochea"
on the rock), Bishop of Durango, visited Zuni in 1737.
Photograph made about 1889 by Ben Wittick.

Looking toward Towayalane. Zuni Pueblo as it
appeared in 1879. Photograph by John K. Hillers.

One of the first suburban houses of Zuni.
Photograph made by John K. Hillers about 1879.

The mission church as it appeared in 1879.
Photograph by John K. Hillers. The restored
mission church is shown on page 94.

Cushing and his Indian escorts in Boston in 1882.
Left to right: Laiiuahtsailunkia, Naiiutchi,
Frank H. Cushing, Palowahtiwa, Kiasi, and Nanake.
Laiiuaitsailu is missing. Photograph by
James Wallace Black.

Pedro Pino, or Laiiuaitsailu, served as governor
from about 1840 to 1875. The two portraits were made
in 1879 by John K. Hillers.

Patricio Pino, or Palowahtiwa, son of Laiiuaitsailu,
was governor from 1875 to 1886. Both men followed
a diplomatic course in guiding the relations
of their tribe with other peoples.

The Zuni Pueblo about 1900. Photographed by
Adam Clark Vroman.

The turquoise-driller. Photographed in 1899
by Adam Clark Vroman.

A gift for design and the use of natural materials
is reflected in the interior of this Zuni home.
Photographed by Adam Clark Vroman about 1900.

The farming village of Ojo Caliente.
Photograph made in 1899 by Adam Clark Vroman.

C. Gregory Crampton

The farming village of Pescado.

An abandoned stone farmhouse at Upper Nutria.

C. Gregory Crampton

Stone houses at the farming village of Lower Nutria.

C. Gregory Crampton

Ovens at Upper Nutria.

C. Gregory Crampton

The restored mission church.

Old and new in the heart of the Zuni Pueblo.

C. Gregory Crampton

The look of the future.

Chapter 7

Zuni Revealed

Trapdoor frame of a Zuni kiva

Although the reports of military explorers brought the Zunis before the reading public, these Indians, unlike the Rio Grande Pueblos, saw comparatively few Americans until the coming of the railroad in the early 1880s. While many of those caught up in the gold rush to California came into the Southwest by the Santa Fe Trail, most of them went on to the golden shores by southern routes through the Gila River Valley opened during the Mexican War. Travelers who might have chosen a more direct route westward from Santa Fe and Albuquerque over the Continental Divide to California were discouraged from doing so by both the Navajo Indians and the Apaches ranging to the south of them. The barrier made by the Navajos was maintained until 1864, when most of the Navajos had to capitulate to the military power of the United States and, in the end, agree to exile. To the south, the Apaches were able to hold out much longer.

The Doniphan treaties had little effect on the Navajos; they continued to raid the Rio Grande towns and settlements — and the Zuni pueblo.[1] In the summer of 1849, according to James S. Calhoun, the first federal Indian agent assigned to New Mexico, the Indians of the territory were in "bad temper." Gold rushers were streaming through the Rio Grande Valley; some of them, seeking a short cut to the gold fields, turned west from Albuquerque and

---

[1] In 1880 Doniphan claimed this 1846 treaty between the Navajos and Zunis had done much to create good will between the latter and the Americans (Connelley, ed., 1907, 588), but warfare between the two tribes after 1846 and until 1868 was probably as intense as it had ever been (U.S. Indian Claims Commission, *The Navajo Tribe of Indians*, n.d., 5: 1199–1212). "Pino correspondence" in the Hodge–Cushing papers, Southwest Museum, contains a number of letters, reports, and treaties, reflecting Zuni–Navajo conflict as well as Zuni activity in support of the United States.

traveled by way of Laguna and Zuni. Determined to break the Navajo power in the west which threatened both settlements and travelers, New Mexico's military governor Lt. Col. John M. Washington put together a large command and in mid-August headed for the Indians' stronghold in the Chuska Mountains.

En route Washington passed by the prehistoric ruins in Chaco Canyon, described in detail by Lt. James H. Simpson of the Topographical Engineers. Simpson, who had read Humboldt, Prescott, and Gregg, hypothesized an Aztec origin for those magnificent ruins.[2]

Washington, upon reaching the Chuskas, held a council with the Navajos. Impressed with the military power confronting them, the Indians signed a treaty of peace and agreed to assemble at a later date in Canyon de Chelly where a general council for the entire tribe would be held. Then there occurred an unfortunate incident involving a stolen horse, and the council broke up in bloodshed when the United States troops opened fire on the Indians, killing one Navajo and mortally wounding six others. It was a tragic beginning to the relations between the two peoples; peace (despite a number of treaties signed subsequently) was delayed for fifteen years.

Washington marched on, scorching the earth as he went, to Canyon de Chelly where another treaty was signed by two local chiefs who promised to convene a general peace meeting. But nothing was done; the promises made by both sides were forgotten. The Navajos kept on raiding the white settlements — and the Pueblos. (One American response to these activities was the subsequent founding of Fort Defiance in 1851, at a point deep in the Navajo country and at an almost equal distance from the Hopi villages to the west and the Zuni pueblo to the south.)[3]

---

[2] Simpson's journal of the 1849 expedition (1850) is one of the classics of Southwestern exploration. I have used the splendid edition of Frank McNitt (1964) whose editorial material and annotations equal Simpson's journal in number of pages. McNitt, however, reproduces only a few of the numerous illustrations and the map is reproduced on a greatly reduced scale. Simpson was familiar with the literature, including that of his army contemporaries, in which appeared the theories ascribing an Aztec origin to Southwestern monuments. See his discussion in McNitt, ed. (1964, 53–56).

[3] See Simpson's journal (McNitt, ed., 1964) for details of Washington's punitive expedition which had been designed to impress the Navajos with the power of the United States. McNitt, ed. (1964, 163), holds that the "campaign was a failure"; certainly it did not bring lasting peace. One problem of course — and United States negotiators were slow to see it — was that the Navajos of that time acknowledged no single chief or head, and the word of one chief was not regarded as binding on the others. See also Underhill (1956, chap. 8). Brandes (1960, 29–32) has details on the founding of Fort Defiance.

Having heard that the Zuni Indians recently had been attacked by the Apaches, Washington, on his return journey to Santa Fe, visited the pueblo to investigate. On September fifteenth the command approached Zuni from the north, passing to the west of the Zuni Buttes and following an easy trail down Bosson Wash. Simpson, whose journal is filled with precious detail, noted that in the clear air the pueblo was visible three miles away, appearing to be only a "low ridge of brownish rocks." Presently a party headed by Pedro Pino, governor of the pueblo, came out to escort Washington and his staff into the village. Before they reached the outskirts, Simpson records, men and boys poured out of the village to welcome the troops with a sham fight. This was an indication of "gratification," Calhoun reported, which they showed in the "most uproarious, wild and undescribable manner." Washington's party was then taken to the governor's house where the members were offered melons, peaches, and three kinds of bread, all of which, Calhoun writes, were "becomingly received." [4]

Simpson described the pueblo as it appeared in 1849. The terraced houses, some built over narrow streets, which thus caused the streets to resemble tunnels, appealed to him; it was, he thought, the "best-built and neatest-looking pueblo" he had seen, though the "ragged picketed sheep and the goat pens" detracted somewhat from the view. The Church of Nuestra Señora de Guadalupe he found bare of any sacred furnishings save two statues and a "miserable painting" of the Virgin of Guadalupe.

Simpson noted the large herds of sheep and horses and the extensive cultivation of the soil. The Indians sold nothing for money but exchanged goods by barter, and they were, as some of Washington's troops discovered, pretty close traders. The Zunis resembled the other Pueblos in their habits and dress but the engineer said somewhat loftily that they had progressed further in the "arts of civilization" than any Indians he had known.

Governor Pedro Pino responded to many questions asked by the visitors. He was "a very interesting man," wrote Simpson, "about six feet high, athletic in

---

[4] J. H. Simpson's journal (1850, and the McNitt edition, 1964) is the best account of Washington's campaign, including the Zuni visit, but J. S. Calhoun, New Mexico's first Indian agent, went along and wrote a short account (1850, 202–10), as did Colonel Washington (1849). The extensive New Mexico correspondence of Calhoun, a dedicated public servant, has been edited by Abel (1915); Calhoun was appointed the first civilian governor of the territory in March 1851. He died en route east in 1852. The complexities of Indian affairs and administration during the first years of American rule in New Mexico are nowhere better illustrated than in Calhoun's extensive correspondence. Dale's (1949) book reviews a century of federal relations with the Southwestern tribes.

structure, uncommonly graceful and energetic in action, fluent in language, and intelligent." The Apaches had not attacked, the governor said, but the Navajos were a constant menace; he probably requested military assistance to protect the pueblo from these raiders.

The governor regaled his audience with accounts of the origins of his people, pointing out that the Zunis had once lived on top of Corn Mountain, east of the village, where the ruins of ancient structures might still be seen. Simpson, who had read Hughes' *Doniphan's Expedition* (Zuni may be the only pueblo "now resembling those of the ancient Aztecs," Hughes had said), probably pumped the governor on the matter of origins. Yes, Pino had seen the ruins in Chaco Canyon, but he knew nothing about them.

Simpson could find little among the Zunis to differentiate them from the other Pueblos. Their language differed, yes. But if the Pueblos spoke different languages, how could they all be descended from the same stock? Simpson was in doubt about Aztec origins. He wondered, "Is there any *satisfactory* basis of hypothecation, that any of them are descended from that remarkable people?" [5]

Staying at Zuni but one night, Washington's command moved out on September sixteenth and in ten days reached Santa Fe. In the first three days after leaving the pueblo, Lt. James H. Simpson, with great profit to history, engaged in a number of explorations. He started to climb Corn Mountain to see the ruins of "Old Zuni" that Pino had mentioned the night before but unfortunately did not allow enough time for it; he visited and described the ruins and Zuni farmlands along the Rio Pescado; he visited, described, and transcribed many of the names on Inscription Rock.

As for the Zuni Indians, Simpson's description, though brief, was one of the best yet written. He was a good observer and put down what he saw without engaging in fanciful speculations. Even the Aztec fantasy, which so much interested him and his contemporaries, was fading from his mind by the time he left

---

[5] Simpson's 1849 journal as edited by McNitt (1964, 110–21) has been used here. Simpson does not refer to the governor of the pueblo by name; that detail is supplied in a letter of October 4, 1849, by Calhoun (1850, 211) who lists the "governor, Pedro Pino; the Captain of War, Salvadore; and the Alcalde, Mariana Vaca; all intelligent men." Simpson learned from the governor that there were seven albinos in the village, "all of pure Zuni blood," but the engineer was not tempted to speculate on "white origins." Simpson had already collected vocabularies of several different Southwestern tribes, including the Zuni (see his appendix B), and he was thus aware of the linguistic differences which weakened the Aztec theory when applied to all Pueblos.

Zuni. His *Journal* was read widely by a public anxious to learn about the new territories so recently acquired from Mexico. Imaginations were quickened to learn of gold on Pacific shores and of peoples of apparently ancient origins living in southwestern deserts. Simpson's book contained over seventy plates, many in color, of views along the way — but only one of Zuni (of no particular credit to the artist) — made by Richard H. Kern, and an accurate map by Edward M. Kern of the country traversed and of the general region.

As he laid before the public a document of enduring significance, Simpson literally put the Navajos and Zunis and their country on modern maps. Knowledge about them derived from Spanish sources had become vague and, anyway, much that the Spaniards learned had never been made public. For most Americans, Simpson's work offered a first look at the land of Cíbola and a people whose way of life had changed but little after centuries of contact with European culture.[6]

Simpson did more than publicize the Zunis and their pueblo. In the concluding paragraphs of his journal he held out an exciting prospect for those

---

[6] See Simpson's journal for September 16–18 (McNitt, ed., 1964, 120–42) for his interesting trip along the Rio Pescado to Inscription Rock. There with artist Richard Kern he copied many of the early names — "hieroglyphics" — on the historic rock, now part of El Morro National Monument. Both Simpson and Kern added their own (still well-preserved) names. See Slater (1961) for a modern study of El Morro's inscriptions. The part played in the Washington campaign by the Kerns has been detailed by Hine (1962) and Taft (1943).

As noted before, the McNitt edition (1964) of the Simpson journal should be consulted for easy reference and interpretation, but it lacks most of the plates and the map has been reduced in scale beyond usefulness. The original journal (1850), or the commercial edition of 1852, should be consulted for the full visual impact of the work. The illustrations are lithographs, many in color, made from sketches in the field, mainly by R. H. Kern. These include Indians, views of the Chaco ruins, potsherds, and a number of foldout reproductions of the inscriptions at El Morro. There is only one plate of Zuni (no. 59, reproduced by McNitt, ed., 1964), a grotesquely distorted view of a part of the pueblo looking east to Corn Mountain. Nevertheless, this may very well have been the first graphic ever made of the pueblo, beyond the infrequently found symbolic representations on Spanish maps; as such, given the popularity of Simpson's narrative, it may have had some impact in creating a popular image of the Zuni Pueblo. The map compiled by Simpson and drawn by Edward Kern was on a large scale and beautifully executed. There is an interesting feature of the map: remembering what Pedro Pino had said about the Zunis once living on Corn Mountain, Simpson had Kern ink in the name "Old Zuni" on the mountain (not named). This designation remained on the maps for many years and confounded later explorers and ethnologists who thought the ruins on Corn Mountain to be related to the Seven Cities of Cíbola. Simpson in a later work (1872, 300) asserted that the mesa top ruins were one of the seven towns of Cíbola. See Spier (1917a, 231) for some references to this matter.

seeking a direct route across the Southwest to California. From some trappers around Santa Fe, Simpson had learned that travel directly west of Zuni to the borders of California was feasible. Water, wood, and grass were to be found en route. Further inquiry revealed that the valley of the Colorado River might be passable. The Zuni River was a tributary of the Colorado. What of the main stream? It ran through a deep canyon, the trappers said, but they seemed to know little else about it.

In view of the lack of information about the Colorado River country, Simpson suggested that the Army's Corps of Topographical Engineers take up the exploration of the region west of Zuni to locate a route suitable for wagons between the pueblo and Los Angeles. Such a route, Simpson believed, might save as much as three hundred miles over the existing trails.

Since its activation in 1838 the Topographical Engineers had functioned as a scientific and exploratory branch of the Army. Some of the most brilliant work of the unit was accomplished in the unexplored sections of the West. With high zeal and a sense of national purpose, the engineers explored and mapped and assembled scientific data and, in several important published reports, they revealed to the world the location and condition of the many tribes and the amazingly diverse geography of the regions west of the Mississippi. Fremont's reports of the 1840s and Simpson's paper on the Navajo campaign are notable examples of these publications.

In view of the need for direct roads across the Southwest, Simpson's proposal met with ready approval. A comprehensive map of the canyon country of the Colorado River prepared by Lt. John G. Parke and published in 1851 revealed that most of the country west of Zuni to California was "unexplored."[7] To find a route between the Rio Grande and the Rio Colorado, Capt. Lorenzo Sitgreaves was directed to explore the Zuni River from the Zuni Pueblo to its junction with the Colorado River, and then he was to follow that river downstream to its mouth. Particular attention, his orders read, should be given to determining the "navigable properties" of the Zuni River.

---

[7] On the last pages of his journal (McNitt, ed., 1964, 160–62), Simpson recommended exploration of the region to the west of Zuni. Goetzmann's book (1959) emphasizes the history of the Topographical Engineers from activation in 1838 to 1863 when the Corps was absorbed into other units of the U.S. Army. Lieutenant John G. Parke's "Map of the Territory of New Mexico," reproduced by Wheat (1957–1963, vol. 3) was issued by the War Department.

Even as late as 1851 some men entertained the hope of finding a commercial water route between the Continental Divide and the Pacific Ocean — and the Colorado River offered the best possibility for such a route. Although his surveying party rendezvoused at the pueblo, Sitgreaves said very little about Zuni in his official report. He did include six lithographs of domestic scenes and the "Buffalo dance," made from drawings by Richard H. Kern, who had also traveled with Simpson. Sitgreaves headed west from the Zuni Pueblo on September 24, 1851, and completed a pioneer traverse across northern Arizona. The Zuni River, which he found a "mere rivulet," was not navigable, but he did locate a route suitable not only for wagons but also for rails. Thirty-two years later the Santa Fe Railway finished laying tracks on its line between Albuquerque and Needles; the Arizona section closely paralleled Sitgreaves' trail of 1851.[8]

Indeed, the publication of Sitgreaves' *Report* in 1853 coincided with a rising national interest in a transcontinental railroad. In that year Congress empowered the War Department to make surveys across the Trans-Mississippi West to locate the best routes for a railroad; Lt. A. W. Whipple, of the Topographical Engineers, was named to investigate a belt of country along the thirty-fifth parallel. West of the Zuni Pueblo Whipple covered much of the same ground explored by Sitgreaves but he made a much more careful study of it, finding the thirty-fifth parallel route not only practicable for a railroad but also "eminently advantageous."

Whipple issued an elaborate report of the exploration in two large quarto volumes, with a detailed itinerary and description of the route. An engraved map portrayed the area surveyed and lithographs and drawings illustrated scenes along the way. The volumes included special sections on geology, biology, and climate, and a long report on the Indian tribes. H. B. Möllhausen, a friend of Alexander von Humboldt, joined the expedition. His *Diary of a Journey* was filled with observations made along the way, including much information on the Indian tribes.

On November 18, 1853, Whipple reached El Morro, and during the next ten days his party made a studiously careful reconnaissance of the Zuni country. The "charming valley" of the Rio Pescado with its ancient ruins set alongside the contemporary farming village, the petroglyphs on the low bluffs, the patina

---

[8] Sitgreaves' official *Report* (1853) was agonizingly brief. Goetzmann (1959) puts the exploration in regional perspective. See Hine (1962) and Taft (1943) for data on Kern's Western art.

and interesting designs on fragments of prehistoric pottery, all caught the explorer's eye. Along the Pescado, camp was made under a cloudless sky in an "atmosphere so pure that stars gleam with a brilliancy unknown upon the Atlantic Coast."

Below the confluence of the Pescado and the Rio Nutria, the command entered the wide valley of the Zuni River and camped for five days at a spot where the stream broke through a lava dike — a place later known as Black Rock. Here Whipple was in sight of the Pueblo of Zuni a few miles away. The twin mesas stood out on the northern horizon, and toward the south towered the lofty Towayalane, where, the explorer remembered, Simpson had said the ruins of "Old Zuni" were located. Möllhausen then sketched what appeared to be a sacred spring surrounded by painted pottery vessels. Below the lava dike springs watered numerous garden patches. But there were no ditches. Irrigation was not necessary in the Zuni country, an Indian guide told the engineers, since rain supplied enough moisture for all the crops.

On the second day Governor Pedro Pino and two of his headmen, José Maria and José Hacha, paid a state visit to Whipple's camp. The project of opening a direct route to the Pacific Ocean "seemed to strike them wonderfully," and before the Americans left the area the tribal government agreed to provide guides who would show them an easy route directly west to the Little Colorado.

While waiting for some of his party to come in from Fort Defiance, Whipple made good use of his time. Wagons and equipment were repaired and put in good condition for the long trip ahead. Lt. J. C. Ives made barometric and meteorological observations. While the geologist and botanist explored the environs, the naturalist reaped a "rich harvest" of new varieties of birds and fish.

The commander meanwhile visited the pueblo. A compact mass, ranging up to five stories in height, the village reminded Whipple of an "immense ant hill." He saw many tame and captive eagles and turkeys, whose feathers were used for ceremonial purposes. From his guides Whipple learned of the legend of the great flood and of certain religious functions held in a court "consecrated to Montezuma dances." The tribal government was described to him and he heard that some of the Zunis (albinos) had fair complexions and light hair, facts that had suggested Welsh origins to some writers. But, Whipple reported, the Zunis denied that the Welsh legend had any foundation in truth.

Smallpox had hit the village; the Zunis were engulfed by an epidemic of the dread disease when Whipple arrived. This seems not to have deterred him from visiting the pueblo where "smallpox had been making terrible ravages among the people." He was prevented from seeing any of the albinos but otherwise he said, "We were soon surrounded by great numbers — men, women, and children — exhibiting this loathsome disease in various stages of progress." The Zunis had been highly selective in their choice of foreign ways and customs, but they had no defense against diseases introduced by outsiders. For the next forty years, smallpox intermittently took a tragic toll among the Indians at Zuni, whose vulnerability was increased by their gregarious community life.

Before continuing the railroad survey, Whipple, the botanist J. M. Bigelow, astronomer Thomas H. Parke, and H. B. Möllhausen climbed Corn Mountain to see the remains of "Old Zuni." At the eastern base of the mesa, where peach orchards grew on the sandy slopes, the explorers met an old man who directed them to the main trail leading up the precipitous eastern slope. From this trail, the old man said, the Zunis years ago "had hurled rocks upon the invading Spaniards." The Americans undoubtedly had followed the same route Vargas had taken in 1692, and once on top they found at the southeastern extremity of the mountain ruins of the many structures which the Zunis had built after the Pueblo Revolt and in which they were living when Vargas arrived.

"Crumbling walls, from two to twelve feet high, were crowded together in confused heaps over several acres of ground," Whipple wrote. The walls, laid with small blocks of sandstone cemented with mud, and the mounds and ruins scattered about, were located in an open piñon–juniper woodland and handsome stands of tree-like, braided cacti. Not far from the ruins, the visitors were shown a sort of shrine, a sacred place, at which the Zunis paid homage to the gods, and over which their guide blew some corn meal as they departed.

Here, to the top of Towayalane, according to ancient legend, the Zunis had fled in the great flood. As the waters continued to rise and lapped at the very rim of the mesa, the people were saved only when the son and daughter of a priest walked out into the menacing sea. Then the waters began to recede and the sacrificial victims appeared in the form of two stone pillars rising from the northeastern slope of the mountain. Before leaving, the explorers were guided to the rim to see the magnificent twin monoliths, five-hundred-foot-high eroded remnants of the mesa itself, which dominated its western face. Leaving the mountains, Whipple and his party caught up with the main command, which was camped at Arch Spring eight miles northwest of the pueblo near the Zuni Buttes.

Before leaving Zuni, Whipple once more returned to the pueblo. This time, in the home of the governor, he was shown some Spanish manuscripts which had been found long ago in the Catholic church; it was correspondence between the governor of New Mexico and the resident priests at Zuni. One paper dated back to 1757. No, in response to Whipple's question, the governor would not part with any of these papers. The manuscripts, Pedro Pino explained, had been handed down from generation to generation. They had taken on a sacred quality and were considered an insignia of the office of governor.

The wagon train started off and, with two Zuni guides, Whipple headed west by way of Jacob's Well and Navajo Springs, thus opening a direct route to the Little Colorado and shortening Sitgreaves' route by a substantial distance. "We have now passed through the ancient country of Cíbola, described by Marco de Nica in 1539, and by Vasquez de Coronado in 1540," Whipple wrote in his journal; he had seen enough to verify the accuracy of the observations of those first visitors. What they had said about the ancient Cíbolans, he thought, was "for the most part applicable to the Zunian of the present day."

Whipple made an important contribution to the documentary history of the Zuni people. His own journal and the reports and accounts issued by the principals of his command, illustrated with maps, charts, sketches and drawings, and colored lithographs by H. B. Möllhausen, were the fullest and most accurate of any yet published. For at least thirty years the reports written by Simpson and Whipple and their associates constituted the main and most reliable and revealing sources of information about the Zuni people, their land, and their way of life.[9]

---

[9] Whipple's "Report" (1856) is a full and interesting account of the railroad exploration along the thirty-fifth parallel. Chaps. 8–9 contain the material on Zuni. A special "Report on the Indian Tribes" (1856) was prepared by Whipple, Ewbank, and Turner. A colored lithograph of the Zuni Pueblo with Towayalane in the background is a somewhat fanciful production. Lithographs in color, by Möllhausen, of the sacred spring at Black Rock and the ruins and shrine on Towayalane, together with drawings and sketches, appear in the second source. The special reports on geology, biology, and climate were published by the U.S. War Department, *Reports of Explorations and Surveys* . . . (1855–1861), but they are not listed separately here. An English translation of Möllhausen's *Diary*, with some additional illustrations, was published in 1858 in two volumes. A handy edition of the Whipple narrative, with a map of the route, was issued by Foreman, ed., in 1941.

These sources have supplied the information contained in my paragraphs above. Whipple was well read on the Zunis and their history and was familiar with narratives of the Coronado expedition and with the speculations on Welsh and Aztec origins. He develops the Aztec-Montezuma theme, together with the Zuni story of the flood and other matters, in the

---

"Special Report on the Indian Tribes," 39–42. See also Möllhausen (1858). The smallpox epidemic reached Zuni some time after the Sitgreaves exploration in 1851. Neither Sitgreaves nor Simpson mention the disease at Zuni. No special report on the epidemic was made by J. M. Bigelow, M.D., who accompanied Whipple's party as physician and botanist. Bigelow published several botanical papers in the final reports of the expedition. At Zuni, he appears to have been more interested in discovering new varieties of cacti than in reporting on the smallpox epidemic. The disease may have been introduced by California-bound emigrant parties.

There are several versions of the Zuni story of the flood, first reported by Whipple and Möllhausen. Reference to these will be found in Benedict (1969), who apparently did not see the first published accounts.

A critical evaluation of the Western art created by the German H. B. Möllhausen appears in Taft (1943). See also E. S. Wallace (1955, chap. 12). Some of the success of the Whipple expedition in locating a suitable railroad route west of Albuquerque, and in other matters, may be attributed to the guide Antoine Leroux who had been with Sitgreaves in 1851. See Foreman, ed. (1941, 10–13), and the biography by Parkhill (1965).

Much ink has been spilled over the location of Coronado's Seven Cities. Not all writers agreed with Whipple. See the notes to Haynes' essay (1886) on the early exploration of New Mexico.

Chapter 8

Troubled Times

A window glazed with selenite

The Topographical Engineers had shown that there was no inhabited place of any size between Zuni and Los Angeles, a distance of about seven hundred miles. The pueblo was a jumping-off place. Travelers heading west had a last chance to obtain food and supplies for the long trek to California, and those traveling eastward had their first chance to get a prepared meal and even a room. One of the first to make the eastward trip was François X. Aubry who arrived in Zuni in September 1853. His party en route from California had subsisted for a month on quarter rations of mule and horse meat. At Zuni, Aubry wrote appreciatively, "We met with a hospitable and civilized population from whom we obtained an abundance of good provisions, over which we greatly rejoiced." [1]

Travel across the Southwestern deserts between inhabited points was a wearing and hazardous venture. Though the railroad surveyors had found practicable routes, everyone in the 1850s knew that the rails were not likely to come for years. The need for wagon roads was much more immediate and pressing, and federal funds were available to build them. Consequently, before the completion of the first transcontinental railroad in 1869, the War Department surveyed and built a number of major roads in several sections of the West. In 1857–1859, Edward F. Beale laid out one such route between Fort Defiance and the Colorado River.

---

[1] Bieber, ed., and Bender (1938) have reproduced Aubry's journal; he arrived at Zuni on September 6, 1853, before going on to Albuquerque where he met Lieutenant Whipple and contributed information useful to the engineer about to head west on the railroad survey (ibid., 56–57).

Old-timers on Southwestern trails — the trappers, now turned guides, prospectors, drovers, or whatever — who had visited the place earlier, or heard of it, stopped in on occasion. Berthrong and Davenport, eds. (1956, xix), refer to a visit in 1850 by Joseph R. Walker.

Heading west from Albuquerque, Beale's party reached the Zuni Pueblo late in August 1857 and from there went on to survey a road closely parallel to Sitgreave's and Whipple's tracks.

Beale's caravan must have been an exciting sight. Pacing alongside the heavy equipment and supply wagons were twenty-five camels sent by the War Department for testing as pack animals for use in the Southwestern deserts. What the Zunis thought of these exotic creatures and their native attendants is not recorded. For Beale, who estimated that two thousand people lived in the pueblo, Zuni was a curious and interesting sight. Among other things, he remarked on the extensive corn fields, the high quality of wheat grown nearby, the albinos, and the carriage of the women, who easily ascended ladders with water-filled vessels balanced on their heads.

Retracing his route from the Pacific coast, Beale again stopped at Zuni in February 1858; he also visited twice in 1859, during the building and improvement of the road between Albuquerque and Beale's Crossing (near Fort Mojave) on the Colorado River. Beale developed a fondness for the Zuni country, particularly the upper valley of the Pescado in the vicinity of Inscription Rock. Grandly rising far above the tips of the tall pines at its base, El Morro seemed to Beale to be an axis for valleys of "marvellous beauty" radiating in all directions. It was the kind of country, he ventured to predict, in which "my people" would build "flourishing settlements and prosperous communities."

Edward F. Beale was extravagant in his praise of much of the country through which the road passed. He knew how valuable the route would be to the overlanders — "this will inevitably become the great emigrant road to California" — and he thought of his work as opening "the way for the railroad" sure to follow. He was right, of course. The Santa Fe Railway and, later, transcontinental highway U.S. 66 (Interstate 40) closely paralleled Beale's road between the Rio Grande and the Rio Colorado.[2]

---

[2] Jackson's scholarly work (1952) reviews federal road-building, 1846–1869; see chap. 11 and notes on pp. 367–69. Beale's official journals and reports (1858, 1860) are detailed documents. Beale's instructions called for a road west from Fort Defiance. Although he visited the post and relied on it for military support, Beale regarded the Zuni Pueblo as the eastern terminus of the route in the survey of 1857; the completed road, which actually extended from Fort Smith in Arkansas on the Arkansas River to the Colorado at Fort Mojave, passed by Inscription Rock and the Zuni Pueblo.

E. F. Beale's Brahminism frequently pops out in his journal. He expected the "enterprise" of "our people" to make the Zuni country and the lands along the thirty-fifth parallel bloom into "prosperous communities." When it came to the Indians who had lived "in what

Certainly Beale's road put Zuni squarely on one of the main lines of American expansion, but for years the travelers were few. To the west, in the 225 miles beyond Zuni to the Colorado River, there were no settlements, there was no military protection, and hostile Indians posed a threat. On July 9, 1858, a large party of emigrants, of which John Udell and L. J. Rose were members, was heading west from Zuni when it was attacked by Mojave Indians near the Colorado River. Having lost eight of their party, with fifteen more wounded, the emigrants turned back. On October twentieth, Udell and the advance group reached Zuni, suffering from hunger and exposure; they stayed in the pueblo two weeks recovering from the ordeal. The "very good bread" and the beans and pumpkins supplied by the Indians helped in their recovery.[3]

The Navajos, however, and not the Mojaves, were the more persistent threat to overland travelers west of Albuquerque. The Navajos ranged from the San Juan River on the north to the Zuni country on the south, and anyone crossing the Continental Divide in these latitudes might expect to encounter them. The Zunis found themselves in almost constant jeopardy from these accomplished raiders and from the Apaches on their southern frontier, both enemies they had known for a long time.

For nearly twenty years after the coming of the Americans to New Mexico, turmoil prevailed more often than peace along the western Indian frontier. During Spain's rule and Mexico's, the Navajos, through well-engineered raids (sometimes in retaliation for slave raids on them), had risen from poverty to riches; they eluded all attempts to bring them under control. The Navajos were scarcely

is now a wilderness," he took a lofty stance. See his report (1860, 36–41), for his exploration and praise of the Pescado country around El Morro.

[3] A record of the Udell–Rose emigrant party was kept by John Udell (Wright, ed., 1946). Some of the members left their names on El Morro, and these names are among the few dating from the decade of the 1850s, a good indication of the extent of travel during that time; see Slater (1961). Despite their hard luck in the first venture, the Udell–Rose party returned over the same road in 1859 and made it safely to California. The emigrants thus saw the Zunis on three separate occasions but John Udell, the principal diarist, has little to say about them.

In 1860 Samuel W. Cozzens visited Zuni; in a book entitled *The Ancient Cibola: The Marvelous Country; or, Three Years in Arizona and New Mexico* (1876), he devotes nine chapters to the pueblo, its people and environs. The account is partly fictional and the chapters seem to be mainly his own personal adventures superimposed on the observations of prior writers. Appearing just before the railroad arrived in New Mexico, however, the work was influential in drawing national attention to the Southwest in general and the Zuni Indians in particular.

ready in 1846 to pay much attention to the Doniphan treaty or to subsequent
treaties with the United States that were not enforced. The founding of Fort
Defiance in the heart of the Navajo country did, for a few years, bring a strained
peace to the frontier, but in 1858 open war broke out between the Navajos and
the United States. It did not end until the fall and winter of 1863–1864 when
eight thousand Navajos capitulated and consented to leave their homelands and
take the "long walk" into exile at Bosque Redondo, at Fort Sumner in eastern
New Mexico. In 1868 the Navajos agreed to a general peace and were permitted
to return to a reservation in their homeland in the Chuska Mountains.[4]

The Zunis did not avoid involvement in the Navajo war. It is apparent that
they quickly embraced the Americans as a welcome ally in their long war against
the Navajos. In September 1849 Washington's command had been given a
"hearty reception" in the pueblo; less than thirty days later, the Zuni governor
and two headmen had gone to Santa Fe to ask the American government for
arms and ammunition and permission to make a war of extermination against
the Navajos. The deputation pleaded that there were 597 Zuni men capable of
bearing arms but that there were only thirty-two muskets and rifles and less than
twenty rounds each for these weapons. As things were, the Zunis had to arm
themselves wherever they went and had to maintain a twenty-four-hour guard
on their horses, mules, and sheep. They wanted to fight, to carry the war to the
Navajos. They were capable of defending themselves against the Navajos and
Apaches, the Zunis said, but they were interested in participating in an alliance
to destroy the enemy.[5]

---

[4] Much has been written on the Navajo wars, 1846–1863, but the last word has not been
said. Bailey (1964) has devoted a book to the subject. See also Spicer (1962, chap. 8) and
Underhill (1956, chaps. 8–12). Frank D. Reeve has done a number of pieces on the Navajos;
his 1939 article is relevant here. Indians hostile to American authority took advantage of the
Civil War in New Mexico to increase their raids and depredations. With the fall of the
Confederates in mid-1962, Union General James H. Carleton opened a vigorous campaign
against the Navajos, resulting in their defeat. Van Valkenburgh (1938, 20) points out that
Carleton employed both Zuni and Ute scouts against the Navajos. The biography of Carleton by A. Hunt (1958) has many details. Kelly, ed. (1970), documents the 1863–1865 campaigns. Keleher's book (1952) is a detailed overview of the tumultuous times. Frazer (1968)
has edited a comprehensive report on military and political conditions in New Mexico made
in 1850 by the War Department's Colonel McCall.

[5] As reported in the correspondence of Indian Agent James S. Calhoun, October 1, 15,
1849, in Calhoun (1850, 206, 219). The American forces mistakenly assumed the existence
of a Navajo state and that the signatures of a few headmen on a treaty bound all Navajos.
Treaty-making was therefore of little avail in quieting the issues between the two peoples.

Their application for arms was denied. Disillusioned as they were by this and subsequent actions of the United States, the Zunis were now caught up in a frontier struggle, and, whether in alliance (as they sometimes were, as "auxiliaries") or not, they had no recourse but to support the Americans.

This gave the Navajos ample excuse (if any were needed) to increase their raids against these Pueblos. E. F. Beale records in February 1857 that the Zunis had recently lost one hundred fifty horses to the raiders. A year later the Zuni governor complained to Beale that the Americans apparently had just made a separate peace with the Navajos, leaving the Zunis to face a powerful foe alone. Beale's unfriendly reply was that the Zunis had been served right for meddling and he warned the governor in the future to avoid "all entangling alliances." [6]

Though they lost heavily, the Zunis survived their war with the Navajos. They devised artful defenses. One consisted of horse traps — ten-foot-deep pits covered with brush and soil located on the main trails leading into the village. When a horse fell into this trap it was impaled on long sharp-pointed stakes. The rider, even if unharmed, was at the mercy of his enemy. The Zunis on occasion allied themselves with some of the Apache bands to strengthen their defenses, but sometimes they fought the enemy alone. In December 1863 three hundred Zunis surprised a band of Navajos in the Datil Mountains seventy-five miles southeast of the pueblo, killing seventeen men and capturing forty-four women and children. A thousand sheep were part of the spoils. [7]

---

[6] See letter of Calhoun, August 12, 1850, in Abel, ed. (1915, 249–50), for the onset of Zuni disillusionment. Beale's remark is recorded in his 1858–1859 journal (1860, 40). The Zunis served at times as guides and spies in the Navajo war. See Horn (1963, 78–79) and U.S. Indian Claims Commission, *The Navajo Tribe of Indians* (n.d., 5: 1199–215). Kelly, ed. (1970), has documented the Zuni participation as has Sabin (1935).

[7] On occasion, officers from Fort Defiance and on tours of duty visited Zuni and wrote accounts of what they saw. Lt. Col. J. H. Eaton, who was much interested in history, assembled a Zuni vocabulary and correctly surmised that the albinos in the village had given rise to the stories of white origins. Dr. P. G. S. Ten Broeck, assistant surgeon, repeated the supposition about Welsh origins and described the horse traps. Both Eaton's account and Ten Broeck's are found in the massive work assembled by Schoolcraft (1851–1857, 4: 72–91, 216–21). More than once American troops were caught in the traps. Rice in 1851 writes of an occasion on which Col. E. V. Sumner fell into one (Dillon, ed., 1970, 67).

During the Navajo wars, the Apaches appear to have been less troublesome to the Zunis. In U.S. Indian Claims Commission, *The Navajo Tribe of Indians* (n.d., 5: 1199–215), there are cited instances of the Zunis forming temporary alliances with the Apaches. Utley (1967, 240) cites the 1863 Zuni campaign against the Navajos; his book is an excellent overview of the subject.

Hostilities between the Zunis and Navajos continued for a time after the "long walk." Not all the Navajos surrendered to the American forces and many — perhaps half of the tribe — escaped the Bosque Redondo captivity by fleeing outward from the traditional homelands. This created pressures on the Zunis that produced some bloody incidents between the two peoples; but after 1868, when the Navajos agreed to live in peace with the United States, conditions improved. Through the efforts of Indian Agents William F. M. Arny and James H. Miller, conferences in May 1871 between the Zunis and Navajos resulted in an agreement that both sides would at least try to coexist and keep the peace.[8]

The war had brought some real benefits. After the founding of Fort Defiance in 1851, the Zunis were engaged to supply corn to feed the "public animals" at the post. The military kept open the road between the fort and the pueblo. In 1856 the Army was paying the Zunis as much as four thousand dollars a year for corn, and as a result, one officer reported, the Indians were in a "thriving condition." This business was probably continued with Fort Wingate when in 1861 Defiance was abandoned at the outbreak of the American Civil War.[9] Moreover, the general calm that came after the peace of 1868 opened the way for intertribal trade and commerce of substantial value to the Zunis, who exported their goods and the products of their farms and fields and shops to Navajos and Apaches alike.[10]

---

[8] Gwyther (1871) reported an assault against some Navajos in 1866 by Pueblos from several villages. One hundred and sixty of the Navajo prisoners, according to a probably apocryphal account, were taken to Zuni Pueblo where they were forced to jump to their deaths from a precipice. See A. Hunt (1958, 278–79) and U.S. Indian Claims Commission, *The Navajo Tribe of Indians* (n.d., 5: 1199–215). The 1871 Zuni–Navajo conferences arranged by Miller and Arny are discussed by McNitt (1962, 124–27). Arny, who reported on the matter in 1871, mentions the slaying by the Zunis of about a hundred captive Navajos in 1863. Arny's diary has been edited and published by Murphy (1967).

[9] Fort Wingate in New Mexico, originally located near Cebolleta, was later moved to a point near San Rafael and still later to its present location, which had been the site of a post founded in 1860 as Fort Fauntleroy, later changed to Fort Lyon. In 1868 the two forts were consolidated under the Wingate name. R. Brandes (1960) has an outline history of Fort Defiance. For details on Fort Wingate, see Pearce, Cassidy, and Pearce, eds. (1965, 59), and U.S. Work Projects Administration (1940, 322–23).

See Eaton (1854, 221) on Zuni as a source of supply for the "public animals" at Fort Defiance. Kendrick (1947 and 1950), written in 1856, describes the "thriving condition" of the Zunis in those years.

[10] During the years of the Navajo wars the Apaches were also at war with the United States, and they found Zuni an excellent source of supplies. A general calm, seldom broken,

Although the conflicts of the 1850s, 1860s, and 1870s were a climax to nearly two hundred years of intermittent warfare, the Zunis, isolated, and more often than not defending themselves without allies, had survived these troubled times. Trouble, danger, and war were not new to them, and they had always found some way to save themselves from physical and cultural extinction and even to benefit from the experience.

Once peace settled over the pueblo, the Zunis found that the alien impact of the Anglo-Americans began to increase. Up to 1871 the most influential Anglos were Army personnel, who, since the first months of the Mexican War, had been frequent visitors to the pueblo.

During that time other contacts were minor, though wandering prospectors and adventurers, guides and scouts on occasion enjoyed Zuni hospitality. Mail carrier Albert Franklin Banta reported years later that in February 1866 he was admitted to membership in the tribe. Banta worked for Sol Barth who had secured the contract to carry government mail from Albuquerque to Prescott, the route passing through Zuni. Barth appears to have mined salt from the Zuni salt lake as a sideline and to have opened a trading establishment in the pueblo. William F. M. Arny in 1871 mentioned that Zuni "was a good place for traders, who sell whiskey and gunpowder to the Southern Apache Indians. At last count one of these traders, Sol Barth, was convicted; the judge sentenced him to twenty-four hours imprisonment and a fine of $25." [11]

Arny was Special Agent for the Indians of New Mexico and his visits to the pueblo in 1870 and 1871 opened formal relations between the Zuni Indians and

---

settled over the relations between the two peoples. As the U.S.–Apache wars intensified in the 1870s and 1880s Zuni became even more important as a supply point. The importance of trade in the economic and cultural life of the Zunis and the Apaches is illustrated by Mendivil (1871, reproduced by Dorr, 1953). For some aspects of Zuni trade of the time see Adair (1944) and McNitt (1962), and on Western Apache raiding and warfare see Basso, ed. (1971), and Ogle (1970).

[11] Banta's reminiscences, containing a number of references to the Zunis, have been edited by Reeve (1953). The Tucson *Arizona Star*, February 25, 1888, contains an article on Banta. In 1881 Bourke met a Charles Franklin in Zuni; see Bloom, ed. (1933–1937, 11: 192–95). The Prescott *Arizonian*, September 4, December 11, 1869, contains articles on visits by prospectors C. E. Cooley and J. C. Handy and others. An obituary on Sol Barth, longtime resident of St. Johns, Arizona, appeared in "Pioneers Pass Away," *Arizona Historical Review* (1929). See also the scholarly article on Barth by Greenwood (1973). Arny's comment on Barth and the Zuni traders appears in his 1872 report. Arny mentions other traders interested in the Zuni traffic. On both Banta and Barth see McClintock (1921, chap. 16). Murphy (1967) has edited Arny's 1870 diary, and in a scholarly monograph (1972) he has summarized the "frontier crusader's" work in the Southwest.

the federal Bureau of Indian Affairs. The encroachments of whites, not only prospectors but also settlers and stockmen, many of them Spanish-speaking New Mexicans, posed a threat to the Zunis. In consideration of this fact Arny recommended that the Indians be given a reservation embracing their traditional homelands. The action was finally taken in 1877 when a reservation was established confirming the Zuni ownership of the land, part of which, presumably, had been granted to them in 1689 by the Spanish government.[12]

During the 1870s new forces impinged on the pueblo: missionary interest was renewed. In 1863 the first bishop of New Mexico, John B. Lamy, had visited the Zunis and had been well received, but apparently nothing was done at the time to reactivate the old Mission of Guadalupe. Then, in response to a request made by the Zunis for an American teacher, Indian Agent Arny wrote to the Presbyterian Board of Missions asking the establishment of a mission at Zuni.

The Presbyterians were interested, but before they reached the vineyard, missionaries of the Church of Jesus Christ of Latter-day Saints had put in an appearance. Since 1847, when they reached the shores of Great Salt Lake, the Mormons had rapidly extended their frontiers through the valleys of the mountains, particularly toward California and the plateau country of the Colorado River. In 1858 a missionary venture headed by Jacob Hamblin had reached the Hopi villages. The Mormons were intrigued by the myth of Welsh origins. But they found no Welsh-speaking Hopis and, like the Spaniards before them, discovered that these Indians were not inclined to change their religious customs. Mormon missionary activity was slowed down by the Navajo wars, but in the mid-1870s permanent settlements were laid out in the basin of the Little Colorado and proselyting among the tribes was renewed.

Missionaries Ammon M. Tenney and Robert H. Smith arrived in Zuni on April 2, 1876. After some initial reticence the Indians appeared to accept the preachments of the Mormons, and after a few weeks in the pueblo 111 baptisms were recorded. A second mission arrived before the end of the year, but by then

---

[12] Arny's recommendation for a reservation is found in his report of 1871 (1872, 806). The Spanish deed to Zuni was one of several apparently spurious grants issued after the Pueblo Revolt by one Cruzate. The reservation of 1877, later enlarged, was not confirmed by Congress until 1931. On the complex matter of Pueblo land titles see Brayer (1938), Jenkins (1961), Twitchell (1914, 1: 451–83) and Cohen, ed. (1958). The documents pertaining to the formation of the Zuni reservation, 1689 to 1931, have been assembled by Fay, ed. (1971). The official file of original land grant and reservation records is in the U.S. Bureau of Land Management, Santa Fe, N. Mex.; see Zuni Pueblo, Land Grant Papers. Dale (1949) summarizes a century of federal relations with the tribes of the Southwest.

the Indians' enthusiasm for Mormon doctrine had been dampened notably by their own spiritual advisers. Undiscouraged, the Mormons returned for a third effort which was more successful. Llewelyn Harris arrived in Zuni in January 1878 to find a smallpox epidemic raging; he turned to faith healing and, as he states in his account of his work among the sick, restored to health some four hundred Indians. Harris, of Welsh ancestry, spent some time looking for evidence of Welsh origins. The Zuni language, he found, contained a "great many words . . . like the Welsh, and with the same meaning."

Among Mormon church officials the news of the missionary's good works aroused enthusiasm for the success of the Zuni mission. Wilford Woodruff, an apostle of the church and later its president, visited the pueblo (and those of Laguna and Isleta) in 1879 and, like the Spanish padres of earlier centuries, was captivated by the village life and the intelligence and achievements of the Pueblos. As it turned out, however, the Mormons' zeal in propagating the faith was not matched by the Zunis' desire to accept it, and the mission languished. An immediate and lasting result of the enterprise, however, was the permanent home for their Indian mission which the Mormons established on the upper reaches of the Pescado, at the foot of the Zuni Mountains. The colony of Savoya, dating from 1876, was the first settlement, but it was eclipsed six years later by Ramah (first called Navajo) located six miles downstream. The Mormons also labored among the Navajos in the area with considerable success.[13]

The Presbyterians, working in the pueblo with the blessing and support of the federal Indian bureau, made somewhat better headway. Beginning in 1877 the missionaries operated a day school at government expense and, as time and the number of converts increased, erected a church building. The first Presbyterian missionary and "United States Teacher" was Dr. H. K. Palmer. He was followed in 1878 by Dr. Taylor F. Ealy, who stayed at Zuni until 1881, teaching, preaching, and practicing medicine. During this time he built a mission of cut stone;

---

[13] See Arny's report (1872, 807). Slater (1961, 46) mentions Lamy's visit. Salpointe (1898) reviews the reorganization of the Catholic establishment in New Mexico and the opening of a new missionary program following the acquisition of the territory by the United States.

Mormon frontier history in the region of the Little Colorado is well documented. I am relying here on a recent scholarly study by Peterson (1967); additional details are supplied by Tietjen (1969), Telling (1953), Jenson (1941, 690), and McClintock (1921), who quotes Harris's views on the similarities between the Zuni and Welsh languages. Harris (1879) tells his own story of the "miraculous healing" of the Zunis.

for the government he put up a school building and teacherage, and served as the pueblo's first postmaster.

It appears from the documents that little love was lost between the Christian missionaries of various sects employed at Zuni in the late 1870s; it was thought that the Presbyterians used their influence as semi-official agents of the government to keep the Mormons from establishing a mission school in the pueblo. This hostility was probably generated by the different policies of the two denominations. The Presbyterians put education first and evangelization second whereas the Mormons held that a better life could come more quickly after conversion. However, few Zunis were found ready to take either road pointed out to them by the missionaries.

Since the Zuni people were themselves thoroughly religious — ceremonialism and ritual permeated their daily lives — they found no compelling reasons for changing any of their beliefs or adding the alien dogma to their very large body of religious knowledge. And thus, as in past centuries, the foreigners' religion made little impact on them.[14]

---

[14] Benjamin M. Thomas (1877), Pueblo Indian Agent, and Taylor F. Ealy (1880, 1881) submitted reports on the opening of Presbyterian missionary activities at Zuni. Ruth R. Ealy (1955) edited her father's diary and correspondence relating to the Zuni adventure. From 1871 the annual reports of the New Mexico Indian agents to the Commissioner of Indian Affairs contain frequent reference to affairs at Zuni; see U.S. Bureau of Indian Affairs, *Annual Reports of the Commissioner of Indian Affairs*. Much more revealing than the published reports is the correspondence of Pueblo Indian Agent Benjamin M. Thomas (1874–1883) on file in the Federal Records Center, Denver. It appears from these papers — the files of the U.S. Bureau of Indian Affairs — that a federal education program was begun at Zuni as early as 1874. There is much material in those files on schools, traders, missionaries, trespass on Zuni lands, and the establishment of the reservation. The more complete files are U.S. Bureau of Indian Affairs, Pueblo and Zuni Agencies, Correspondence, 1874–1917, National Archives, Washington, D.C.

Chapter 9

The Coming of the Rails

Wooden pivot hinges of a door

The inscriptions on El Morro tell us that during the 1860s and 1870s few transients passed through the Zuni country. Among the more interesting names left on the great rock during this time were those of some members of the surveying parties employed in 1867 and 1868 by the Union Pacific Railway Company (not to be identified with the Union Pacific Railroad) to run an instrumental survey for a railroad along the thirty-fifth parallel of north latitude.

Two members of the survey team stopped at Zuni to try their hands at trading. From Santa Fe they had brought a bagful of trinkets and cheap merchandise expecting to barter this "sham bijouterie" (our informant reports) for Zuni robes, weapons, and handicrafts. But these offerings and the would-be traders' "best speeches failed to raise the bartering emotions of the tribe." After "infinite bargaining" the Anglos did manage to obtain two small sheep. The surveyors left, "fully persuaded that the Zunians were the 'smartest' traders west of the Mississippi."

West of Albuquerque the Union Pacific survey crews, headed by General William J. Palmer, discovered that a line running north of the Zuni Mountains crossed the Continental Divide at a lower elevation and offered a better grade than the route passing El Morro and the Zuni Pueblo marked out by Sitgreaves, Whipple, and Beale.[1]

---

[1] Slater (1961, 46) lists the names found on El Morro of the Union Pacific railroad survey members. In 1867 the eastern division of the Union Pacific considered the possibility of extending its lines from Kansas through the Southwest to southern California. W. J. Palmer was placed in charge of the survey and feasibility study; he submitted a report in 1869. Bell (1870, 405–6), who was attached to the survey, reported the bartering episodes. During the course of his survey in 1853 Whipple found that the grade over the Continental Divide at Campbell's Pass (Navajo Pass in Palmer's day — where U.S. Interstate 40 and the

But the rails were slow in reaching the Southwest. Though Palmer had located an excellent route to the Pacific, his line, now called the Kansas Pacific, crossed into Colorado instead. The Atlantic and Pacific Railroad was chartered in 1866 to construct a line from Missouri along the thirty-fifth parallel to the Pacific, but the corporation foundered in the Panic of 1873. In 1880 a half interest in the Atlantic and Pacific was acquired by the aggressive Atchison, Topeka, and Santa Fe Railway whose tracks had already reached Albuquerque.

The agreement called for the construction of a line from Albuquerque to California under a federal charter held by the Atlantic and Pacific. Surveyors and graders were soon at work. Before the end of 1883, A & P tracks, closely following the Palmer route, had reached the Colorado River opposite Needles. Bridging the Colorado, the company linked its rails with the Southern Pacific which had already laid tracks to Needles. Thus the Atlantic and Pacific (renamed the Santa Fe Pacific in 1897 and in 1903 given the name of the parent company — Atchison, Topeka, and Santa Fe Railway), with transcontinental connections, put the Southwest in fast and easy communication with the rest of the world. New Mexico was no longer land-bound, remote, and isolated, and the life of nearly everyone was touched if not transformed by the railroad.[2]

The Pueblo Indians of New Mexico might well have preferred to remain in the relative seclusion they had enjoyed before the railroad era, but they had no voice in the matter. They watched as waves of traders, stockmen, miners, lumbermen, and farmers washed over the territory. The towns along the railroad were built up with warehouses, corrals, offices, stores, shops, and eating and drinking establishments offering, as the trade demanded, a variety of entertainment. The railroad brought Anglo-America to New Mexico in full flood.

West of Albuquerque the railroad followed the easy grade found by the Palmer survey. El Morro and Zuni, for so long major stopping places for overland travelers, were henceforth bypassed. The railroad towns of Grants, east of the Continental Divide, and Gallup, west of it, now became the stations, the supply and distribution points, for the Zuni country.

Santa Fe Railway cross the Continental Divide) was better than the Zuni route and he recommended it as preferable; see Foreman, ed. (1941, 154).

[2] Lamar (1966) from a broad regional perspective, writes of the building of the railroads and their impact, as does Meinig (1971). Greever (1954) writes of the land problems encountered by the Santa Fe in New Mexico and Arizona. One year before the completion of the Santa Fe route the Southern Pacific and Texas Pacific had joined rails, thus opening a second transcontinental route across the Southwest.

To celebrate the opening of the railroad era in 1883, the citizens of Santa Fe promoted and staged an elaborate exposition, the "Tertio-Millennial," in which New Mexican history over three centuries was presented in a series of parades and pageants. As the exposition opened, the "quiet Pueblo, the valiant Spaniard, the aggressive Anglo-American" filled the ancient capital of Santa Fe and turned out ten thousand strong to enjoy the festivities. "In regal magnificence and barbaric splendor," Ralph Twitchell wrote with enthusiasm, "this historical presentation has never been equalled on the American continent." The theme, of course, was the commemoration of the Spanish conquest and the planting of "the first seed of civilization" in New Mexico.

The pages of history were reopened with color and music, salutes and salvos, and a reenactment of the siege of Hawikuh by Coronado's army. The Pueblo Indians (fifty Zunis marched in the parade "on foot, with their bows and arrows, and brilliant head-bands of red, green and yellow" in company with about a hundred and fifty Pueblos from the Rio Grande) took a position on top of the old state house (later the federal building), used on this occasion to simulate the Pueblo of Hawikuh. Then, in the presence of "the assembled thousands," the Spaniards, after "a beautiful and realistic combat," demanded surrender of the Indians and an oath of allegiance.

Following the "battle" all parties retired to the exposition hall for speech-making. After a number of dignitaries had spoken in English, the Governor of the Zunis, Palowahtiwa, was invited to respond. Taking the platform, Palowahtiwa in his native tongue addressed the "immense audience." His remarks were interpreted by Frank H. Cushing, who represented the Bureau of Ethnology in the Smithsonian Institution.

True it was, when the world was young, he began, the white man had "discovered how to make marks with meaning," but, "is not the tongue of the Zuni his writing-stick and are not the ears and hearts of his listeners, his books and paper?" Through tradition the Zunis were mindful of history. They remembered the first coming of the strangers "nine, ten and even twelve generations" gone by. With arrows and stones and war clubs they had fought Coronado, but later, the governor continued, "we found them to be our brothers."

Palowahtiwa made no reference to the arrogance of those who glorified the conquerors as the sole carriers of civilization to New Mexico, nor did he dwell on the cultural strength of the Pueblos, who for three centuries had lived side by side with the Spaniards without losing their identity. Perhaps he thought the fact of survival was itself worth celebrating.

And what of the future? Since he had already traveled to the eastern cities and had seen something of the power of the United States, Palowahtiwa could easily see that Zuni survival depended on a continuing policy of diplomacy, peace, and good will. Near the end of his speech the governor spoke the bitter truth: "I am told that this is a feast of my father in Washington — that he approved it; therefore have I come with all my children and I now speak, for I know that my people are poor among men, and if they do not smile on Washington and his children, and he not smile on them, they will pass away or, like dogs, lie hungry at the doors of strangers."

In an impressive conclusion, the governor reminded his audience that *all* of the people of New Mexico were members now of the American union. "We are the children of one father, are we not? And that father is Washington, the great chief of the land of the Daybreak, therefore have I called you brothers, and may we smile one upon the other and be happy forever and through all days. This much I have spoken."

Palowahtiwa, said one reporter, "created a deep and lasting impression" upon his hearers, and one wonders if any of those on the program of the "Tertio-Millennial" who spoke of "conquest" and "civilization," of "regal magnificence and barbaric splendor" had said as much.[3]

The coming of the Anglos caused many problems for the Pueblos. The land-hungry Americans were aggressive competitors for the available natural resources. The Eastern Pueblos were the most exposed but the Western Pueblos did not escape these pressures, particularly those from the stockmen. The railroad brought the national market within reach, and as the tracks were laid across the pristine ranges of northern New Mexico and Arizona the sheepmen and cattlemen were quick to follow.

Ranchers, both Mexican and Anglo, from little towns like Cubero and San Rafael moved west into the country beyond the Continental Divide. Already on hand were the soldiers at Fort Wingate, some of whom were tempted by the

---

[3] The proceedings of the "Tertio-Millennial" were reported by Twitchell, ed. (1925, 401–9); Palowahtiwa's speech, as interpreted by Cushing, is there reproduced. The translation was corrected by the chief, who hoped it would be sent on to the "land of the day," that is, to the East.

good money to be made in cattle. Gallup, reached by the rails in 1881, quickly became the region's industrial, trading, and shipping center when important coal mines were discovered nearby.

The Zuni Mountains, which run southeast of Fort Wingate and Gallup for seventy miles and rise to elevations just over nine thousand feet, offered the best range in the region, and it was not long before conflict developed over the use of land and water. The situation was complicated by the fact that lands granted to the railroad as a federal subsidy for building the line blanketed in a checkerboard fashion most of the Zuni Mountains. Although the railroad sold thousands of acres to legitimate grazing interests, many other stockmen ranged their animals over railroad lands without permission or payment of fees.

As the Americans and Mexicans scrambled to reap high profits from uncontrolled grazing of the virgin grasslands, the native Indians became involved in the struggle. The Navajos, who for years had roamed at will through the Zuni Mountains, resisted white encroachments by using their well-tried tactics of raiding and rustling. The Zunis, whose reservation reached the western foothills of the Zuni Mountains, attempted to defend themselves against both the aggressive stockmen and their old enemies, the Navajos. For ten years and more after the coming of the railroad, the Zuni–Gallup country was plagued with an intermittent range war. When Indians were involved in serious encounters — as they usually were — "peace" was restored by the troops at Fort Wingate.[4]

During the range war the Zunis were harassed and victimized by trespassers and rustlers, both Indian and white. The broad grasslands along the upper reaches of the Nutria and Pescado, some distance from the Pueblo, were particularly vulnerable. On one occasion Navajos, trespassing on the Zuni reservation, butchered some animals branded with the Bar S, the mark of the Cibola Cattle Company owned by soldiers at Fort Wingate. The Zunis fought back. The trespassers and thieves were found dead in and near the reservation, but the Zunis lost several of their number to the bullets of rustlers.

Far from the Pueblo agency at Santa Fe, the Zunis were accorded very little direct federal supervision. On occasion, however, troop detachments from Fort

---

[4] For each mile of track laid the railroad was granted forty odd-numbered sections of land on either side of the line. The railroad had difficulty in selling the lands, at least in some areas, and was plagued with unauthorized use by interlopers. See Greever (1954, chap. 4). Telling (1952) details the growth of the pastoral industries in the Zuni–Gallup area and the conflicts between red men and white (chap. 4) following frontier expansion.

Wingate were ordered to the pueblo to consult with the Indians, assist them in various ways, and provide them with some show of protection.[5] Such visits were not entirely welcome since the soldiers had shown a willingness to victimize the Indians when the opportunity arose.

After 1882 the Puebloans were especially wary, for in that year they nearly lost the headsprings of the Nutria River, one of the most valuable assets of the Zuni homelands. The springs and adjacent lands had long been used by the Indians for grazing and farming; nearby a small village of stone houses served as living quarters during the times of planting and harvest. The springs were mentioned in the presidential order of 1877 describing the boundaries of the Zuni reservation. But the description was inexact and this valuable property seems not to have been included in the subsequent survey.

The error was discovered by the officers at Fort Wingate about the time that Illinois Senator John A. Logan stopped off at the post. The senator, one of the more powerful political figures of his day, visited with his son-in-law, Maj. William F. Tucker, one of the owners of the Bar S. In September 1882 these men and a large party traveled to the Zuni Pueblo, stopping en route to look over Nutria village and the adjacent springs. Two months later, Major Tucker, Capt. Henry W. Lawton, and a civilian, Orrin B. Stout, entered claims for land at Nutria Springs in order to make use of the springs as a primary source of water for the Bar S. Each man filed for 160 acres under the Homestead Act and 640 acres under the Deseret Land Act. These claims seem not to have come to the attention of the Zunis until early in 1883 when the three men appeared at the springs to begin ranching operations. Thunderstruck at this invasion of what they supposed was their own property, the Indians held excited councils.

"My heart is sick with anxiety for my people," said the old priest Naiiutchi. "What do you suppose we can do? It is easy for the Zuni to grow poor and have trouble. It is easy for the American to grow rich and take our lands away. If there be one thing upon which we depend for our lives, and our cattle, and our corn, it is the four springs [Nutria and three others, including Pescado, also threatened]. Take these away and you take away the life of the Zuni." Continuing, the priest said, "The land of the Zuni is dry and sandy, and those springs are all we have. We want the water to make food. We do not want to keep others away, but we want the water from the springs in order that we may live."

---

[5] Telling (1952, chap. 4), and the U.S. Bureau of Indian Affairs, Pueblo and Zuni Agencies, letters sent, 1883–1890 (MSS, National Archives, Federal Records Center, Denver).

Through the assistance of friends, namely Frank H. Cushing, the ethnologist, and Pueblo Agent Ben M. Thomas, the matter was started up through channels. President Chester A. Arthur on May 1, 1883, issued an executive order incorporating Nutria and Pescado Springs and the adjacent settlements into the reservation. The claims of Tucker, Lawton, and Stout were disallowed since they were on Indian land. Two newspaper men, Sylvester Baxter of the Boston *Herald* and William E. Curtis of the *Chicago Inter-Ocean*, both associates of Cushing and sympathetic to the Zuni cause, gave the case national publicity. Senator Logan, who was regarded by some as a likely prospect for the presidency, was said to share an interest with his son-in-law in the Nutria cattle ranch.

Logan took little notice of these reports until President Arthur extended the boundaries of the Zuni reservation, thus restoring the contested lands to the Indians. Then the senator addressed an indignant letter to the press. He denied any personal interest in the Nutria property but implied the right of his son-in-law to claim public land. Besides, the Zunis already had more than enough land — "1036 acres and a fraction to each head of a family," he reckoned. "Will any man who believes in fair dealing with the government as well as the Indians say that these few indolent Indians living in a little town or village, with but few cattle or horses, require any such amount of the public domain to the exclusion of all other citizens." He went on, "If a civilized Indian who makes his living by peaceful and agricultural pursuits, being the head of a family, is entitled to over 1000 acres of land gratuitously without being required to live on or cultivate it, how much land ought a civilized white man to be entitled to, provided he cultivate and pay the Government price for it?" And finally he asked, "Who has the best right to the land in controversy, a soldier by paying for it, or the Indians by asking for it?"

Naturally, Logan's enemies, crying "land grabber" and the like, made political capital of the matter. The senator blamed Frank Cushing for this unfavorable turn of events. Cushing had been sent to the pueblo by John Wesley Powell, director of the newly-formed Bureau of Ethnology, to make ethnological studies. Cushing's interest and assistance certainly had helped the Indians win their case. Put into an embarrassing political position by the affair, Senator Logan threatened the life of the Bureau of Ethnology unless Cushing were removed from the pueblo.

The Zuni Indians "shouted for joy" when they learned of President Arthur's proclamation. Old Naiiutchi, the priest, sent for Cushing and dictated to him a graceful letter thanking the president. In Cushing's translation it read in part: "Father, through your will we are this day happy, when but for your will we had been heavy with thoughts." One writer, who knew the Zunis and who was familiar with all aspects of the case, felt called upon to discuss some of the attributes of civilization — "liberty, morality, industry, humanity and justice; generosity to the weak, resistance to oppression, and self confidence toward the strong." If these are the qualities of civilization, he concluded, then the "Zunis have it to a higher degree than some of our law-givers." [6]

---

[6] The Nutria case attracted much attention in large part owing to the national publicity given it and to Senator Logan's involvement and Frank Cushing's. The basic documents — homestead and desert land claims, Arthur's proclamation, etc. — were published as "Zuni Indian Reservation in New Mexico and Arizona" in 1885. These and other pertinent documents are reproduced in Fay, ed. (1971). Correspondent W. E. Curtis of the Chicago *Inter-Ocean* investigated the threatened "land grab," and a section in his book (1883, chap. 3) is one of the best accounts of it. Sylvester Baxter, correspondent for the Boston *Herald* also wrote an account (1883). Baxter had already given national publicity to Cushing's work at Zuni. Cushing's involvement is covered by the unpublished works of his biographers (Fuller, 1943, and Brandes, 1965). In his introduction to Cushing's *My Adventures in Zuni*, DeGolyer, ed. (1941), touches on the matter. Senator Logan's letter to the press appears in part in the New York *Times*, May 29, 1883; according to this newspaper the full text of the letter was to be published in the Chicago *Tribune*, May 30, 1883. Logan was bitter in his denunciation of Cushing. The insinuation that Logan was trying to steal Indian land was overdrawn; he was, however, exercised by the president's order which added Nutria Springs to the reservation and thus closed it to entry. It seems clear that the original claims made by Tucker, Lawton, and Stout were proper entries on what was presumed to be public land.

The Nutria case did not end in 1883. Captain Lawton on behalf of the other claimants appealed the president's order of May first; the New Mexico press sided against the "lazy" Zunis. On March 3, 1885, President Arthur issued another order amending the second one to allow the three entrées. But the Zunis and the Pueblo Indian Agency protested and the General Land Office cancelled the entrées. The claimants again appealed and the issue was settled in 1891 when the claims of the three men for land within the Zuni Reservation were finally cancelled. See Fuller (1943, 81–83) and Fay, ed. (1971). By 1891 the reservation boundaries were secure but trespassers continued to plague the Indians.

Chapter 10

Kushy

Incised decoration on a window sash

Alien pressures on the Zuni people were light compared to those suffered by Indians elsewhere. The vigorous, unrelenting sweep of the whites across the continent — accelerated in the mid-nineteenth century by the gold rush to California — devastated the native Americans. Intimidation and exile, dissolution and destruction of resources, pestilence and war, threatened many of the tribes with extermination. The Navajos and Apaches capitulated to American power, but others suffered even more than they. By the 1870s deterioration of the tribes across the land had gone far enough seemingly to confirm predictions, made by many for nearly a century, that the Indians would soon vanish; certainly their culture, their traditional lifeway, was doomed.

A few humanitarians and reformers tried to stem the decline of the red men by arousing the national conscience and demanding a policy of justice and fair play. One of these, early in 1881, published a telling book whose title characterized federal policy toward the Indians as *A Century of Dishonor*. The author was Helen Hunt Jackson, who hoped she could do as much for the Indian as Harriet Beecher Stowe had done for the American Negro. Her crusade peaked in 1884 when she published *Ramona*, an immensely popular novel depicting the destruction of the California Mission Indians at the hands of land-grabbing whites. Helen Jackson and the reformers succeeded in pricking the national conscience and awakening public concern over Indian welfare to the extent that Congress responded with the Dawes Act intended (though it failed) to integrate the Indians into the American system.[1]

---

[1] The reform movement of the post–Civil War era is a large chapter in American history with a correspondingly large literature. Rolle, ed. (1965), in his edition of *A Century of Dishonor*, has shown Jackson's impact on the attempted reform in Indian welfare. Rolle

Scientifically-minded men argued that legislation would scarcely solve the "Indian question." If the Indian is to survive, their argument went, he must be exposed to the civilizing influences of more advanced peoples; all societies evolve and pass through the same stages of development, and the nineteenth-century American Indians, they said, were in an early, or primitive, stage of development. These Darwinian ideas appeared in the pages of *Ancient Society* published in 1877 by the pioneer American anthropologist Lewis Henry Morgan. Among those strongly influenced by Morgan was John Wesley Powell, who found himself in 1879 at the head of a new federal agency — the Bureau of Ethnology — organized for the purpose of carrying on "anthropologic researches" among the American Indians.[2]

For nearly a decade after his celebrated descent through the Grand Canyon in 1869, Powell studied the Indians of the Colorado River region as part of his work as director of the Geographical and Geological Survey of the Rocky Mountain Region. The Powell Survey was one of four great surveys set up by the federal government after the Civil War to study, describe, and map the western territories being overrun and exploited by swarming frontiersmen. The other surveys were headed by George M. Wheeler, Clarence King, and Ferdinand V. Hayden. During their years in the field these men produced a magnificent shelf of reports covering the ground from fossil animals and archeology to mining camps and the western Indians.

The page count on geology and geography in these reports may have bulked larger than that on the Indians, but there were some good accounts of the tribes; Powell regarded Indian studies as an important part of his field work. Much intrigued by the Hopis (he referred to them as Moquis) living in "the ancient province of Tusayan," Powell in 1870 spent nearly two months among these Indians where he marveled to see an agricultural people in a desert land living in stone houses up to six stories high, people skilled as potters and weavers, people possessing an "elaborate, ceremonious" religion and a "vast store" of mythology.[3]

has changed the subtitle of the original to "The Early Crusade for Indian Reform," from "A Sketch of the United States Government's Dealings with Some of the Indian Tribes."

[2] Lewis Henry Morgan's influential *Ancient Society* (1877) and other works and their author's place in American scholarship have been appraised by Resek (1960), Eggan (1966), and by sociologist Bernhard J. Stern (Charlotte Stern and others, eds., 1959, 163–90), and undoubtedly by a number of other scholars. See Darrah (1951) for Morgan's influence on Powell.

[3] Powell in 1875 reported his trip to the Hopi villages in 1870; his use of "Tusayan" revived the Spanish name for Hopiland. Powell's writings and those in which he is a subject

Lt. George M. Wheeler, whose survey operated under the War Department, was the only one of the four to visit the Zuni Pueblo. During the summer of 1873 Wheeler's reconnaissance and survey parties criss-crossed the Zuni country. One result of this activity was the publication of a very useful hachured map of the region, the first based on actual survey. The Zuni territory was covered in Wheeler's atlas of the western territories on sheets 76 and 77 issued separately about 1875 and 1879, respectively. Some splendid photographs — probably the first — of the pueblo and the people were made by Timothy O'Sullivan and also published separately by the Wheeler Survey.

The reports covering the reconnaissance of 1873 carried eyewitness accounts of the Zunis' gardens, fields, and flocks, of the farming villages, and of the pueblo and its inhabitants which then numbered some two thousand souls. The writers described domestic scenes, the captive eagles and "sparrow hawks," and the old church with its two bells, the altar still covered with a "profusion of carving" that showed traces of "gilding and colors." Wheeler's men witnessed a "cachina" dance and described in detail the elaborate dress of the dancers. They took notes on government, language, traditions, and ruins and concluded that it was "quite probable" that the Zuni country was identical with the Cíbola of Coronado.

Assistant topographer and clerk Francis Klett was much impressed with the Zunis. He listened to the white-haired Governor, Pedro Pino, profess hatred for the Mexicans and friendship for the Americans. Klett thought the Zuni Indians "showed marked and distinctive peculiarities"; he singled out originality in dress, strong conservatism, and industriousness. Exuberantly, Klett wrote of his hosts as "descendants of a race long freeholders of the soil of the North American continent." Surely "they are among Nature's Noblemen." [4]

---

form lengthy bibliographies. Darrah's biography (1951) is standard; see Fowler, Euler, and Fowler (1969) for recent scholarship on Powell's anthropological researches. Bartlett (1962) has a balanced history of the four great surveys. Goetzmann (1966) pointed out the impact of the survey on the nation at large.

[4] The publications issued by the Wheeler Survey — normally the United States Geological Surveys West of the One Hundredth Meridian — constitute a bibliographical nightmare. Schmeckebier (1904) has compiled a list of the publications of the Wheeler, Powell, Hayden, and King surveys but it is not complete, particularly when it comes to the Wheeler maps and atlases as Wheat (1957–1963, 5: 340–42) attests. The maps covered the entire area; the earlier railroad and road surveyors had published strip maps only. Wheeler's ponderous final *Report* (1889) summarizes the entire work of his survey with some reference to the Zuni reconnaissance in 1873 on pages 59–62 and elsewhere. Wheeler (1875) contains more detailed reports of the 1873 reconnaissance. See Schmeckebier (1904) for reference to occasional reports touching the Zuni region published as late as 1878. Francis Klett, one of

In 1879 Congress replaced the Powell, Wheeler, Hayden, and King surveys with a new agency, the United States Geological Survey. While this move was being considered, John Wesley Powell lobbied, argued, and pleaded for federal support of Indian studies, a project only just begun by the earlier surveys. Ethnological research should be pushed with vigor, he said, since the Indian cultures were disappearing. Primitive men cannot be transformed by law or conversion, Powell insisted. Echoing Lewis Henry Morgan, he wrote that we must "deal with the Indian as he is, looking to the slow but irresistible influence of civilization . . . to effect a change." The Indians could be helped along the road of social progress, Powell thought, if the white man knew enough about them to provide intelligent guidance. Knowledge, acquired through serious study of Indian language, mythology, social organization, arts, and history, was essential if the Indian "problem" were to be resolved.

Moreover, if all men evolve and progress along similar lines, then the living nineteenth-century American Indian offered a wonderful laboratory. "In studying the condition of the Indian tribes," Morgan said in a work Powell published, "we may recover some portion of the lost history of our own race."

Powell got his wish. In the act which created the Geological Survey, Congress established the Bureau of Ethnology (in 1894 changed to the Bureau of American Ethnology) under the Smithsonian Institution. And Powell, named the first director, set about with vigor to learn about the "Indian as he is" and "to organize anthropologic research in America." [5] The director launched a pro-

Wheeler's men, in 1873 wrote a detailed article (1874) of value for a picture of Zuni in that year. His illustrations are probably based on photographs by O'Sullivan. Klett also wrote a brief article on the "Cachina" dance which appeared in a final volume devoted to archeology, edited by F. W. Putnam of the Peabody Museum at Harvard and issued by Wheeler in 1879. The frontispiece of the volume depicts a colored lithograph of three of the dancers as Klett saw them in 1873. There are additional scattered ethnological references to Zuni in this volume. W. C. Manning (1875), who probably traveled with Wheeler, wrote some sketches on the pueblos, including Zuni. O'Sullivan's photographs of Zuni in 1873 were probably the first made of the pueblo and its people; Horan (1966, 297–303) in his biography of the photographer, reproduces seven of them. Some of the O'Sullivan photographs were distributed publicly as large (about 8″ × 11″) mounted views and as stereographs.

[5] Darrah (1951) has a detailed coverage of Powell and the formation and direction of the Bureau of American Ethnology. I have quoted here from Powell's report to the Secretary of the Interior which Darrah has reproduced in part, pp. 16–17. Judd's (1967) "partial history" of the BAE is an excellent reference; half of the work is taken up with a listing of the Bureau's many publications. Morgan's work on the "Houses and House-life of the American Aborigines" (1881) was written as a part of his *Ancient Society* but was not published with that work. At Powell's request it was included as vol. 4 of the *Contributions to North Ameri-*

gram of bibliographic, linguistic, and tribal studies; he initiated the preparation of a series of anthropological manuals to guide researchers, as well as a systematic linguistic classification of the North American Indians.

As for the pueblos of the Southwest, national interest in the prehistoric ruins and the living Pueblos, aroused during the Mexican War, had been kept alive by the writers of the Pacific Railroad surveys in the 1850s and by the Powell, Wheeler, and Hayden surveys of the 1870s. Indeed, Lewis H. Morgan had directed attention to the Southwest in 1869 when he published a lengthy article on the "Seven Cities of Cibola" in the *North American Review*. In the Southwest Powell saw an excellent opportunity to prove the Darwinian evolutionary theory of man's progress from "barbarism" toward "civilization." The older ruins were of rude construction; the more recent ones were larger and more sophisticated in design. The living Pueblos, though speaking different languages, had reached "a somewhat homogeneous stage of culture." The evidence of both the ruins and the people seemed to prove the point.

One of his earliest actions as head of the new bureau was to make arrangements to continue the explorations in the Pueblo country which he had begun ten years before. In August 1879 James Stevenson and a party which included Frank H. Cushing, an ethnologist in the Smithsonian Institution, and John K. Hillers, photographer, were sent off to the Southwest. The first major target was the Zuni Pueblo, still little touched by "the advancing wave of Caucasian settlement."

Here Stevenson and his wife, Matilda Coxe ("Tilly") Stevenson spent about a month assembling a collection of fourteen hundred articles embracing "almost every object necessary to illustrate the domestic life and art" of the Zunis. The cataloged collection contained over a thousand articles made of clay: water vases, jars, jugs, canteens and pitchers, cups, bowls, cooking vessels, ladles, clay baskets, paint pots, and ornamental vessels. There were also over a hundred stone items: axes, hammers, mauls, mortars, pestles, and miscellaneous objects. The articles made of basketry, fabric, horn, and bone and those of wood — furniture, implements, weapons, toys, and ceremonial objects — ran into the hundreds. Crating up several wagonloads and addressing them to the United States National Museum, a division of the Smithsonian Institution, the Stevensons went on to

---

can Ethnology issued by the Powell Survey. The frontispiece of the work was a colored lithograph of a "Zuni Water Carrier" made from a drawing by W. H. Holmes.

collect in the Hopi villages, Laguna, Acoma, and the Rio Grande pueblos before returning to Washington. Powell reported that Jack Hillers, who had served under him since 1871, had turned in an "excellent suite of photographs." [6]

After the Stevensons left, Cushing, the ethnologist, stayed on at Zuni to study the language, mythology, sociology, history, ceremonies, and art of "that most interesting pueblo." Though only twenty-two and far from robust, Cushing succeeded remarkably well in his studies. He ingratiated himself with the Zunis and was soon noting and sketching everything he saw, including the various ceremonies and activities of the secret societies. Cushing got on well with Governor Patricio Pino, better known as Palowahtiwa, who had recently replaced his father, Pedro Pino, the governor of Zuni for thirty years. Cushing was adopted by Patricio and shared for a time the living quarters of the governor's family. The governor's wife, herself a hypochondriac, pampered the young ethnologist and tried to make his stay comfortable.

By mid-1880 Cushing had acquired a conversational knowledge of the Zuni language. This skill widened his acceptance by the villagers, admitted him to secret councils, and enabled him to acquire a wide range of information, including data on the killing of the Negro Estevan and the location of nearly all of the ancient cities of Cíbola.

Before the end of his second year Cushing, by then an expert in the Zuni language, acquired a Zuni name — Tenatsali, translated as "A Flower," or "Medicine Flower." A more familiar name was taken from his own — "Kushy"

---

[6] Powell tells of his plans for field studies and for the organization of "anthropologic research in America" in his *First Annual Report of the Bureau of Ethnology* (1881). His evolutionary thinking is expressed in a number of places here. See particularly his comments on the planned investigations of C. C. Royce, pp. xxvii–xxx; then read his views on the prehistoric and living Pueblos in his remarks on the explorations of James Stevenson, pp. xxx–xxxii. Stevenson prepared an illustrated catalog of the 1879 collections published in 1883; see n. 7 of this chapter. See also Powell's "Report of the Director" in the *Second Annual Report of the Bureau of Ethnology* (1883), as well as Darrah (1951) and Judd (1967). Tilly Stevenson wrote a privately printed descriptive sketch of the Zuni Pueblo in 1879 and gave some account of the Stevensons' collecting activities. She mentions that two of the carved wooden statues of saints, "still remarkably preserved," were removed from the Spanish-built church and added to the collection sent to the National Museum. One of the statues is portrayed in her work (1881, 10).

Jack Hillers, who joined Powell's second Colorado River expedition in 1871, stayed on as photographer for the Powell Survey, the Bureau of Ethnology, and the U.S. Geological Survey. His work, some of which was published here and there in government reports, was brilliantly done. A sampling of the 1879 Zuni photos has been published by Fowler, ed. (1972). A number of the views in V. Mindeleff's fine report (1891) are from Hillers' lens.

or "Cushy." He had been admitted to the war society, the Priesthood of the
Bow; he had ranged some distance out from the pueblo to examine religious and
mythological sites; he had visited the Hopi Indians and the Havasupai Indians
living in Grand Canyon who for many years had carried on trade with the Zunis;
and he had made copious notes on everything he observed. Furthermore, he had
written a paper on "Zuni Fetiches" which Powell published in the second annual
report of the Bureau of Ethnology.

Cushing was on hand when the Stevensons returned in the summer of 1881
to make another collection of "archaeologic and ethnologic specimens" for the
U.S. National Museum. Perhaps as many as three thousand items of stone, pottery, and wood — utensils, weapons, clothing, ceremonial objects — were collected with the help of Cushing, who included the Zuni names for most of the
articles. This material was later published in the illustrated catalog of the
collection.[7]

Frank Hamilton Cushing's presence among the Zuni Indians strongly influenced the course of their history. That he had entered fully into the life of the
Zunis, that he had, to all intents and purposes, become an Indian, was a broadly
publicized fact which caught the imagination of many people at a time when the
nation was beginning to feel conscience-stricken over its treatment of the American Indians.

Cushing's work at Zuni reached a wide audience in 1882. During the spring
and summer the ethnologist escorted five headmen of the Zunis and one Hopi
on a tour of the eastern cities. For some years the Indians had dreamed of going

---

[7] The literature on Cushing at Zuni is large. His own publications are numerous. "Zuñi
Fetiches" (1883) was issued with a number of illustrations including three colored plates;
two of the plates were included in an edition published by Bahti (1966). Commenting on
Cushing's "Fetiches," Powell (1883, xxviii) treated his readers to these words: "The philosophy of the Zunis is an admirable example of that state in savagery where transition is shown
from zootheism into physitheism, with survivals of hekastotheism. In this stage fetichism is
the chief religious means of obtaining success and protection." See subsequent notes for
reference to Cushing's other Zuni books.

Two unpublished biographies, focusing primarily on Cushing's researches at Zuni, have
been written by Fuller (1943) and Brandes (1965). Woodward (1939) wrote of Cushing's
eccentricities and contributions as "war chief of the Zunis."

The catalog of the collections made at Zuni in 1881 was published by James Stevenson
in 1884. Practically all the items collected are identified by Zuni names. The catalogs compiled by Stevenson in 1879, 1880, and 1881, published in 1883 and 1884, were extensively
illustrated, with a number of colored plates. These undoubtedly are some of the earliest
exact illustrations of Zuni pottery and other objects.

to see for themselves the fabled land on the shores of the Atlantic Ocean — "the Ocean of Sunrise." Hoping that the Indians would benefit from the trip and that good will for his own projects would be generated, Cushing obtained funds from the Smithsonian Institution to pay their expenses. Old Pedro Pino, or Laiiuaitsailu, his son Governor Palowahtiwa, Bow priests Naiiutchi and Kiasi, Laiiuahtsailunkia, and Nanake, the Hopi, made up the party.

Cushing and the Indians took the Santa Fe Railway to Chicago, stayed at the Palmer House, and then boarded the Baltimore and Ohio for Washington, where they were received by President Chester A. Arthur. In Boston the Indians were treated to a round of activities — a reception at Old South Meeting House, a minstrel show, a visit to Harvard University and the Peabody Museum. At a public reception held for them in Salem, the Zunis praised the colonial New Englanders for their punishment of witches. When called on for comment, Kiasi delivered a sermon on witchcraft which, one reporter remarked, "would have pleased old Cotton Mather himself."

The most important event of the trip took place on an island in Boston Harbor. After appropriate ceremony the Zunis filled a number of containers with precious sea water. The ancestral gods, the Indians believed, had once lived in the ocean. These gods had taught their people the prayers and songs that brought rain to their desert home. The effectiveness of the rain ceremonies might be increased if a few drops from the "Ocean of Sunrise" were sprinkled about.

Cushing, who wore a picturesque Western–Spanish costume bedecked with silver, and the Zuni Indians were well received by learned societies and public gatherings alike, and their appearances were covered extensively by the press. They were featured in popular magazines. Cushing's lecture on "The Zuni Social, Mythic, and Religious Systems," delivered before the National Academy of Sciences in Washington, appeared in *Popular Science Monthly* for June 1882. Sylvester Baxter, correspondent for the Boston *Herald*, covered the highlights of the trip in "An Aboriginal Pilgrimage" published in *Century Magazine* for August 1882.[8]

Cushing and his Indian friends were given very favorable publicity by Baxter. He had visited Cushing at Zuni in 1881 and collected material for a

---

[8] Cushing's lecture at the National Academy is a remarkable summary of his knowledge of the Zuni mind, acquired over a period of three years. Baxter's piece was illustrated with pictures of all the pilgrims, including Cushing in full regalia. Gilbert (1961) is an adaptation from Baxter. Brandes (1965) devotes a chapter to the pilgrimage and refers to a number of newspaper articles.

detailed account of the Indians and the ethnologist's life among them. This appeared in *Harper's Magazine* for June 1882, when the Zunis and Cushing were in the East, and it also helped to publicize their tour.

Cushing himself wrote several popular accounts of his adventures in the Southwest. "My Adventures in Zuni" ran in three numbers of *Century Magazine* between December 1882 and May 1883. An article on his visit to the Havasupai Indians had appeared in *Atlantic Monthly* in September and October 1882. The articles in prominent national magazines, illustrated by first-class artists like W. L. Metcalf and Henry F. Farny, and the eastern pilgramage itself, gave the Zuni story (and Cushing's) the widest publicity it had ever known.[9] Indeed, by the end of the year 1882, the Zunis were probably the best known of the peaceful Indians in the Southwest, if not in the United States. And the events of the next year — their participation in Santa Fe's "Tertio-Millennial" and the controversy over Nutria Springs — kept them in the public view.

Frank Hamilton Cushing was a central figure in these events, all of which benefited his Pueblo hosts. Although the pilgrimage to the Atlantic Ocean was memorable, his greatest contribution to the welfare of the Zunis was starting the action that saved Nutria Springs. The consequences of that action, as noted above, stirred up a political tempest which threatened the existence of the Bureau of Ethnology. Although he was not to be bullied by Senator Logan, Powell became increasingly annoyed by Cushing's failure to write up the results of his researches. The frail Cushing, who had suffered failing health in the pueblo, found it difficult to write, let alone to compose an acceptable synthesis of his findings. In March 1884 Powell ordered Cushing to return to Washington, thus terminating his five-year sojourn with the Zuni Indians.[10]

Cushing's works tower above nearly everything else written about the Zuni people. He wrote to be read. The easy, entertaining style of his magazine articles carried over to the studies of Zuni fetiches (1883) and pottery and cul-

---

[9] After being guided about the Zuni Pueblo by Cushing, Baxter wrote a detailed and highly informative piece called "The Father of the Pueblos" about the people, their village and environs, and about Cushing. Baxter and Cushing became good friends with important consequences for Cushing and the Indians: Baxter played a significant role in the Nutria controversy; see Chapter 9. Cushing related his own adventures for the *Century Magazine*, 1882–1883; the trip to the Havasupais was reported in the *Atlantic Monthly* (1882a). The first has been reproduced by Euler, ed. (1965), and the second by both DeGolyer, ed. (1941), and Jones, ed. (1967). On Metcalf and Farny see Taft (1943); Metcalf visited Zuni and Cushing in company with Sylvester Baxter.

[10] Brandes (1965, chap. 6) has details on Cushing's health and departure for Zuni.

ture growth (1886) which were published by Powell in the early Reports of the Bureau of Ethnology. His popular articles and serious papers revealed to the world in intimate detail many facets of the Zuni culture. Cushing found inappropriate terms like "primitive," "barbarism," and "savage," words conspicuous in the writings of men like Morgan and Powell. He seemed little concerned about cultural evolution. His descriptions of Zuni institutions suggest that he found this culture impressive; he once referred to the Indians' mythological tradition as the "Zuni Iliad." [11]

Cushing wrote, not as a student reporting from a laboratory, but as a man reflecting on his fellow man. His articles and papers, still read eagerly today, soon after their publication began to lead a succession of students to New Mexico to see for themselves the fascinating Zuni people. Before long the pueblo had become the happy hunting ground for the anthropologists.[12]

---

[11] Cushing's paper "A Study of Pueblo Pottery as Illustrative of Zuni Culture Growth" (1886b) appeared in the *Fourth Annual Report of the Bureau of Ethnology, 1882–83*. In the early work "Zuñi Fetiches," Cushing dignifies the Indians' oral traditions with terms like the "Zuñi Iliad." Cushing wrote an interesting paper on "The Need of Studying the Indian in Order to Teach Him" (1897, 109). Those who would understand the Indian, he wrote, "must go to him as brothers," and "be in thought and act his equal only."

[12] Anyone who writes on Zuni history will find an abundance of materials for the Cushing era. Cushing, of course, had projected the Zuni people into a position of national prominence and, for much of the time since, they have retained it. One may hazard the guess that if any college junior could name one of the Southwestern Pueblos, it would be the Zuni. If that is something the Zunis find comforting they may give Frank Hamilton Cushing much of the credit.

Although Cushing left the pueblo in 1884 he did return a few years later at the head of the Hemenway Expedition (see Chapter 11). Brandes (1965), emphasizing the work done at Zuni, refers to Cushing as a "pioneer Americanist." Brandes lists the unpublished and published writings of the ethnologist as well as his correspondence. Cushing died while still a young man at age forty-three. Memorial articles by Chamberlain (1900) and by W. J. McGee, W. H. Holmes, J. W. Powell, and others (1900) give his essential bibliography and reflect the high opinion of the man held by his professional colleagues. Powell, who had suffered a good number of Cushing's eccentricities, called him a genius. Bandelier (1889, 4: 5) wrote that Cushing's Zuni researches "will serve as a model for all times to come."

After he left the pueblo Cushing wrote two important works about Zuni: *Zuñi Breadstuff* was published 1884–1885 (new edition, 1920), and the "Outlines of Zuñi Creation Myths" appeared in 1896. A third writing, *Zuñi Folk Tales*, perhaps his best known work, was published after his death in 1901. The book carried a foreword by John W. Powell. A later edition (1931) was introduced by Mary Austin who wrote that Cushing was the only man not of Indian blood "who understands completely the soul of such lore" among the Indians of the Southwest.

Cushing left many papers including numbers of unpublished manuscripts. Most of these will be found in the National Anthropological Archives of the Smithsonian Institution in Washington; Archives of the Peabody Museum, Harvard University; and the Southwest

Museum, Highland Park, Los Angeles. The most extensive collection, assembled by F. W. Hodge, who knew Cushing from his Zuni era, is in the Southwest Museum.

The Gilcrease Institute of American History and Art, Tulsa, Okla., possesses a large oil painting of Cushing done about 1895 by the celebrated American artist, Thomas Eakins (Wenger, 1959). Cushing helped the artist convert his studio into a replica of a typical room in the Zuni pueblo as a background for the portrait. The ethnologist posed in a flamboyant costume of his own making, one not distinctly Zuni by any means. Of an earlier outfit, one Cushing wore on the eastern tour in 1882, Woodward (1939) wrote that "his costume of knee trousers, elaborately trimmed with small silver buttons, his long blouse-like shirt, similarly ornamented, even to his shoes, were vestigial remnants of the Spanish-Mexican costume of the late 18th century." Woodward concluded that his coarse footless socks and the "twisted fillet of cloth wound about his head" were probably the only distinctively Indian items in his regalia.

Chapter II

Exposure

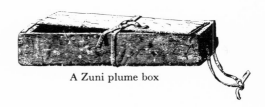

A Zuni plume box

After the coming of the railroad, the Zuni cultural fabric was constantly affected by the alien influence of traders, missionaries, government agents, teachers, and students of anthropology who were drawn to the pueblo like quicksilver to gold.

Frank Cushing's well-publicized researches not only caught the public fancy but inspired four generations of scholars to follow him to Zuni and the Southwest. Even before he left New Mexico Cushing had entertained several persons interested in his Zuni studies. Among them was Dr. Washington Mathews, stationed at Fort Wingate, a student of the Navajos. Others were John G. Bourke, the Dutch scholar H. F. C. ten Kate, and A. F. Bandelier, all of whom wrote papers on the Zuni Indians based on their own studies.[1]

---

[1] Mention has also been made of James and Tilly Stevenson who accompanied Cushing to Zuni in 1879. Cushing's relations with them, at least with Tilly, were anything but friendly. Brandes (1965) refers to Cushing's scholarly associates in New Mexico. Mathews published on the Navajos; see listings in Saunders, comp. (1944), and Murdock (1960). Bourke's account of his ethnological peregrinations in the Southwest was edited by Bloom (1933–1938). Bourke visited Zuni in 1881 and jotted down several pages of data most of which appeared in his diary entries for May 18–21. Articles on the Zuni by H. F. C. ten Kate are listed in Saunders, comp. (1944), and Murdock (1960). Bandelier's works on Zuni and the Southwest, a number of which have been cited here, are extensive and important. Saunders, comp. (1944), lists many of them. Burrus, ed. (1969), has issued the first volume of Bandelier's hitherto unpublished seven-part history of the Southwest (originally in French) covering the time to 1700. In this introductory volume Burrus describes Bandelier's extensive researches and lists the illustrations accompanying the history, now in the Vatican Library. A number of these illustrations, drawings from Bandelier's own hand that portray Zuni ruins and symbols, are reproduced in the supplement to volume 1. Bandelier visited the pueblo and environs in 1883; his private journal of that year, reflecting a close observation of Zuni, has been elaborately edited by Lange and Riley (1970).

Powell, of the Bureau of Ethnology, continued sending his people to Zuni. He was deeply interested in comparisons between prehistoric and modern Pueblo architecture in the Southwest. On the surface it appeared to him that there had been a progression in building techniques which illustrated man's evolution toward civilization. Moreover, he was convinced that the architecture of the pueblos was a product of the Southwestern environment, not an importation from distant regions. To test these views Powell in 1881 sent Victor Mindeleff to make a detailed instrumental survey of the Zuni Pueblo, the first part of a program of studies of Pueblo architecture, both ancient and modern. Later, from Mindeleff's measurements, the Bureau of Ethnology laboratory constructed a model of the pueblo in papier mâché one sixtieth its actual size. The model, done in "the true colors of the village as well as of all the details" was placed on exhibition in the U. S. National Museum in Washington.[2]

Assisted by his brother Cosmos, Victor Mindeleff spent several seasons in the Southwest gathering data for a monograph which appeared in 1891 under the title, "A Study of Pueblo Architecture: Tusayan and Cibola." In introducing the work, Powell noted that aboriginal architecture in the United States had reached "its culmination in the large communal villages of many-storied terraced buildings which were in use at the time of the Spanish discovery, and which still survive in Zuni." Mindeleff showed that Powell was right. Modern Pueblo architecture indeed was not only an outgrowth of, but also an improvement upon, the building arts of the Anasazis. Its distinguishing characteristics were determined by the need for defense and the abundance of excellent building materials everywhere available in the desert. Mindeleff concluded by observing that since Pueblo architecture had originated locally, there was no longer any need to drag in some extinct race to account for it, and thus he laid to rest a popular theory, current since the Mexican War, which had held that the Aztecs were the first architects of the Southwest.[3]

---

[2] The model was on display in the U.S. National Museum when Powell submitted his third annual report of the Bureau of Ethnology in 1883. See Powell (1884, xxi). The model may still exist among the treasures of the museum.

[3] The Mindeleff brothers spent less time in Cíbola than Tusayan, but the monograph issued in the *Eighth Annual Report of the Bureau of Ethnology, 1886–87* (1891) contains many illustrations (including some Hillers photos) of Zuni architecture and ground plans of the old "Cities of Cíbola" as they were in 1881, and of other villages. Cosmos published a number of papers including one on the ruins in Canyon de Chelly (1897).

Mindeleff ventured to predict (quite accurately) that as defensive require-
ments lessened the Pueblos would abandon the many-storied structures and
return to the more convenient system of scattered houses, thus returning in full
circle to the mode of building probably dominant in the early days when peace
prevailed throughout the land. (Indeed the move to the "suburbs" was already
underway in Mindeleff's day. By then, at least one small house, the subject of
a photograph by Jack Hillers, had been built outside the main pueblo.)[4]

Before he left Zuni, Frank Cushing himself began the break with the defensive
mode in architecture when he installed a ground level door in his pueblo apart-
ment. This of course eliminated the inconvenience of climbing a ladder in order
to enter his chamber through the roof, a defensive measure used everywhere in
the village. Cushing painted the door vermilion and set it against the dull-colored
adobe wall. The Indians thought it beautiful. The style quickly spread and soon
many houses had installed ground level doors, many of them bought ready-made
from lumber merchants in Albuquerque.[5]

Cushing also furthered the trend to the suburbs when he built a house across
the river, south of the main pueblo. This was in 1883, just prior to his departure
from the pueblo. He used this building as his headquarters when he returned to
Zuni in 1888 as director of the Hemenway Southwestern Archaeological Expedition. At that time he enlarged the structure and, while digging the foundations,
unexpectedly laid bare the walls of some ancient rooms, once a part of the Zuni
Pueblo. Usually called by the name of Halona, the Spanish designation for the
Zuni Pueblo, this building had been levelled to the ground, probably at the opening of the eighteenth century. Since his mission was archeological research,
Cushing spent several months uncovering old Halona as he completed his house,
which was the only one on the south bank.[6]

The Hemenway Expedition grew out of the enlightened philanthropy of
Mary (Mrs. Augustus) Hemenway of Boston whose interest in Southwestern

---

[4] V. Mindeleff (1891), particularly his concluding remarks, pp. 223–28. And see the
introductory remarks by Powell (1891, xxx–xxxiv). The small house is shown opposite p. 170
of that work and on p. 81 of the present volume.

[5] Cushing relates this experience in his essay on the need for studying the Indian (1897,
112).

[6] Old Halona originally occupied both banks of the Zuni River. The section on the south
bank was probably razed about 1700 when the Zunis consolidated their numbers at Zuni after
the Pueblo Revolt; see Chapter 5. Victor Mindeleff (1891, 88) published an 1886 photo of
the Zuni house (and the excavations), the only one in sight; Mindeleff's remarks on old
Halona, pp. 88–89, are instructive.

archeology and ethnology was kindled in large measure by Frank H. Cushing and three Zuni Indians. During the summer of 1886, while recuperating from his chronic illness, Cushing was invited by Mrs. Hemenway to spend some time at her retreat, Manchester-by-the-Sea near Boston. Cushing moved into a private cottage, promptly naming it "Casa Ramona" in honor of Helen H. Jackson's novel, then a runaway best seller. Shortly he was joined there by three Zuni headmen whose trip East Frank had been trying to arrange for some time. His old friend, Governor Palowahtiwa, who had made the eastern trip in 1882, was one of the visitors; the others were Waihusiwa and Heluta.[7]

Cushing and his Zuni friends made the most of their stay with Mrs. Hemenway. Near the seashore the Indians practiced with bow and arrow while Henry Sandham, the artist, made sketches for a painting of the sport. With these ready informants at hand, Cushing was able to fill gaps in his Zuni research. Mrs. Hemenway and occasional guests listened with great interest as Cushing translated the lively tales and stories told by the Indians.

The Zunis often commented on the strange ways of the Americans. Why, they asked, do Americans "gather around us and come into our country continually, and even strive to get our land from us? Is it possible for anyone to say what they want? Where is there a country more beautiful than this one we are sitting in now? Is there any water needed here? Without irrigation, on the very tops of the mountains and hills things grow green. Yes, the Americans have all of this; they have enough to eat and to spare. Though their houses and villages lie scattered over the land as thickly as the pine woods and sage brush in Zuni land, still they have enough to eat and enough to wear, and what they eat and what they wear are also the best."

Why, indeed, with all of this should the Americans encroach on a poor people far away in a desert land? The Zunis attempted to answer their own questions. Of the Americans: "The sentiment of home affects them not; the little bits of land they may own, or the house they may have been bred in, are as nothing to them. Their thoughts do not seem to dwell contentedly even on their own wives and children, for they wander incessantly, wander through all difficulties and dangers to seek new places and better things. Why are they so unceasingly unsatisfied?"

---

[7] Details on the background and achievements of the Hemenway Southwestern Archaeological Expedition are found in Brandes (1965, chaps. 7–8) and Haury (1945, 5–9). A brief "official" history is Gilman and Stone (1908).

Palowahtiwa said, "Above every people they are a people of emulation; above every kind of man or being, a people of fierce jealousies. Is not this an explanation? If one American goes one day's journey in the direction of a difficult trail, it is not long ere another American will go two day's journey in the direction of a more difficult one. One American cannot bear that another shall surpass him. Ah, the Gods know full well the passions of the Americans."

It is not recorded how the whites reacted to these astute evaluations of the American character. We do know that Cushing, one of those "unsatisfied" Americans, longed to return to the Zuni country to finish work begun but not completed and spent many hours discussing his ethnological studies with Mrs. Hemenway. In the Southwest where the Indians live amid the relics of their past, Cushing said, we have an unparalleled opportunity to extend our knowledge of the Zunis back through millennia. What we would learn through further study of Zuni culture would apply (given the ideas then current on cultural evolution) to other Indian peoples. Our understanding of the Indian as he is would rest on firm foundations and programs of assistance might be designed with sympathy and enlightenment.

Mrs. Hemenway, undoubtedly impressed by her guests, agreed to Cushing's suggestion that she support a scientific expedition for an elaborate study of prehistoric and living cultures of the Southwest. Cushing assembled a large staff to undertake ethnological, anthropological, historical, and archeological studies, and reached the field before the end of 1886.[8]

The Hemenway Expedition spent a year and a half excavating ruins near Phoenix in the Salt River Valley before moving to the Zuni Pueblo in mid-1888. It was while enlarging his old home — now christened "Hemenway House" — that Cushing discovered the sub-surface ruins of old Halona. He decided to excavate these and also the ruins at Heshotauthla, fifteen miles up the Pescado, as the first of a series of explorations into Cíbola's ancient history. After making a good start, Cushing fell ill once more. He was unable to continue his work and went east to recuperate; he never returned again to Zuni.

---

[8] Details about the summer at Casa Ramona come from Brandes (1965, chap. 7) and Cushing's own unpublished "Notes" (1886a) made at the time, preserved in the Southwest Museum. Cushing's expectations for the Hemenway venture on the Southwest were elaborated by him in a paper read before the International Congress of Americanists in 1888 (1890). A brief account of the formation of the expedition with a bibliography of resulting publications is in Gilman and Stone (1908).

The Hemenway Expedition was later reorganized under the direction of J. Walter Fewkes, who spent the summer of 1890 at Zuni. He made a study of the summer ceremonials and recorded the music on the newly-invented phonographic cylinders. He also undertook a reconnaissance of various ruins in the region. After one season at Zuni he devoted himself to the study of the ethnology of the Hopi Indians.[9]

Zuni, Pueblo, and Southwestern history generally were well served by the Hemenway Expedition through the publications of A. F. Bandelier. Already a competent historian when he met Cushing at Zuni in 1883, Bandelier was engaged as the expedition's "historiographer." Drawing upon manuscript and published sources, he brought out in 1892 *An Outline of the Documentary History of the Zuni Tribe*, a work of lasting importance. The study carries Zuni history from Fray Marcos to the Pueblo Revolts; an unpublished portion continues the narrative to about 1780, near the end of the Spanish period. These were followed by additional papers illuminating related chapters in Southwestern history.[10]

The Hemenway Southwestern Archaeological Expedition attracted attention to the possibilities for historical and archeological research in the Southwest and to the abundant prehistoric remains and historical documents available for that study. Papers by both Cushing and Bandelier were read before the International Congress of Americanists meeting in Berlin in 1888. Fewkes' paper, pinpointing nearly thirty ruins near Zuni Pueblo, was published in 1891, the same year that Mindeleff's elaborate study on the Pueblo architecture of Cíbola and

---

[9] Haury (1945), who completed the archeological work begun by Cushing in the Salt River Valley, dedicated his monograph to the memory of Mary Hemenway "whose initiative, generosity, and understanding set in motion the first organized archaeological work in the Southwest"; see Amsden (1949, 22–29). Cushing's old friend and "home secretary" of the expedition, Sylvester Baxter, published an account of the Salt River Valley explorations (1888). Excavations by the Hemenway Expedition at Zuni were noticed by Fewkes (1891b), Cushing's successor. Fewkes later (1909) published a technical paper on "Ancient Zuni Pottery" based on the excavations at Heshotauthla. His observations of the summer ceremonial were published in 1891(a). The interesting matter of recording Zuni music on phonographic cylinders was reported by Gilman (1891).

[10] Bandelier's scholarly papers have been much used in this work and are listed in the bibliography. Two of them (1890b and 1892b) were brought out under the auspices of the Hemenway Expedition. See the introduction by Lange and Riley, eds. (1966–1970), for Bandelier's many activities and publications. Bandelier summarized his work for the Hemenway Expedition in a paper read before the International Congress of Americanists in 1888 (1890c).

Tusayan appeared. It was Frederick Webb Hodge, Cushing's assistant, whose imagination was most fired by the prehistoric Zuni towns. Hodge had supervised the digs at Halona and Heshotauthla for the Hemenway Expedition. Years later, in 1917, he came back to excavate the largest of the "Seven Cities" — Hawikuh.[11]

In American anthropology it would be difficult to name a more powerful lodestone than the land of Cíbola. The Zuni people have had to endure on-the-ground microscopic examinations by an apparently endless stream of zealous students of man and his culture. Mindeleff, Cushing, Fewkes, and Hodge had no more than left the pueblo when Matilda Coxe Stevenson arrived.

"Tilly," who had first visited Zuni in 1879 with her husband and Frank Cushing, came back in 1891 for Powell and the Bureau of Ethnology. Strong-willed and aggressive, she must have appeared to the Zunis to be one of those "unsatisfied Americans" as she went about collecting information on everything from mythology and ceremonials to beadmaking and salt gathering, from witchcraft and medicine to history and art. Her prodigious research over several seasons resulted in a heavy volume of 608 pages published by the Bureau of American Ethnology in 1904. As she completed her study, Mrs. Stevenson complimented her subjects by writing: "The field ethnologist must realize that a lifetime is not sufficient to fully understand a people as profuse in legend and ritual as the Zuni." [12]

In 1917, Hodge returned. It was his ambition to tackle a site known to have been inhabited from prehistoric times well into the historic period. There was no

---

[11] Hodge (1937, xv) briefly mentions his identification with the expedition at Zuni, 1888–1889.

The field work of the expedition came to an end with Mrs. Hemenway's death in 1894. A list of publications resulting from the expedition and running through the years 1889–1908, was issued by Gilman and Stone (1908). The archives of the Hemenway Southwestern Archaeological Expedition (1886–1959) at the Peabody Museum at Harvard contain much unpublished material on the work done in Arizona and at Zuni. Additional material will be found in the Hodge–Cushing papers at the Southwest Museum, Los Angeles.

One of the more interesting publications to emanate from the Hemenway Expedition was a long poem by Edna Dean Proctor, *The Song of the Ancient People* (1893). It contained preface and notes by the prominent historian John Fiske and commentary by F. H. Cushing, who signed himself "A Zuni Familiar." The book, handsomely published, was illustrated with aquatints by Julian Scott. The work draws on Zuni and Hopi mythology as recorded in the studies of Cushing and Fewkes.

[12] M. C. Stevenson (1904), as far as I know, is the largest single volume devoted to the culture of the Zuni people. A supplementary paper on the ethnobotany of the Zuni Indians was issued by Stevenson in 1915. Her compliment to the Zunis is in a letter to J. W. Powell, August 15, 1900, in her papers (1890–1918).

better place than Hawikuh, which had fallen into ruins and lain undisturbed since the Zunis abandoned it after the Pueblo Revolt. Backed by the Museum of the American Indian, Heye Foundation, of New York City, Hodge in six field seasons carried out the "most extensive archaeological investigation of a single site undertaken up to that time in the United States." Revealed were the broad outlines of prehistory and varied aspects of the Zuni lifeway during the first century and a half of the Spanish epoch. As a complement to the archeological findings, Hodge went to the Spanish documents and prepared a distinguished history of Hawikuh, carrying the narrative down to 1680.[13]

Other students of anthropology followed Stevenson and Hodge: Leslie Spier, A. L. Kroeber, Elsie Clews Parsons, Ruth Benedict, Ruth Bunzel, John Adair, and a number of scholars associated with cooperative programs conducted by Harvard University and the University of Chicago. Adding the names of Stevenson and Hodge, the list — far from complete — is a sampling of those scientists and institutions whose interests took them to the Zuni country during the seventy years following the departure of the Hemenway Expedition. The resulting publications would fill a very long shelf indeed. Their authors have made the Zuni Indians one of the best known peoples in North America.[14]

---

[13] Hodge's history (1937), owing much to Bandelier's earlier (1892b) work, was one of the best things to come out of his Zuni experiences. Hodge was a rare person whose outlook was broad enough to include the methods of diverse disciplines in his quest for knowledge. He wrote many books and papers. Those pertaining to Zuni are listed in Smith, Woodbury, and Woodbury (1966, 298–301), the final report on the Hawikuh excavation and the source of my quotation on its national importance. An obituary notice by Cole (1957) credits Hodge with more than three hundred fifty published items. See J. A. Carroll (1959). One of Hodge's monuments was the editorial preparation of the *Handbook of American Indians North of Mexico* (1907–1910) to which he contributed the article on "Zuni" (1910).

[14] Murdock (1960, 354–58) lists the Zuni titles by these and many other authors. Most of the major works will be found in the bibliography in this book. It is interesting to note that much of the scholarship on Zuni produced in the years from 1889 to 1960 was done by women. I have already noticed Stevenson's volume (1904) and supplement (1915). Parsons wrote dozens of titles and a two-volume work on *Pueblo Indian Religion* (1939b). Benedict is perhaps best known in Zuni literature for her two-volume *Zuni Mythology* (1939). However, see her *Patterns of Culture* (1934, 57–129), a work more widely read, in which she calls the Zunis "Apollonian" in character, a much-disputed term; see Dozier (1970, 200–203). Bunzel has contributed a number of papers ranging from Pueblo pottery to Zuni ritual poetry. Another woman, March (1941), one of the few to have written of the literary quality of Zuni tradition, has studied the Zuni myths as literature. Leighton and Adair (1966) report the results of a joint project of the University of Chicago and the Bureau of Indian Affairs; Vogt and Albert, eds. (1966), report the "Comparative Studies of Values in Five Cultures" project of Harvard University, in which Zuni was one of the five cultures studied.

The writing about Zuni has been dominated by the astonishing productivity of the anthropologists. One wonders why the historians have not done more. The Pueblos in general, and the Zunis particularly, are as interesting historically as any of the American Indians, yet the historians have been timid in their approach to them. Perhaps fearing to be called "local" and "provincial," the scholars have preferred to take on larger subjects, leaving the study of man in microcosm to others.

While the historians appear to have felt no compulsion to investigate Zuni history, the mass of anthropological literature about the Zuni people seems to convey a feeling of urgency in this field. The long shadows of Morgan and Powell seem to play over the volumes. The Zuni Pueblo, its people little affected in 1879 by the "advancing wave of Caucasian settlement," was a laboratory, and a study of Zuni society could throw light on man's progress toward civilization. But would these Indians survive the impact of "civilization" suddenly thrust upon them? Would their culture change radically? Would they vanish along with other Indians less advanced than they?

Fearing the answers to their own questions, the anthropologists appear to have felt obligated to press on with their studies while there was still time. Some thought was even given to protecting the pueblo from the contamination of outside influences. On one occasion the Bureau of American Ethnology was asked if one of its zealous students was attempting to freeze the Indian culture for museum purposes and make of it an "ethnologist's paradise." [15] This idea seemed to have some currency. Concerning the Zuni and Hopi Indians, John Fiske, prominent evolutionist and historian, in 1893 wrote: "We have still much to learn from them concerning ancient society, and we ought not to be in too great a hurry to civilize them, especially if they do not demand it of us." [16]

The Zuni Indians had never demanded any brand of civilization but their own. All they had ever wanted was to live under their own sky and at peace with their neighbors. Yet as the decades passed the Zunis found themselves caught between two worlds. The struggle to preserve their own way grew increasingly

---

Newman (1965, 9) reports a Zuni bibliography compiled by John M. Roberts that contains some four hundred titles. Anthropological studies at Zuni continue: Tedlock, "The Ethnography of Tale-telling at Zuni" (1968), is the most recent study I know.

[15] In 1907. See Wilken (1953) regarding some of the activities of Matilda Coxe Stevenson.

[16] In the preface of Edna Dean Proctor's *The Song of the Ancient People* (1893, xv).

difficult as they were exposed to the encompassing power of the American national economic and political system. And the attractions of the material wealth of the Anglos posed a threat to the structure of their society and even to the very survival of the Zunis.

Any contact was bound to produce some change. The Pueblos emerged from an amalgam of prehistoric culture and over the centuries they have borrowed from each other and from neighboring tribes; they have never been static. The Spanish intrusion brought fundamental changes in Pueblo living and, as might be expected, the Americans brought more, particularly after the railroad was built. The most obvious changes occurred in the economy but the traditional organization of society, religion, and civil government were also affected. The Zuni Indians were exposed to new ways chiefly through the agents of contact — missionaries, traders, teachers, government people, and the students of man and his culture.

Anthropologists are seldom cast in the role of historians. But they seem to deserve the name here, not so much as agents of change — though not forgetting Cushing and the vermilion-painted ground-floor doors! — but as recorders of change taking place in the traditional life of the Zuni people. The anthropologists' works, written in such quantity over so many years, are the best measure we have of the extent of that change.[17]

The sum total of anthropological research at Zuni, with all of its clinical intimacies and apparent irrelevancies, constitutes an imposing document, one which may have a stabilizing influence on the culture itself. The anthropologists have held up a mirror by which, in a rapidly-changing world, the Zunis may be made aware of their own unique heritage. Anthropological monographs are seen occasionally in Zuni homes today. Tilly Stevenson's "The Zuni Indians" is well known in the pueblo. Furthermore, from the anthropologists the outside world has an opportunity to learn something of a people whose lifeway has impressed four generations of scholars. These outsiders may find themselves in the position of many of those in the past who have studied other peoples — the student often may become the convert.

---

[17] The historian who writes of the Zunis and the other Pueblos, and for that matter of any of the Indian peoples, must always be grateful to the researches of anthropologists. In this instance I refer to the study of Leighton and Adair, *People of the Middle Place* (1966), who have introduced some measure of historical perspective into their work, a rare occurrence in anthropological literature.

A Zuni chair

Chapter 12

Between Two Worlds

Anglo-American influences reached the Zuni Pueblo by a number of routes. Education in the white man's style was one. The beginnings of formal education date back to 1877 when the Presbyterian Church established a day school supported in part by federal funds. For the first few years the school seems not to have made much headway. The teachers must have encountered strong hostility and suffered from communication problems; turnover in the early days was high. The early teachers, who doubled as missionaries, also found it difficult not to involve themselves in the life of the pueblo.

Dr. Taylor F. Ealy, who served his church as "medical missionary" and his government as "United States Teacher" for two and a half years, 1878–1881, found himself much concerned with the matter of Zuni "progress." The rains came in abundance during the summer of 1880 and this, he reported, produced a "general encouragement to all to push forward." There was only one plow on the reservation and not a single "fanning mill" to winnow wheat. Ealy tried unsuccessfully to persuade the Indians to build a dam at Black Rock. The extra water, he reckoned, would support a population five times that then living in the pueblo. Dr. Ealy felt compelled to report that he had heard that someone in the village had been executed for witchcraft. As for education, a little progress was being made: "Some of their children have come to school." [1]

During the early years, as they labored at propagating the faith among the Zunis, some hostility appears to have developed between the Presbyterians and the Mormons. However, the missionaries abandoned their differences when they discovered that they had to compete with Frank Cushing for favor with the

---

[1] See Chapter 8. I am citing Ealy's 1880 report (1881); see also his 1879 report (1880) and Ruth Ealy (1955) for some of the trials and tribulations of a pioneer school teacher.

Indians. Since Cushing, a member of the tribe in good standing, apparently felt no need to foster good will between his fellow tribesmen and the missionaries, an unsettling conflict developed in 1881.

Involved were the Board of Home Missions of the Presbyterian Church, the Church of Jesus Christ of Latter-day Saints, the Smithsonian Institution, and the Bureau of Ethnology. Cushing, aided by John G. Bourke, an army officer and also a student of Indians, tilted against the Reverend S. A. Bentley of the Presbyterian Church and Tilly Stevenson, who had no particular regard for Cushing and his eccentric ways. Although this affair seems to have blown over without serious consequences, it did have the effect of disquieting the Zunis and damaging the Anglo position in the village. The subsequent need to improve good will was one of the objectives Cushing had in mind when he took the five headmen East in 1882. Moreover, as he wrote at the time, he wanted "to show them the wisdom of consenting to education." [2]

Despite these inauspicious beginnings, in 1882 education for Zuni children was opened on a regular basis and has been in continuous operation since.[3] In 1897, after twenty years of pioneering effort, the Presbyterian Church gave up the Zuni school and mission. During the last years of the church's tenure, education at the pueblo was enlivened by the presence of Miss Mary E. DeSette, who had taught at Haskell Institute and the "Ramona School" at Santa Fe before coming to Zuni. Miss DeSette felt that if the Indians were to have faith in her then she must "stir up the authorities" in their behalf.

Arriving at her post in 1889, the teacher embarked upon a crusade in the interest of "law, order and morality" and did not hesitate to pry busily into pueblo affairs. She "stirred up" her superiors in the Indian service through a stream of letters reporting conditions at Zuni and demanding action against alleged criminals, "witch-hangers," and liquor peddlers at the Shalako dances. In 1897, in answer to one of these reports, several Zuni men were charged with murdering a witch. As the sheriff arrived to make the arrests, the army moved in to cover the situation. Three troops of cavalry (two from Fort Wingate, one

---

[2] In a long letter of December 4, 1884, Cushing explained the complex situation at Zuni to Spencer Baird, Secretary of the Smithsonian Institution. In a letter of December 24, 1881, to J. C. Pilling of the same agency, Cushing explained the desirability of maintaining the good will of the Zunis which would come with the trip east. These letters are in Cushing, Letters Received, 1879–1899, National Anthropological Archives, Smithsonian Institution.

[3] Leighton and Adair (1966, 87). The first day school, they say, opened in 1882. "Education has been continuous but by no means universal since that date."

from Fort Apache) were on hand to protect the arresting officer and the Indian witnesses in case of trouble, which did not develop, however. One troop was left at Zuni to keep an eye on the situation and to "protect" the teachers and other whites in the pueblo.

Within a few months the case against the Zunis was annulled upon motion of the government itself. The troops were withdrawn from the pueblo. Early in the "campaign" one of the commanding officers said that "influence rather than force" might work better. Throughout the affair the Zunis remained calm, though they may well have had some misgivings about future trends in education.

In 1897, the government stopped subsidizing the mission-school system and opened a regular day school. Miss DeSette, expecting transfer, stayed on through the winter of 1898–1899, working heroically to help fight a smallpox epidemic that killed over four hundred Zunis. Then she was quietly assigned to another post.[4] The events of 1897 and the smallpox epidemic made the federal government feel the need for a closer tie with the Zunis. About 1902, a Zuni sub-agency of the federal Indian Service was established near the pueblo at Black Rock.

Educational facilities were gradually increased over the next twenty-five years. In 1907 the government opened a boarding school at Black Rock. The following year the Christian (Dutch) Reformed Church, which had sent Andrew VanderWagen to establish a mission at Zuni in 1897, opened a mission

---

[4] My account of Miss DeSette's ten-year encounter with the Zuni Indians is distilled from correspondence in U.S. Bureau of Indian Affairs, Pueblo and Jicarilla and Zuni Agencies, Record Group 75, in the National Archives, Washington, D.C., and the Federal Record Center of the Archives in Denver. In the latter collection reference is made to letters sent as follows: August 18, 1897, to Commissioner of Indian Affairs: DeSette's information provides the basis for prosecution of Zunis; February 21, 1898, to Commissioner of Indian Affairs: DeSette is to be transferred; January 19, 1899: DeSette is to stay on for a time as nurse. Reference is made to letters in the National Archives, Washington, D.C., as follows: December 2, 1889: DeSette and Carrie B. Pond are referred to as teachers at Zuni; July 23, 1892, Dorchester to Commissioner of Indian Affairs: Dorchester recommends DeSette as field matron at Zuni and gives DeSette's background; April 5, 1893, DeSette to Commissioner of Indian Affairs: DeSette declares it is necessary to "stir up authorities" to insure Zuni "faith"; August 28, 1896, Smith to Commissioner of Indian Affairs: Presbyterians are ready to give up Zuni mission; October 5, 1897, Secretary of War to Secretary of Interior regarding military actions at Zuni in September 1897; August 10, 1899, Pueblo and Jicarilla Agency to Commissioner of Indian Affairs, p. 21: the case against the Zunis was annulled and the smallpox epidemic reported. Telling (1952, 133–35) covers the 1897 incident, using War Department documents in the main.

Photographer Ben Wittick photographed Troop K, 2nd Cavalry, from Fort Apache, in their encampment near the south bank of the Zuni River in full view of the pueblo. Photo is in the Museum of New Mexico, Santa Fe (Wittick, vol. 5, no. 62).

school.[5] Then in 1921, after a century of absence, the Franciscans came back to found a new mission — St. Anthony's — for the Catholic Church. A mission school was started in 1923.[6]

Despite the behavior of early educators whose zeal to reform carried them far beyond the classroom, the Zuni people generally seem to have accepted the idea of formal education for their children. This was the case, at any rate, after 1900. Perhaps the availability of three different schools in the pueblo helped foster this acceptance since children were permitted to transfer from one to another if there were difficulties in adjustment. In any event, in 1942 an educational research team found that schooling in the pueblo had been compulsory for some years. The parents recognized that even a few years of formal education gave the children an advantage in bridging the gap between their own and the white man's world.[7] Perhaps they also recognized that education — and Americanization — had an erosive effect on the structure of their own culture.[8]

In the twentieth century the forces of change have been as constant as the winds of spring. Perhaps the most radical transformations have occurred in the economy. Since the coming of the rails the age-old subsistence agriculture largely has been replaced; self-sufficiency has given way to dependency on outside markets and sources of supply. The fields along the Zuni River and its branches, once heavily planted in corn and grain, are now given over to growing alfalfa for the outside market or for consumption by local herds. Many of the picturesque stone summer houses at Nutria, Pescado, Tekapo, and Ojo Caliente have fallen into ruin.

---

[5] Andrew VanderWagen left the mission to go into trading and ranching before the school was opened in 1908. Details from VanderWagen and VanderWagen (1926), a document supplied by Gertrude VanderWagen Wall, Zuni, New Mexico. DeKorne (1947) is a fuller treatment of the first fifty years of the Christian Reformed mission at Zuni. A book by Kuipers (1946), principal of the Christian Reformed mission school, is a candid account of Zuni resistance to the ways of the white man.

[6] St. Anthony's Mission was authorized by the Franciscan Order in 1921 and dedicated in 1923, when the mission school was opened. The founding was carried out by Father Anthony Kroger, O.F.M. Details are from his journal in Cooper, ed. (1955, 26–27).

[7] Leighton and Adair (1966, all of pt. 2). See Spicer (1962, 360–67) on the "bearers of Anglo culture."

[8] See Parsons (1917 and 1939b, chap. 9) for early comment on this matter. Steps to reverse the trend and repair the losses are much in the minds of contemporary Zuni leaders who have advanced plans to include Zuni culture and language in the school curriculum. One move in this direction is the publication of *Self-portrayals* (Quam, trans., 1972), written by the Zunis themselves and designed in large part for the edification of their young people.

Even the peach trees grown in the sands at the base of Towayalane and the twin buttes north of the pueblo have been left to die, and the picturesque "waffle gardens" — once spread along the river on the north edge of the Zuni pueblo, where the Indian women hand-irrigated small plots of onions, chiles, and other vegetables — have disappeared. On the other hand, the raising of livestock, notably sheep, has become a major enterprise.

Economic changes at Zuni rapidly followed the coming of the railroad. As we noted in Chapter 9, the railroad sparked a race for the virgin grassland, and profit-hungry cattlemen crowded hard on the Zuni range. Even after the settlement of the reservation boundary in 1883, the Zunis were plagued by trespassers both Anglo and Indian. In an affair of violence in 1889, three Indians were killed when they pursued some Anglos caught rustling cattle at Nutria.[9]

But the Indians also capitalized on the livestock market. Dealing mainly through trading companies operated by Anglos, the Zunis gradually went into stock raising to develop their first big cash crop. Additions to the reservation since 1883 partially reflect the Indians' need for more grazing land to support this growing industry.[10]

Although itinerant traders had been known in the pueblo since the early days of Mexican rule, Douglas D. Graham was the first to move in with a permanent business operation. Graham opened shop about 1878, and he stayed on at Zuni as trader for twenty years. A versatile character, he later served as teacher in the pueblo, as government farmer, and as federal agent. Trader Graham is mentioned by nearly every sojourner in Zuni from Cushing to Mary DeSette.[11]

Not long after Graham's departure, three more trading houses set up in business — VanderWagen, Kelsey, and Wallace. Andrew VanderWagen, the

----

[9] Telling (1952, 132–33) covers this and other incidents. The Zunis themselves have preserved several stories about the rustler era; see Quam, trans. (1972, pt. 6).

[10] Congress in 1931 finally confirmed the executive land grant established by President Arthur in 1883. Subsequent additions and leases brought the reservation and land-use areas of the Zuni Indians, as of about 1940, to 412,983 acres (Aberle, 1948, 83). In 1974 the land-use area was 407,247 acres.

[11] During twenty years or so Graham's name appeared frequently in the accounts of visitors and in government correspondence but I have found nothing of consequence written about the man. The Zunis referred to him as "Blackbeard." McNitt (1962, 239–40) finds that one August Lacome was licensed to trade at Zuni in 1872; he was followed by William and John Burgess, the first "nailed-down counter and shelf" traders who, however, spent but a year or two at the pueblo. See chap. 12 of McNitt (1962) for reference to traders at Zuni before 1878.

Christian Reformed missionary turned trader, was somewhat more successful trading with the Zunis than converting them.[12] He opened shop on the south side of the river in Cushing's "Hemenway House."

Business at the trading posts involved the exchange of livestock and farm products for hundreds of manufactured items — matches, lamps, stoves, iron cooking ware, rope, harness, horseshoes, wagons, and luxury items like coffee and tobacco.[13] Naturally, the traders encouraged the Indians to improve their stock and increase their herds since this swelled the volume of over-the-counter trade. The Zunis generally preferred sheep, as they had in the past, and their constantly increasing herds finally depleted the range and accelerated soil erosion. In 1942, the federal government began a five-year stock-reduction program which brought the number of animals down to the carrying capacity of the reservation ranges. This worked hardship on the Indians and traders alike, but it saved the land.

Actually, the first cash crop raised by the Zuni Indians was corn supplied to the army posts at Fort Defiance and Fort Wingate, but in the modern economy, income from the range has consistently towered over that from the farm. Zuni life for centuries was based upon agriculture, and much of the elaborate ceremonial ritual was organized around the production of crops. The traditional Zuni, uninterested in efficiency or scientific agriculture, has been slow to change his ways in farming, especially in the growing of the traditional foods — corn, beans, and squash.[14]

Trying to increase the farm production of the Zunis, the federal government has developed the water resources on the reservation. Shortly after the Indian service established its sub-agency at Zuni, the Black Rock dam was built across the Zuni River. Earth-filled and braced by blocks cut from black basalt found nearby, the dam was completed in 1908, a monument to engineer John B. Harper and the Zuni workmen who performed much of the labor by hand. Zuni sheep were drafted to puddle the clay wall on the retaining face of the structure. Ten years after the dam had filled the canals carrying water to irrigated fields on

---

[12] Leighton and Adair (1966, 24), McNitt (1962, 240–44). McNitt relates some stories about the colorful Dan DuBois, sometime trader and a legendary character in the Navajo and Zuni country.

[13] For the intricacies of trading post operation, historically considered, one should turn to McNitt's splendid book on *The Indian Traders* (1962).

[14] Leighton and Adair (1966). Chap. 3 is an excellent summary of economic changes at Zuni.

the north side, Bunzel observed that corn was still being raised by the old method of dry farming on the south bank.[15] Indeed, it is still grown that way, though today one sees very little corn being grown at all.

During the Depression years more government dams were built on Nutria and Pescado creeks; another, constructed by the Zunis themselves at Ojo Caliente, was enlarged. As a result agricultural production climbed until 1943, but then a decline set in, brought on by World War II. Over two hundred men left the pueblo to fight in the U.S. Army. When the veterans returned, they found little incentive to return to the fields. Running sheep or making silver jewelry paid better.[16]

Silver-crafting at Zuni dates back to the 1880s when a few smiths worked in the medium using techniques acquired from the Navajo Indians. However, the Navajos practically monopolized the silver jewelry business through World War I. Then they were forced to share the market with Zuni silversmiths who had developed their own distinctive hallmark. The Navajos had traditionally used heavy silver set with large pieces of turquoise. The Zunis developed a lighter style, making use of small sets of turquoise and adding elaborate inlay work of shell and a variety of stones. Between the wars this craft boomed, the cash inflow reaching nearly a million dollars in the peak years, 1945–1946. Since that time the income from silver and curios has declined but the craft remains one of the main sources of tribal income.[17]

During the war years the booming economy was further strengthened by dependency allotments paid to the families of Zuni servicemen and by wages paid to those who worked in a variety of occupations outside the pueblo.

Prosperity brought change, rapid change. Why subsist on the products of the field when with the income from sheep, or silver, or wages, you could buy the necessities in the pueblo trading post, or in the Gallup supermarket, and even have some money left over? Why indeed? With the surplus you could buy good clothes, furniture, appliances, gadgets, a refrigerator, a new automobile, and in more recent days, a television set. To the extent that now they are con-

---

[15] Bunzel (1932a, 474). Bohrer and others (1960) describe agriculture and agricultural practices as of 1956–1957. Similar research carried out twenty years later would undoubtedly reveal quite different results.

[16] Leighton and Adair (1966, 26–30).

[17] Adair (1944) in a deservedly popular book devoted three chapters to the history of Zuni silversmithing.

cerned with wage increases, profits, capital, leisure time, and prestige buying, the Zunis have become Americanized.[18]

Changes in traditional Zuni society followed gradually upon the rise of the new economy. Men of property began to assume more prominent positions in a power structure once dominated by the priests. At times breaking with tradition, they became the primary advocates and instruments of change. The separation of state and church at Zuni was one result of this cleavage.

Political differences at Zuni can be traced back to the 1880s when Cushing escorted tribal leaders to the Atlantic seaboard. Apparently, new ideas introduced then produced a mild factionalism.[19] However, since the government of the pueblo at that time was in the hands of an inner council of priests, there was little prospect of change not in accord with the wishes of the priestly authority. Men did not seek office; governors were appointed and served at the pleasure of the religious leaders.

After the turn of the century, cracks in the theocracy began to develop when the priests found themselves caught up in political crosscurrents generated by outside influences. The cracks widened when the Catholics returned to Zuni. Remembrance of the Spanish yoke was strong, and when the church applied to reestablish a mission the pueblo was divided in its opinions. The pro-Catholics were in the minority, but apparently they were supported by a government agent, himself a Catholic, and the mission was accepted and reopened.

Continuing factional division was insured when the members of the council of priests found themselves divided on the Catholic issue. In exercising their power of appointment they often disagreed on suitable candidates. One governor served an over-long seven-year term since no replacement could be agreed upon. In 1934, the cane — his symbol of office — of a newly-appointed governor, a pro-Catholic, was taken from him by the priests. This crisis occurred just at the time the United States government embarked on a "New Deal" for the American Indians.

By the 1930s, the government's drive to "Americanize" the Indians, long implicit in the educational policy of the Bureau of Indian Affairs and neatly

---

[18] Much of this is taken from Leighton and Adair (1966, chap. 3). The authors report the remark of a government worker who said in 1947 that "Zuni has changed more in the last ten years than during the whole preceding twenty-year period."

[19] Spicer (1962, 199) makes this assertion, placing Pedro Pino in the center of the controversy.

typified by the aggressions of Mary DeSette, was abandoned. The Indian Reorganization Act, passed by Congress in 1934, set the government on a new course: Indian culture should be preserved, not dissipated in the melting pot; let the government shun paternalism; let the Indians manage their own affairs.

The agent at Black Rock suggested that the Zunis resolve their political impasse by forming a nominating committee who would in turn select candidates to be voted upon in public meeting. The system was accepted and in principle has continued to this writing. By this action the priests were removed from direct political authority; secularization had been achieved, thanks in large part to those who sought to bring the Zunis' external affairs into closer harmony with the American system at large. At present the formal political organization of the Zuni Pueblo consists of a council of eight members, including a governor and lieutenant-governor elected by secret ballot for a term of four years. Political procedure and rights (all eighteen-year-olds, including women, have the franchise) were formalized in a Zuni constitution adopted by the people in 1970.

The transition from a theocratic form of government to one based on popular consent was not achieved without much division and debate, anxiety, stress, tension, and soul-searching.[20] People still take sides on the form of government the Zunis should have. The conservatives deplore the losses to Zuni culture which secularization brought. The progressives argue that bettering the economic level of the people and improving the conditions of life are worthy goals. Change in the structure of government, and of the Zuni society as a whole, as in the past, may be expected in the future.

---

[20] The political agony suffered by the Zuni people through the first six decades of the twentieth century has not been written about in detail. Most scholarly attention focuses on the period before about 1950. My own treatment is a bald summary of a very complex matter involving all segments of Zuni society. The following sources have been consulted: Parsons (1917, 1939a, 1939b); Aberle (1948); Eggan (1950); Smith and Roberts (1954), an excellent analysis of the political structure with historical data; Leighton and Adair (1966) for broad coverage and implications. Pandey (1968) analyzed the Zuni tribal council elections of 1965. A good many authors discuss American Indian policy. Hagan (1961) is a convenient, broad review through the New Deal era. John Collier, architect of the New Deal for the American Indians, was highly knowledgeable about the Southwestern tribes. His autobiographical memoir (1963) is essential to an understanding of the entire Indian reform movement and his own long term as U.S. Commissioner of Indian Affairs. Some years before that he had championed Indian rights and had helped defeat the Bursum Bill, a measure that threatened Pueblo land titles. He ran a series of articles in *Sunset* magazine (not listed here) opposing the measure; see Fergusson (1951, chap. 4). The controversy prompted Mary Austin (1924) to write on the prehistoric and historic Pueblos, emphasizing the Zuni and Hopi villages.

Whatever the shape of the future the historian of the Zunis can say with some assurance that these people will do most of the shaping of their own destiny. They were living in well-established towns along the Zuni River before the Middle Ages waned in Europe. Flourishing when Columbus arrived in America, they successfully fended off the imperialist Spaniard and, for the most part, kept him at bay. They were veterans in the struggle for freedom when the liberty bell rang out in Philadelphia in 1776. They weathered the aggressions of the Anglo-American pioneers. It was only as the pressure of American influence closed in tightly that the probably inevitable changes were forced upon them. But there is little in this situation to suggest that American civilization will dissolve such a tough and refractory human spirit.

If anything, the Anglo-American impact may have the effect of intensifying the Zunis' sense of national purpose. The present government has an elaborate and diversified development plan which, when fully implemented, will turn the Zuni Pueblo into a modern New Mexican town.

"But," said the governor in 1970, "it will differ from all other towns in that it will be uniquely Zuni. It will remain the only place on earth where the Zuni language is spoken, the only place on earth where the Zuni religion is practiced, and the only place on earth where the themes of Zuni culture find expression in the art forms and crafts of the people." [21] These words emphasize that the Zuni do not wish to enter the American mainstream at the expense of their own identity. That is the way it has been with them: Accept the alien ways that enrich, not destroy.

Learn more of these people from the books about them. But realize that the writers, as some of them have admitted, have only passed the threshold of understanding. Read about the ways in which the Zuni Indians lived close to the land and close to the sky, the source of life. Survival in a desert land came by ritual and the planting stick, the one no less vital than the other. Man was brought closer to man as they danced together in the plaza and worked together in the field. Society counted for more than the individual.

Read those who have written of society, kin and clan, family, to learn that the "total socio-religious structure of Zuni is a most intricate network" surpassing in

---

[21] Lewis (1971). The way in which the Zunis have resisted outside influences is nicely illustrated in their treatment of the returning World War II veterans. Two hundred and thirteen men — about one-tenth of the total population — went to war, yet when they returned, social controls and religious activities effectively prevented the introduction of any significant non-Pueblo traits. See also Adair and Vogt (1949).

"complexity of structure and function . . . that of any other Indian group in the United States." Many have written of the tightly-knit group in Zuni society, of social controls, of endogamy and matrilocality; fewer have written of the sensitive and generous and humor-loving people who comprise the social whole.

Learn something of the great body of religious knowledge, the ritual poetry, the cycle of songs, the folktales, and the myths of origin. Religion is a central theme of life, not something reserved for special occasions. Many of the writers have extolled the richness, variety, and beauty of the ceremonials; few have seen them as the expressions of the soul and as beautifully orchestrated works of art.

Learn of the Zunis' feeling of oneness with the natural world and of their tolerance for the differences among men. Rather than control and exploit, they would cooperate and reciprocate with plants and animals and with other men.[22]

Learn that the Zuni sky is good to those who live under it.

---

[22] The thoughts here expressed, which touch only a few aspects of the Zuni lifeway, are synthesized from the Zunis' own book, *The Zunis: Self-portrayals*, translated by Quam (1972), and from Kroeber (1916b), Bunzel (1932a), Collier (1963), Leighton and Adair (1966), particularly the observations on the "total socioreligious structure," Parsons (1939b), Underhill (1938), and from my own reflections upon reading in the works listed in the bibliography and upon conversations with a number of Zuni Indians, not all of whom are known to me by name.

Bibliography

A Zuni stool

ABEL, ANNIE HELOISE, ED.

1915 *The Official Correspondence of James S. Calhoun While Indian Agent at Santa Fé and Superintendent of Indian Affairs in New Mexico.* U.S. Office of Indian Affairs. Washington: Government Printing Office.

ABERLE, S. D.

1948 *The Pueblo Indians of New Mexico: Their Land, Economy and Civil Organization.* Memoir Series of the American Anthropological Association, no. 70.

ABERT, J. W.

1848 "Report of His Examination of New Mexico in the Years 1846–'47." *In* W. H. Emory, *Notes of a Military Reconnaissance, from Fort Leavenworth, in Missouri, to San Diego, in California, Including Parts of the Arkansas, Del Norte, and Gila Rivers. Made in 1846–7 with the Advanced Guard of the "Army of the West,"* pp. 417–548. Washington: Wendell and Van Benthuysen.

ADAIR, JOHN JOSEPH

1944 *The Navajo and Pueblo Silversmiths.* Norman: University of Oklahoma Press.

1948 "A Study of Culture Resistance: The Veterans of World War II at Zuni Pueblo." Ph.D. dissertation, University of New Mexico.

ADAIR, JOHN JOSEPH, AND EVON VOGT

1949 "Navaho and Zuni Veterans: A Study of Contrasting Modes of Culture Change." *American Anthropologist* 51: 547–61.

ADAMS, ELEANOR B., ED.

1954 *Bishop Tamarón's Visitation of New Mexico, 1760.* Historical Society of New Mexico Publications in History, vol. 15. Albuquerque, N. Mex.

1963   "Fray Silvestre and the Obstinate Hopi." *New Mexico Historical Review*
        38: 97–138.

ADAMS, ELEANOR B., AND ANGELICO CHAVEZ, EDS. AND TRANS.
1956   *The Missions of New Mexico, 1776: A Description by Fray Francisco
        Atanasio Domínguez, with Other Contemporary Documents.* Albuquer-
        que: University of New Mexico Press.

AMSDEN, CHARLES AVERY
1949   *Prehistoric Southwesterners from Basketmaker to Pueblo.* Los Angeles:
        Southwest Museum.

ARIZONA HISTORICAL REVIEW
1929   "Pioneers Pass Away: Hon. Sol Barth." 1: 5–6.

ARNY, W. F. M.
1872   "[Annual Report in Reference to the Pueblo Indians of New Mexico,]
        August 18, 1871." In *Report of the Commissioner of Indian Affairs,
        1871.* U.S. 42nd Cong., 2nd Sess., House Ex. Doc. 1, 3: 796–811.
        Washington: Government Printing Office.

AUSTIN, MARY
1924   "The Days of Our Ancients." *Survey* 53: 33–38, 59.

AYER, MRS. EDWARD E., TRANS., AND FREDERICK W. HODGE
AND CHARLES F. LUMMIS, EDS.
1916   *The Memorial of Fray Alonso de Benavides, 1630.* Chicago: privately
        printed.

BAHTI, TOM, ED.
1966   *Zuñi Fetishes* by Frank Hamilton Cushing. Flagstaff, Ariz.: K. C. Pub-
        lications.

BAILEY, L. R.
1964   *The Long Walk: A History of the Navajo Wars, 1846–68.* Los Angeles:
        Westernlore Press.
1966   *Indian Slave Trade in the Southwest: A Study of Slave-taking and the
        Traffic of Indian Captives.* Los Angeles: Westernlore Press.

BALDWIN, GORDON C.
1963   *The Ancient Ones: Basketmakers and Cliff Dwellers of the Southwest.*
        New York: W. W. Norton.

BANCROFT, HUBERT HOWE
1889   *History of Arizona and New Mexico, 1530–1888.* San Francisco: His-
        tory Company.

BANDELIER, A. F.

1889 "An Outline of the Documentary History of the Zuñi Tribe, 1680–1846." Chaps. 3–4. MS, Peabody Museum Archives, Harvard University, Cambridge. Another copy is in History Library, Museum of New Mexico, Santa Fe. The unpublished continuation of Bandelier 1892b.

1890a *Final Report of Investigations among the Indians of the Southwestern United States, Carried on Mainly in the Years from 1880 to 1885.* Pt. 1. Papers of the Archaeological Institute of America, American Series, vol. 3. Cambridge, Mass.: John Wilson and Son.

1890b *Hemenway Southwestern Archaeological Expedition: Contributions to the History of the Southwestern Portion of the United States.* Papers of the Archaeological Institute of America, American Series, vol. 5. Cambridge, Mass.: John Wilson and Son.

1890c "The Historical Archives of the Hemenway Southwestern Archaeological Expedition." In *Congrès International des Américanistes: Compte-rendu de la Septième Session, Berlin, 1888,* pp. 449–59. Berlin: W. H. Kühl.

1892a *Final Report of Investigations among the Indians of the Southwestern United States, Carried on Mainly in the Years from 1880 to 1885.* Pt. 2. Papers of the Archaeological Institute of America, American Series, vol. 4. Cambridge, Mass.: John Wilson and Son.

1892b "Hemenway Southwestern Archaeological Expedition. I, An Outline of the Documentary History of the Zuni Tribe." *Journal of American Ethnology and Archaeology* 3: 1–115.

1893 *The Gilded Man (El Dorado) and Other Pictures of the Spanish Occupancy of America.* New York: D. Appleton.

BARTH, A. W.

1933 "New Notes on El Morro." *Art and Archaeology* 34: 147–56.

BARTLETT, RICHARD A.

1962 *Great Surveys of the American West.* Norman: University of Oklahoma Press.

BASSO, KEITH H., ED.

1971 *Western Apache Raiding and Warfare from the Notes of Grenville Goodwin.* Tucson: University of Arizona Press.

BAXTER, SYLVESTER

1882a "An Aboriginal Pilgrimage." *Century Magazine* 24: 526–36.

1882b "The Father of the Pueblos." *Harper's Magazine* 65: 72–91.

1883 "Zuñi Revisited." *American Architect and Building News.* 13: 124–26.

1888   *The Old New World: An Account of the Explorations of the Hemenway Southwestern Archaeological Expedition in 1887–88, under the Direction of Frank Hamilton Cushing.* Salem, Mass.: Salem Press.

BEALE, E. F.

1858   *Wagon Road from Fort Defiance to the Colorado River.* U.S. 35th Cong., 1st Sess., House Ex. Doc. 124. Washington: James B. Steedman.

1860   *Wagon Road — Fort Smith to Colorado River.* U.S. 36th Cong., 1st Sess., House Ex. Doc. 42. Washington: Thomas H. Ford.

BELL, WILLIAM A.

1870   *New Tracks in North America: A Journal of Travel and Adventure Whilst Engaged in the Survey for a Southern Railroad to the Pacific Ocean During 1867–8.* London: Chapman and Hall; New York: Scribner, Welford.

BENEDICT, RUTH

1934   *Patterns of Culture.* Boston and New York: Houghton Mifflin.

1939   *Zuni Mythology.* 2 vols. Reprint. New York: AMS Press, 1969.

BERTHRONG, DONALD J., AND ODESSA DAVENPORT, EDS.

1956   *Joseph Reddeford Walker and the Arizona Adventure* by Daniel Ellis Conner. Norman: University of Oklahoma Press.

BIEBER, RALPH P., ED.

1936   *Marching with the Army of the West, 1846–1848, by Abraham Robinson Johnston, Marcellus Ball Edwards, Philip Gooch Ferguson.* Glendale, Calif.: Arthur H. Clark.

BIEBER, RALPH P., ED., WITH AVERAM B. BENDER

1938   *Exploring Southwestern Trails, 1846–1854, by Philip St. George Cooke, William Henry Chase Whiting, François Xavier Aubry.* Glendale, Calif.: Arthur H. Clark.

BLOOM, LANSING BARTLETT

1913–   "New Mexico under Mexican Administration, 1821–1846." *Old Santa
1915   Fe* (Santa Fe, N. Mex.), vols. 1–2.

1933   "Fray Estevan de Perea's Relacion." *New Mexico Historical Review* 8: 211–35.

BLOOM, LANSING BARTLETT, ED.

1933–   "Bourke on the Southwest." *New Mexico Historical Review*, vols. 8–13.
1938

BOAS, FRANZ

1922 "Tales of Spanish Provenience from Zuñi." *Journal of American Folklore* 35: 62–98.

BOAS, FRANZ, AND ELSIE CLEWS PARSONS

1920 "Spanish Tales from Laguna and Zuñi, N. Mex." *Journal of American Folk-lore* 33: 47–72.

BOBB, BERNARD E.

1962 *The Viceregency of Antonio María Bucareli in New Spain, 1771–1779.* Austin: University of Texas Press.

BOHRER, VORSILA L., AND OTHERS

1960 "Zuni Agriculture." *El Palacio* 67: 181–202.

BOLTON, HERBERT

1939 *Outpost of Empire: The Story of the Founding of San Francisco.* New York: Alfred A. Knopf.

1949 *Coronado on the Turquoise Trail: Knight of Pueblos and Plains.* Reprinted in 1964. Albuquerque: University of New Mexico Press.

BOLTON, HERBERT, ED.

1916 *Spanish Exploration in the Southwest, 1542–1706.* New York: Charles Scribner's Sons.

BOLTON, HERBERT, ED. AND TRANS.

1950 *Pageant in the Wilderness: The Story of the Escalante Expedition to the Interior Basin, 1776, Including the Diary and Itinerary of Father Escalante.* Salt Lake City: Utah State Historical Society.

BRANDES, RAYMOND STEWART

1960 *Frontier Military Posts of Arizona.* Globe, Ariz.: Dale Stuart King.

1965 "Frank Hamilton Cushing: Pioneer Americanist." Ph.D. dissertation, University of Arizona.

BRAYER, HERBERT O.

1938 *Pueblo Indian Land Grants of the "Rio Abajo," New Mexico.* University of New Mexico Bulletin no. 334.

BRUGGE, DAVID M.

1968 *Navajos in the Catholic Church Records of New Mexico, 1694–1875.* Window Rock, Ariz.: Navajo Tribe.

1969 "Pueblo Factionalism and External Relations." *Ethnohistory* 16: 191–200.

BUNZEL, RUTH

1929 *The Pueblo Potter: A Study of Creative Imagination in Primitive Art.* Columbia University Contributions to Anthropology, edited by Franz Boas, vol. 8. New York: Columbia University Press.

1932a "Introduction to Zuñi Ceremonialism." In *Forty-seventh Annual Report of the Bureau of American Ethnology, 1929–1930*, pp. 467–544. Washington: Government Printing Office.

1932b "Zuñi Origin Myths." In *Forty-seventh Annual Report of the Bureau of American Ethnology, 1929–1930*, pp. 545–609. Washington: Government Printing Office.

1932c "Zuñi Ritual Poetry." In *Forty-seventh Annual Report of the Bureau of American Ethnology, 1929–1930*, pp. 611–835. Washington: Government Printing Office.

1932d "Zuñi Katcinas, an Analytical Study." In *Forty-seventh Annual Report of the Bureau of American Ethnology, 1929–1930*, pp. 837–1086. Washington: Government Printing Office.

1933 *Zuni Texts.* Publications of the American Ethnological Society, no. 15. New York: Stechert.

1935 "Zuni." In *Handbook of American Indian Languages*, edited by Franz Boas, 3: 389–415. New York: J. J. Augustin.

BURRUS, ERNEST J., ED.

1969 *A History of the Southwest: A Study of the Civilization and Conversion of the Indians in Southwestern United States and Northwestern Mexico from the Earliest Times to 1700 by Adolph F. Bandelier. Volume I. A Catalogue of the Bandelier Collection in the Vatican Library. Supplement to Volume I. Reproduction in Color of Thirty Sketches and Ten Maps.* Rome: Jesuit Historical Institute; St. Louis, Mo.: St. Louis University.

CALHOUN, JAMES S.

1850 Letters to W. Medill, Commissioner of Indian Affairs, April–October, 1849. *In* U.S. 31st Cong., 1st Sess., House Ex. Doc. 17, pp. 198–229. Washington: House of Representatives.

CALVIN, ROSS

1965 *Sky Determines: An Interpretation of the Southwest.* Rev. ed. Albuquerque: University of New Mexico Press.

CAMP, CHARLES L., ED.

1966 *George C. Yount and His Chronicles of the West Comprising Extracts from His "Memoir" and from the Orange Clark "Narrative."* Denver: Old West Publishing Co.

CANNON, CARL L., ED.
1932 *A Journal of the Santa Fe Expedition under Colonel Doniphan by Jacob S. Robinson.* Princeton: Princeton University Press.

CARROLL, H. BAILEY, AND J. VILLASANA HAGGARD, EDS. AND TRANS.
1942 *Three New Mexico Chronicles: The Exposición of Don Pedro Bautista Pino, 1812; the Ojeada of Lic. Antonio Barreiro, 1832; and the Additions of Don José Agustín de Escudero, 1849.* Albuquerque: Quivira Society.

CARROLL, JOHN A.
1959 "Frederick Webb Hodge, 1864–1956." *Arizona and the West* 1: 202–5.

CAYWOOD, LOUIS R.
1972 *The Restored Mission of Nuestra Senora de Guadalupe de Zuni, Zuni, New Mexico.* St. Michael's, Ariz.: St. Michael's Press.

CHAMBERLAIN, ALEX F.
1900 "In Memoriam: Frank Hamilton Cushing." *Journal of American Folklore* 13: 129–34.

CHAPMAN, CHARLES E.
1916 *The Founding of Spanish California: The Northwestward Expansion of New Spain, 1687–1783.* New York: Macmillan.

CHAVEZ, ANGELICO
1957 *Archives of the Archdiocese of Santa Fe, 1678–1900.* Washington: Academy of American Franciscan History.
1968 *Coronado's Friars.* Washington: Academy of American Franciscan History.

CLELAND, ROBERT GLASS
1952 *This Reckless Breed of Men: The Trappers and Fur Traders of the Southwest.* New York: Alfred A. Knopf.

COHEN, FELIX S., ED.
1958 *Handbook of Federal Indian Law.* Washington: Government Printing Office.

COLE, FAY-COOPER
1957 "Frederick Webb Hodge, 1864–1956." *American Anthropologist* 59: 517–20.

COLLIER, JOHN

1962   *On the Gleaming Way: Navajos, Eastern Pueblos, Zunis, Hopis, Apaches, and Their Land; and Their Meanings to the World.* Denver: Sage Books.

1963   *From Every Zenith: A Memoir; and Some Essays on Life and Thought.* Denver: Sage Books.

CONNELLEY, WILLIAM E., ED.

1907   *War with Mexico, 1846–1847: Doniphan's Expedition and the Conquest of New Mexico and California. Includes a Reprint of the Work of Col. John T. Hughes.* Topeka, Kans.: the author.

COOLIDGE, DANE, AND MARY ROBERTS COOLIDGE

1930   *The Navajo Indians.* Boston and New York: Houghton Mifflin.

COOPER, ELIZABETH ANN, ED.

1955   "Dedication, Cathedral of the Sacred Heart, Gallup, New Mexico, 1955." Gallup *New Mexico Register*, June 17.

COUES, ELLIOTT, ED. AND TRANS.

1900   *On the Trail of a Spanish Pioneer: The Diary and Itinerary of Francisco Garcés in His Travels through Sonora, Arizona, and California, 1775–1776; Translated from an Official Contemporaneous Copy of the Original Spanish Manuscript.* 2 vols. New York: Francis P. Harper.

COZZENS, SAMUEL WOODWORTH

1876   *The Ancient Cibola: The Marvellous Country; or, Three Years in Arizona and New Mexico.* Boston: Lee and Shepard.

CRAMPTON, C. GREGORY

1965   *Standing Up Country: The Canyon Lands of Utah and Arizona.* New York: Alfred A. Knopf; Salt Lake City: University of Utah Press; in Association with the Amon Carter Museum of Western Art.

CURTIS, EDWARD S.

1926   *The North American Indian: Being a Series of Volumes Picturing and Describing the Indians of the United States, the Dominion of Canada, and Alaska.* Edited by Frederick Webb Hodge. Vol. 17. Cambridge: Harvard University Press.

CURTIS, WILLIAM E.

1883   *Children of the Sun.* Chicago: Inter-Ocean Publishing.

CUSHING, FRANK HAMILTON

1879–   Letters Received, 1879–1899. National Anthropological Archives,
1899   Smithsonian Institution, Washington, D.C.

1882a "The Nation of the Willows." *Atlantic Monthly* 50: 362–74, 541–59.

1882b "The Zuñi Social, Mythic, and Religious Systems." *Popular Science Monthly* 21: 189–92.

1882– "My Adventures in Zuñi." *Century Magazine,* vols. 25–26.
1883

1883 "Zuñi Fetiches." In *Second Annual Report of the Bureau of Ethnology, 1880–81*, pp. 3–45. Washington: Government Printing Office.

1885 "The Discovery of Zuni; or, the Ancient Province of Cibola." MS, Cushing Papers, Southwest Museum, Los Angeles.

1886a "Notes on the Zuñi Made During the Visit of Palowahtiwa, Waihusiwa and Heluta, at Manchester-by-the-Sea in 1886." MS, Cushing Papers, Southwest Museum, Los Angeles.

1886b "A Study of Pueblo Pottery as Illustrative of Zuñi Culture Growth." In *Fourth Annual Report of the Bureau of Ethnology, 1882–83*, pp. 467–521. Washington: Government Printing Office.

1890 "Preliminary Notes on the Origin, Working Hypothesis and Primary Researches of the Hemenway Southwestern Archaeological Expedition." In *Congrès International des Américanistes. Compte-rendu de la Septième Session, Berlin, 1888*, pp. 149–94 and pl. 4. Berlin: W. H. Kühl.

1894 "Primitive Copper Working: An Experimental Study." *American Anthropologist* 7: 93–117.

1896 "Outlines of Zuñi Creation Myths." In *Thirteenth Annual Report of the Bureau of Ethnology, 1891–92*, pp. 321–447. Washington: Government Printing Office.

1897 "The Need of Studying the Indian in Order to Teach Him." In *Twenty-eighth Annual Report of the Board of Indian Commissioners*, pp. 109–15. Washington: Government Printing Office.

1920 *Zuñi Breadstuff*. Indian Notes and Monographs, vol. 8. Originally published in the Indianapolis *Millstone*, January 1884–August 1885.

1931 *Zuñi Folk Tales* with a foreword by J. W. Powell. With an introduction by Mary Austin. Originally published in 1901 by G. P. Putnam's Sons. New York: Alfred A. Knopf.

DALE, EDWARD EVERETT

1949 *The Indians of the Southwest: A Century of Development under the United States*. Norman: University of Oklahoma Press.

DARRAH, WILLIAM CULP

1951 *Powell of the Colorado*. Princeton: Princeton University Press.

DARTON, NELSON H.
1905   "The Zuni Salt Lake." *Journal of Geology* 13: 185–93.

DARTON, NELSON H., AND OTHERS
1915   *Guidebook of the Western United States: Part C. The Santa Fe Route with a Side Trip to the Grand Canyon of the Colorado.* U.S. Geological Survey Bulletin no. 613. Washington: Government Printing Office.

DAVIS, WILLIAM W. H.
1938   *El Gringo; or, New Mexico and Her People.* Santa Fe: Rydal Press.

DeGOLYER, EVERETT L., ED.
1941   *My Adventures in Zuni* by Frank Hamilton Cushing. Santa Fe: Peripatetic Press.

DeKORNE, JOHN C., ED.
1947   *Navajo and Zuni for Christ: Fifty Years of Indian Missions.* Grand Rapids, Mich.: Christian Reformed Board of Missions.

DICKEY, ROLAND F.
1970   *New Mexico Village Arts.* Albuquerque: University of New Mexico Press.

DILLON, RICHARD H., ED.
1970   *A Cannoneer in Navajo Country: Journal of Private Josiah M. Rice, 1851.* Denver: Old West Publishing Co. for the Denver Public Library.

DONALDSON, THOMAS
1893   *Moqui Pueblo Indians of Arizona and Pueblo Indians of New Mexico.* Extra Census Bulletin, Eleventh Census of the United States. Washington: United States Census Printing Office.

DORR, HERBERT C.
1953   "A Ride with the Apaches on a Visit to the Zunis." In *Primitive Heritage, an Anthropological Anthology,* edited by Margaret Mead and Nicolas Calas, pp. 355–62. New York: Random House.

DOZIER, EDWARD P.
1954   *The Hopi–Tewa of Arizona.* University of California Publications in American Archaeology and Ethnology, vol. 44, no. 3. Berkeley: University of California Press.
1970   *The Pueblo Indians of North America.* New York: Holt, Rinehart and Winston.

DUTTON, CLARENCE E.

1885   "Mount Taylor and the Zuñi Plateau." In *Sixth Annual Report of the United States Geological Survey, 1884–85*, pp. 105–98. Washington: Government Printing Office.

EALY, RUTH R.

1955   *Water in a Thirsty Land.* [n.p.].

EALY, TAYLOR F.

1880   "Annual Report of Day School of the Pueblo of Zuni, 1879." In *Report of the Commissioner of Indian Affairs, 1879.* U.S. 46th Cong., 2nd Sess., House Ex. Doc. 1, 9: 226–28. Washington: Government Printing Office.

1881   "[Annual Report,] 1880." In *Report of the Commissioner of Indian Affairs, 1880.* U.S. 46th Cong., 3rd Sess., House Ex. Doc. 1, 9: 256–57. Washington: Government Printing Office.

EATON, J. H.

1854   "Description of the True State and Character of the New Mexican Tribes." *In* Henry R. Schoolcraft, *Historical and Statistical Information Respecting the History, Condition and Prospects of the Indian Tribes of the United States*, 4: 216–21. Philadelphia: Lippincott, Grambo.

EGGAN, FRED

1950   *Social Organization of the Western Pueblos.* Chicago: University of Chicago Press.

1966   *The American Indian: Perspectives for the Study of Social Change.* Chicago: Aldine Publishing.

ESPINOSA, GILBERTO, ED.

1964   *The Expedition of Don Diego Dionisio de Peñalosa, Governor of New Mexico, from Santa Fe to the River Mischipi and Quivira in 1662, as Described by Father Nicolas de Freytas, O.S.F., by John Gilmary Shea.* Originally printed in 1882 by John G. Shea. Reprint. Albuquerque: Horn and Wallace.

ESPINOSA, J. MANUEL

1942   *Crusaders of the Rio Grande: The Story of Don Diego De Vargas and the Reconquest and Refounding of New Mexico.* Chicago: Institute of Jesuit History.

ESPINOSA, J. MANUEL, ED. AND TRANS.

1940   *First Expedition of Vargas into New Mexico, 1692.* Albuquerque: University of New Mexico Press.

EULER, ROBERT C., ED.

1965   *The Nation of the Willows* by Frank H. Cushing. Flagstaff, Ariz.: Northland Press.

EULER, ROBERT C., AND HENRY F. DOBYNS

1971   *The Hopi People.* Phoenix, Ariz.: Indian Tribal Series.

FAY, GEORGE E., ED.

1971   *Treaties, Land Cessions, and Other U.S. Congressional Documents Relative to American Indian Tribes. Zuni Indian Pueblo, New Mexico.* Part 1: U.S. Congressional Documents, 1877–1967. University of Northern Colorado, Museum of Anthropology, Occasional Publications in Anthropology, Ethnology Series, no. 20. Greeley: University of Northern Colorado.

FENNEMAN, NEVIN M.

1931   *Physiography of Western United States.* New York and London: McGraw-Hill.

FERGUSSON, ERNA

1931   *Dancing Gods: Indian Ceremonials of New Mexico and Arizona.* Albuquerque: University of New Mexico Press.

1951   *New Mexico: A Pageant of Three Peoples.* New York: Alfred A. Knopf.

FEWKES, J. WALTER

1891a   "A Few Summer Ceremonials at Zuñi Pueblo," *Journal of American Ethnology and Archaeology* 1: 1–62.

1891b   "Reconnaissance of Ruins in or near the Zuñi Reservation." *Journal of American Ethnology and Archaeology* 1: 92–132.

1909   "Ancient Zuni Pottery." In *Putnam Anniversary Volume: Anthropological Essays Presented to Frederic Ward Putnam in Honor of His Seventieth Birthday, April 16, 1909*, edited by Franz Boas and others, pp. 43–82. New York: G. E. Stechert and Son.

FORBES, JACK D.

1960   *Apache, Navaho and Spaniard.* Norman: University of Oklahoma Press.

FOREMAN, GRANT, ED.

1941   *A Pathfinder in the Southwest: The Itinerary of Lieutenant A. W. Whipple During His Explorations for a Railway Route from Fort Smith to Los Angeles in the Years 1853 & 1854.* Norman: University of Oklahoma Press.

FORREST, EARLE R.

1929 *Missions and Pueblos of the Old Southwest: Their Myths, Legends, Fiestas and Ceremonies, with Some Accounts of the Indian Tribes and Their Dances; and of the Penitentes.* Cleveland: Arthur H. Clark.

FORRESTAL, PETER P., TRANS., AND CYPRIAN J. LYNCH, ED.

1954 *Benavides' Memorial of 1630.* Washington: Academy of American Franciscan History.

FOSTER, ROY W.

1958 *Southern Zuni Mountains.* Socorro, N. Mex.: State Bureau of Mines and Mineral Resources.

FOWLER, DON D., ED.

1972 *"Photographed All the Best Scenery": Jack Hillers's Diary of the Powell Expeditions, 1871–1875.* Salt Lake City: University of Utah Press.

FOWLER, DON D., ROBERT C. EULER, AND CATHERINE S. FOWLER

1969 *John Wesley Powell and the Anthropology of the Canyon Country.* U.S. Geological Survey Professional Paper no. 670. Washington: Government Printing Office.

FRAZER, ROBERT W., ED.

1968 *New Mexico in 1850: A Military View* by Colonel George Archibald McCall. Norman: University of Oklahoma Press.

FULLER, CLARISSA PARSONS

1943 "Frank Hamilton Cushing's Relations to Zuñi and the Hemenway Southwestern Expedition, 1879–1889." Master's thesis, University of New Mexico.

GALVIN, JOHN, ED., AND ADELAIDE SMITHERS, TRANS.

1963 *The Coming of Justice to California: Three Documents Translated from the Spanish.* San Francisco: John Howell.

GILBERT, HOPE

1961 "Zuni Pilgrimage to the Atlantic Ocean." *Desert Magazine* 24: 12–15.

GILMAN, BENJAMIN IVES

1891 "Zuñi Melodies." *Journal of American Ethnology and Archaeology* 1: 63–91.

GILMAN, BENJAMIN IVES, AND KATHERINE H. STONE

1908 "The Hemenway Southwestern Expedition." *Journal of American Ethnology and Archaeology* 4: 227–35.

GOETZMANN, WILLIAM H.

1959   *Army Exploration in the American West, 1803–1863.* New Haven: Yale University Press.

1966   *Exploration and Empire: The Explorer and the Scientist in the Winning of the American West.* New York: Alfred A. Knopf.

GOLDMAN, IRVING

1937   "The Zuni Indians of New Mexico." In *Cooperation and Competition among Primitive Peoples,* edited by Margaret Mead. New York and London: McGraw-Hill.

GOODWIN, GRENVILLE

1969   *The Social Organization of the Western Apache.* With a Preface by Keith H. Basso. Tucson: University of Arizona Press.

GREENWOOD, N. H.

1973   "Sol Barth: A Jewish Settler on the Arizona Frontier." *Journal of Arizona History* 14: 363–78.

GREEVER, WILLIAM S.

1954   *Arid Domain: The Santa Fe Railway and Its Western Land Grant.* Stanford, Calif.: Stanford University Press.

GWYTHER, GEORGE

1871   "Pueblo Indians." *Overland Monthly* 6: 260–67.

HACKETT, CHARLES WILSON, ED. AND TRANS.

1923–   *Historical Documents Relating to New Mexico, Nueva Vizcaya and*
1937   *Approaches Thereto, to 1773. Collected by Adolph F. A. Bandelier and Fanny R. Bandelier. Spanish Texts and English Translations.* 3 vols. Washington: Carnegie Institution.

HACKETT, CHARLES WILSON, ED., AND CHARMION S. SHELBY, TRANS.

1942   *Revolt of the Pueblo Indians of New Mexico and Otermin's Attempted Reconquest, 1680–1682.* 2 vols. Albuquerque: University of New Mexico Press.

HAFEN, LEROY R., AND ANN W. HAFEN

1954   *Old Spanish Trail, Santa Fé to Los Angeles, with Extracts from Contemporary Records Including Diaries of Antonio Armijo and Orville Pratt.* Glendale, Calif.: Arthur H. Clark.

HAGAN, WILLIAM T.

1961   *American Indians.* Chicago and London: University of Chicago Press.

HALLENBECK, CLEVE
1949   *The Journey of Friar Marcos de Niza.* Dallas, Tex.: University Press.

HAMMOND, GEORGE P., AND AGAPITO REY, EDS. AND TRANS.
1929   *Expedition into New Mexico Made by Antonio de Espejo, 1582–1583, as Revealed in the Journal of Diego Pérez de Luxán, a Member of the Party.* Los Angeles: Quivira Society.
1940   *Narratives of the Coronado Expedition, 1540–1542.* Albuquerque: University of New Mexico Press.
1953   *Don Juan de Oñate, Colonizer of New Mexico, 1595–1628.* 2 vols. Albuquerque: University of New Mexico Press.
1966   *The Rediscovery of New Mexico, 1580–1594, the Explorations of Chamuscado, Espejo, Castaño de Sosa, Morlete, and Leyva de Bonilla and Humaña.* Albuquerque: University of New Mexico Press.

HARRIS, LLEWELLYN
1879   "Miraculous Healing among the Zunis." *Juvenile Instructor* (Salt Lake City) 14: 173–76.

HAURY, EMIL H.
1945   *The Excavation of Los Muertos and Neighboring Ruins in the Salt River Valley, Southern Arizona. Based on the Work of the Hemenway Southwestern Archaeological Expedition of 1887–1888.* Harvard University, Papers of the Peabody Museum of American Archaeology and Ethnology, vol. 24, no. 1. Cambridge, Mass.: The Museum.

HAYNES, HENRY W.
1886   "Early Explorations in New Mexico." In *Narrative and Critical History of America*, edited by Justin Winsor, vol. 2, chap. 7. Boston and New York: Houghton Mifflin.

HEMENWAY SOUTHWESTERN ARCHAEOLOGICAL EXPEDITION
1886–   Archives, 1886–1894, and related papers in the "X" files, 1897–1959.
1959   MSS, Peabody Museum, Harvard University, Cambridge, Mass.

HESTER, JAMES J.
1962   *Early Navajo Migrations and Acculturation in the Southwest.* Museum of New Mexico Papers in Anthropology, no. 6. Santa Fe: Museum of New Mexico Press.

HEWETT, EDGAR L., AND REGINALD G. FISHER
1943   *Mission Monuments of New Mexico.* Albuquerque: University of New Mexico Press.

HINE, ROBERT V.

1962 *Edward Kern and American Expansion.* New Haven and London: Yale University Press.

HODGE, FREDERICK W.

1910 "Zuni." In *Handbook of American Indians North of Mexico,* edited by Frederick W. Hodge, 2: 1015–20. Washington: Government Printing Office.

1920 *The Age of the Zuni Pueblo of Kechipauan.* Indian Notes and Monographs, vol. 3, no. 2. New York: Museum of the American Indian, Heye Foundation.

1924 "Snake-pens at Hawikuh, New Mexico." *Indian Notes* (Museum of the American Indian) 1:111–19.

1926 "The Six Cities of Cíbola, 1581–1680." *New Mexico Historical Review* 1: 478–88.

1937 *History of Hawikuh, New Mexico, One of the So-called Cities of Cíbola.* Los Angeles: Southwest Museum.

HODGE, FREDERICK W., ED.

1907– *Handbook of American Indians North of Mexico.* 2 pts. Bureau of
1910   American Ethnology Bulletin no. 30. Washington: Government Printing Office.

HODGE, FREDERICK W., AND FRANK H. CUSHING

1848– Papers. MSS, Southwest Museum, Los Angeles.
1956

HODGE, FREDERICK W., ED., AND GILBERTO ESPINOZA, TRANS.

1933 *History of New Mexico, by Gaspar Pérez de Villagrá, Alcalá, 1610.* Los Angeles: Quivira Society.

HODGE, FREDERICK W., GEORGE P. HAMMOND, AND AGAPITO REY, EDS. AND TRANS.

1945 *Fray Alonso de Benavides' Revised Memorial of 1634; with Numerous Supplementary Documents Elaborately Annotated.* Albuquerque: University of New Mexico Press.

HODGE, FREDERICK W., AND THEODORE H. LEWIS, EDS.

1965 *Spanish Explorers in the Southern United States, 1528–1543.* 1907. Reprint. New York: Barnes and Noble.

HOLLON, W. EUGENE

1961 *The Southwest: Old and New.* New York: Alfred A. Knopf.

HORAN, JAMES D.

1966   *Timothy O'Sullivan, America's Forgotten Photographer.* New York: Bonanza Books.

HORN, CALVIN

1963   *New Mexico's Troubled Years: The Story of the Early Territorial Governors.* With a Foreword by John F. Kennedy. Albuquerque: Horn and Wallace.

HUFF, J. WESLEY

1951   "A Coronado Episode." *New Mexico Historical Review* 26: 119–27.

HUGHES, JOHN T.

1848   *Doniphan's Expedition: Containing an Account of the Conquest of New Mexico; General Kearney's Overland Expedition to California; Doniphan's Campaign against the Navajos.* . . . Cincinnati: J. A. and U. P. James.

HUMBOLDT, ALEXANDER VON

1811   *Political Essay on the Kingdom of New Spain.* . . . 4 vols. and atlas. London: Longman, Hurst, Rees, Orme and Brown.

HUNT, AURORA

1958   *Major General James Henry Carleton, 1814–1873, Western Frontier Dragoon.* Glendale, Calif.: Arthur H. Clark.

HUNT, CHARLES B.

1967   *Physiography of the United States.* San Francisco and London: W. H. Freeman.

JACKSON, W. TURRENTINE

1952   *Wagon Roads West: A Study of Federal Road Surveys and Construction in the Trans-Mississippi West, 1846–1869.* Berkeley and Los Angeles: University of California Press.

JENKINS, MYRA ELLEN

1961   "The Baltasar Baca 'Grant': History of an Encroachment." *El Palacio* 68: 47–64, 87–105.

JENNINGS, JESSE D., AND EDWARD NORBECK, EDS.

1964   *Prehistoric Man in the New World.* Chicago: University of Chicago Press for William Marsh Rice University.

JENSON, ANDREW

1941   *Encyclopedic History of the Church of Jesus Christ of Latter-day Saints.* Salt Lake City: Deseret News Publishing Co.

Jones, Oakah L., Jr.
1966   *Pueblo Warriors and Spanish Conquest.* Norman: University of Oklahoma Press.

Jones, Oakah L., Jr., ed.
1967   *My Adventures in Zuñi* by Frank H. Cushing. Palmer Lake, Colo.: Filter Press.

Judd, Neil M.
1967   *The Bureau of American Ethnology: A Partial History.* Norman: University of Oklahoma Press.

Keleher, William A.
1952   *Turmoil in New Mexico, 1846–1869.* Santa Fe: Rydal Press.

Kelly, Lawrence C.
1968   *The Navajo Indians and Federal Indian Policy, 1900–1935.* Tucson: University of Arizona Press.

Kelly, Lawrence C., ed.
1970   *Navajo Roundup: Selected Correspondence of Kit Carson's Expedition against the Navajo, 1863–1865.* Boulder, Colo.: Pruett Publishing.

Kelsey, Shirley Newcomb
1958   "The Santo Nino of Zuni." *New Mexico* 36: 45–47, 73.

Kendrick, H. L.
1947   H. L. Kendrick to D. Meriwether, Governor and Superintendent of Indian Affairs, Santa Fe, Fort Defiance, August 22, 1856. *New Mexico Historical Review* 22: 178–80.
1950   H. L. Kendrick to D. Meriwether, Governor and Superintendent of Indian Affairs, Santa Fe, Fort Defiance, June 12, 1856. *New Mexico Historical Review* 25: 331–33.

Kinnaird, Lawrence, ed. and trans.
1958   *The Frontiers of New Spain: Nicolás de Lafora's Description, 1766–1768.* Berkeley: Quivira Society.

Kirk, Ruth F.
1940   "Little Santu of Cibola." *New Mexico* 18: 16–17, 35–36, 38.

Klett, Francis
1874   "The Zuñi Indians of New Mexico." *Popular Science Monthly* 5: 580–91.

1879 "The Cachina: A Dance at the Pueblo of Zuñi." In *Report upon United States Geographical Surveys West of the One Hundredth Meridian*, edited by George M. Wheeler, 7: 332–36. Washington: Government Printing Office.

KLUCKHOHN, FLORENCE ROCKWOOD, FRED L. STRODTBECK, WITH OTHERS

1961 *Variations in Value Orientations*. Evanston, Ill., and Elmsford, N.Y.: Row, Peterson and Co.

KROEBER, A. L.

1916a "The Oldest Town in America and Its People." *American Museum Journal* 16: 81–86.

1916b "Thoughts on Zuñi Religion." In *Holmes Anniversary Volume: Anthropological Essays Presented to William Henry Holmes in Honor of His Seventieth Birthday, December 1, 1916, by His Friends and Colaborers*, edited by F. W. Hodge, pp. 269–77. Washington: James William Bryan Press.

1916c "Zuñi Potsherds." *Anthropological Papers of the American Museum of Natural History*, vol. 18, pt. 1, pp. 1–37.

1917 "Zuni Kin and Clan." *Anthropological Papers of the American Museum of Natural History*, vol. 18, pt. 2, pp. 37–205.

KUBLER, GEORGE

1940 *The Religious Architecture of New Mexico in the Colonial Period and Since the American Occupation*. Colorado Springs, Colo.: Taylor Museum.

KUIPERS, CORNELIUS

1946 *Zuni Also Prays: Month-by-Month Observations among the People*. [n.p.:] Christian Reformed Board of Missions.

LAMAR, HOWARD ROBERTS

1966 *The Far Southwest, 1846–1912, a Territorial History*. New Haven and London: Yale University Press.

LANGE, CHARLES H., AND CARROLL L. RILEY, EDS.

1966– *The Southwestern Journals of Adolph F. Bandelier, 1880–1884*. 2 vols.
1970 Albuquerque: University of New Mexico Press.

LATON, FRANCIS M., ED.

1971 *Old Zuni Mission*. Zuni, N. Mex.: St. Anthony's Indian Mission.

LEIGHTON, DOROTHEA C., AND JOHN ADAIR.

1966 *People of the Middle Place: A Study of the Zuni Indians*. New Haven, Conn.: Human Relations Area Files Press.

LEONARD, IRVING, ED. AND TRANS.

1932   *The Mercurio Volante of Don Carlos de Sigüenza y Góngora: An Account of the First Expedition of Don Diego de Vargas into New Mexico in 1692.* Los Angeles: Quivira Society.

LEWIS, ROBERT

1971   "The Role of the Indian in New Mexico." In *Environment, People, and Culture: Addresses Presented at the Inaugural Symposium of President Gerald W. Thomas.* 1: 6–8. Las Cruces: New Mexico State University Press.

McCLINTOCK, JAMES H.

1921   *Mormon Settlement in Arizona: A Record of Peaceful Conquest of the Desert.* Phoenix: Manufacturing Stationers.

McGEE, W. J., W. H. HOLMES, J. W. POWELL, AND OTHERS

1900   "In Memoriam: Frank Hamilton Cushing." *American Anthropologist* n.s. 2: 354–80.

McGREGOR, JOHN C.

1965   *Southwestern Archaeology.* 2nd ed. Urbana: University of Illinois Press.

McNITT, FRANK

1962   *The Indian Traders.* Norman: University of Oklahoma Press.

McNITT, FRANK, ED.

1964   *Navaho Expedition: Journal of a Military Reconnaissance from Santa Fe, New Mexico, to the Navaho Country Made in 1849 by Lieutenant James H. Simpson.* Norman: University of Oklahoma Press.

MANNING, WILLIAM C.

1875   "Ancient Pueblos of New Mexico and Arizona." *Harper's Magazine* 51: 327–33.

MARCH, ELIZABETH JEAN

1941   "A Study of Zuñi Myths as Literature." Ph.D. dissertation, University of New Mexico.

MARTIN, PAUL S., GEORGE I. QUIMBY, AND DONALD COLLIER

1947   *Indians before Columbus: Twenty Thousand Years of North American History Revealed by Archeology.* Chicago: University of Chicago Press.

MEINIG, D. W.

1971   *Southwest: Three Peoples in Geographical Change, 1600–1970.* New York: Oxford University Press.

MENDIVIL, JOSE

1871 "A Ride with the Apaches." *Overland Monthly* 6: 341–45.

MILICH, ALICIA RONSTADT, TRANS. AND ED.

1966 *Relaciones: An Account of Things Seen and Learned by Father Jerónimo de Zárate Salmerón from the Year 1538 to Year 1626.* Foreword by Donald C. Cutter. Albuquerque: Horn and Wallace.

MINDELEFF, COSMOS

1897 "The Cliff Ruins of Canyon de Chelly, Arizona." In *Sixteenth Annual Report of the Bureau of American Ethnology, 1894–95*, pp. 73–198. Washington: Government Printing Office.

MINDELEFF, VICTOR

1891 "A Study of Pueblo Architecture: Tusayan and Cibola." In *Eighth Annual Report of the Bureau of Ethnology, 1886–87*, pp. 3–228. Washington: Government Printing Office.

MOLLHAUSEN, BALDWIN

1858 *Diary of a Journey from the Mississippi to the Coasts of the Pacific with a United States Government Expedition.* With an Introduction by Alexander von Humboldt. Translated by Mrs. Percy Sinnett. 2 vols. London: Longman, Brown, Green, Longmans, and Roberts.

MONTGOMERY, ROSS GORDON, WATSON SMITH, AND JOHN OTIS BREW

1949 *Franciscan Awatovi: The Excavation and Conjectural Reconstruction of a 17th-Century Spanish Mission Establishment at a Hopi Indian Town in North-Eastern Arizona.* Harvard University, Papers of the Peabody Museum of American Archaeology and Ethnology, vol. 36. Cambridge, Mass.: The Museum.

MOORHEAD, MAX L.

1968 *The Apache Frontier: Jacobo Ugarte and Spanish–Indian Relations in Northern New Spain, 1769–1791.* Norman: University of Oklahoma Press.

MOORHEAD, MAX L., ED.

1954 *Commerce of the Prairies* by Josiah Gregg. Norman: University of Oklahoma Press.

MORGAN, LEWIS HENRY

1869 "The 'Seven Cities of Cibola.'" *North American Review* 108: 457–98.

1877 *Ancient Society, or, Researches in the Lines of Human Progress from Savagery, through Barbarism to Civilization.* New York: Henry Holt and Co.

1881   *Houses and House-life of the American Aborigines.* U.S. Geographical and Geological Survey of the Rocky Mountain Region, Contributions to North American Ethnology, vol. 4. Washington: Government Printing Office.

MORISON, SAMUEL ELIOT
1971   *The European Discovery of America: The Northern Voyages, A.D. 500–1600.* New York: Oxford University Press.

MURDOCK, GEORGE PETER
1960   *Ethnographic Bibliography of North America.* 3rd ed. New Haven, Conn.: Human Relations Area Files Press.

MURPHY, LAWRENCE R.
1972   *Frontier Crusader — William F. M. Arny.* Tucson: University of Arizona Press.

MURPHY, LAWRENCE R., ED.
1967   *Indian Agent in New Mexico: The Journal of Special Agent W. F. M. Arny, 1870.* Santa Fe: Stagecoach Press.

NEWMAN, STANLEY
1958   *Zuni Dictionary.* Indiana University Research Center in Anthropology, Folklore, and Linguistics, no. 6. [Bloomington, Ind.].
1965   *Zuni Grammar.* University of New Mexico Publications in Anthropology, no. 14. Albuquerque: University of New Mexico Press.

OGLE, RALPH HEDRICK
1970   *Federal Control of the Western Apaches, 1848–1886.* With an Introduction by Oakah L. Jones, Jr. Albuquerque: University of New Mexico Press.

PALMER, WILLIAM J.
1869   *Report of Surveys across the Continent, in 1867–'68, on the Thirty-fifth and Thirty-second Parallels, for a Route Extending the Kansas Pacific Railway to the Pacific Ocean at San Francisco and San Diego. December 1st, 1868.* Philadelphia: W. B. Selheimer.

PANDEY, TRILOKI NATH
1968   "Tribal Council Elections in a Southwestern Pueblo." *Ethnology* 7: 71–85.

PARKHILL, FORBES
1965   *The Blazed Trail of Antoine Leroux.* Los Angeles: Westernlore Press.

PARSONS, ELSIE CLEWS

1916 "A Few Zuñi Death Beliefs and Practices." *American Anthropologist* n.s. 18: 245–56.

1917 *Notes on Zuñi*. Memoirs of the American Anthropological Association, no. 4. 2 pts.

1918a "Pueblo-Indian Folk-tales, Probably of Spanish Provenience." *Journal of American Folk-lore* 31: 216–55.

1918b "Nativity Myth at Laguna and Zuñi." *Journal of American Folk-lore* 31: 256–63.

1923 "The Origin Myth of Zuñi." *Journal of American Folklore* 36: 135–62.

1924 *The Scalp Ceremonial of Zuñi*. Memoirs of the American Anthropological Association, no. 31.

1927 "Witchcraft among the Pueblos: Indian or Spanish?" *Man* 27: 106–12, 125–28.

1930 "Spanish Elements in the Kachina Cult of the Pueblos." In *Proceedings of the Twenty-third International Congress of Americanists, 1928,* pp. 582–603. New York: [Science Press].

1936 *Hopi Journal of Alexander M. Stephen*. 2 vols. New York: Columbia University Press.

1939a "Franciscans Return to Zuni." *American Anthropologist* n.s. 41: 337–38.

1939b *Pueblo Indian Religion*. 2 vols. Chicago: University of Chicago Press.

PEARCE, T. M., INA SIZER CASSIDY, AND HELEN S. PEARCE, EDS.

1965 *New Mexico Place Names: A Geographical Dictionary*. Albuquerque: University of New Mexico Press.

PERRIGO, LYNN I.

1971 *The American Southwest: Its Peoples and Cultures*. New York: Holt, Rinehart and Winston.

PETERSON, CHARLES S.

1973 *Take Up Your Mission: Mormon Colonizing along the Little Colorado River, 1870–1900*. Tucson: University of Arizona Press.

POWELL, JOHN WESLEY

1875 "The Ancient Province of Tusayan." *Scribner's Monthly* 11: 193–213.

1881 "Report of the Director." In *First Annual Report of the Bureau of Ethnology, 1879–80*, pp. xi–xxxiii. Washington: Government Printing Office.

1883   "Report of the Director." In *Second Annual Report of the Bureau of Ethnology, 1880–81*, pp. xv–xxxvii. Washington: Government Printing Office.

1884   "Report of the Director." In *Third Annual Report of the Bureau of Ethnology, 1881–82*, pp. x–lxxiv. Washington: Government Printing Office.

1891   "Report of the Director." In *Eighth Annual Report of the Bureau of Ethnology, 1886–87*, pp. xiii–xxxvi. Washington: Government Printing Office.

PRESCOTT, WILLIAM HICKLING

1892   *History of the Conquest of Mexico.* Edited by John Foster Kirk. Rev. ed. Philadelphia: J. B. Lippincott.

PRIESTLEY, HERBERT I.

1916   *José de Gálvez, Visitor-general of New Spain, 1765–1771.* Berkeley: University of California Press.

PRINCE, L. BRADFORD

1912   *A Concise History of New Mexico.* Cedar Rapids, Iowa: Torch Press.

PROCTOR, EDNA DEAN

1893   *The Song of the Ancient People.* With Preface and Notes by John Fiske and Commentary by F. H. Cushing. Illustrated with Eleven Aquatints by Julian Scott. Boston and New York: Houghton Mifflin.

PUEBLO OF ZUNI

1973a   *A Glossary of Common Zuni Terms.* [Salt Lake City:] The Pueblo of Zuni.

1973b   *The Zunis: Experiences and Descriptions.* [Salt Lake City:] The Pueblo of Zuni.

PUTNAM, FREDERIC W., AND OTHERS

1879   "Reports upon Archaeological and Ethnological Investigations from Vicinity of Santa Barbara, California, and from Ruined Pueblos of Arizona and New Mexico, and Certain Interior Tribes." *In* George M. Wheeler, *Report upon United States Geographical Surveys West of the One Hundredth Meridian . . . ,* vol. 7. Washington: Government Printing Office.

QUAIFE, MILO MILTON, ED.

1966   *Kit Carson's Autobiography.* Lincoln: University of Nebraska Press.

QUAM, ALVINA, TRANS.
1972   *The Zunis: Self-portrayals* by the Zuni People. Albuquerque: University
       of New Mexico Press.

REED, ERIK K.
1955   "Painted Pottery and Zuñi History." *Southwestern Journal of Anthro-
       pology* 11: 178–93.

REEVE, FRANK D.
1939   "The Government and the Navaho, 1846–1858." *New Mexico His-
       torical Review* 14: 82–114.

REEVE, FRANK D., ED.
1953   *Albert Franklin Banta, Arizona Pioneer.* Historical Society of New
       Mexico Publications in History, vol. 14. Albuquerque: University of
       New Mexico Press.

RESEK, CARL
1960   *Lewis Henry Morgan, American Scholar.* Chicago: University of Chi-
       cago Press.

RILEY, CARROLL L.
1971   "Early Spanish–Indian Communication in the Great Southwest." *New
       Mexico Historical Review* 46: 285–314.

RINALDO, JOHN B.
1964   "Notes on the Origins of Historic Zuni Culture." *Kiva* 29: 86–98.

ROBERTS, FRANK H. H., JR.
1931   *The Ruins at Kiatuthlanna, Eastern Arizona.* Bureau of American Eth-
       nology Bulletin no. 100. Washington: Government Printing Office.
1932   *The Village of the Great Kivas on the Zuñi Reservation in New Mexico.*
       Bureau of American Ethnology Bulletin no. 111. Washington: Govern-
       ment Printing Office.

ROBINSON, ELLA L., TRANS., AND F. W. HODGE, ED.
1944   "Troubles at Zuñi in 1702–03." *Masterkey* 18: 110–16.

ROLLE, ANDREW F., ED.
1965   *A Century of Dishonor: The Early Crusade for Indian Reform* by Helen
       Hunt Jackson. New York: Harper and Row.

SABIN, EDWIN L.
1935   *Kit Carson Days, 1809–1868: "Adventures in the Path of Empire."* Rev.
       ed. 2 vols. New York: Press of the Pioneers.

SALPOINTE, J. B.
1898   *Soldiers of the Cross: Notes on the Ecclesiastical History of New-Mexico, Arizona and Colorado.* Banning, Calif.: St. Boniface's Industrial School.

SAUNDERS, LYLE, COMP.
1944   *A Guide to Materials Bearing on Cultural Relations in New Mexico.* Albuquerque: University of New Mexico Press.

SCHMECKEBIER, L. F.
1904   *Catalogue and Index of the Publications of the Hayden, King, Powell, and Wheeler Surveys.* U.S. Geological Survey Bulletin no. 222. Washington: Government Printing Office.

SCHOLES, FRANCE V.
1929   "Documents for the History of the New Mexican Missions in the Seventeenth Century." *New Mexico Historical Review* 4: 45–58, 195–201.

1932   "Problems in the Early Ecclesiastical History of New Mexico." *New Mexico Historical Review* 7: 32–74.

1936–   "Church and State in New Mexico, 1610–1650." *New Mexico Histori-*
1937   *cal Review,* vols. 11–12.

1937–   "Troublous Times in New Mexico, 1659–1670." *New Mexico Histori-*
1941   *cal Review,* vols. 12–16.

SCHOOLCRAFT, HENRY R.
1851–   *Historical and Statistical Information Respecting the History, Condition*
1857   *and Prospects of the Indian Tribes of the United States, Collected and Prepared under the Direction of the Bureau of Indian Affairs.* 6 vols. Title and publisher varies. Philadelphia: Lippincott, Grambo.

SCHROEDER, ALBERT H.
1968   "Shifting for Survival in the Southwest." *New Mexico Historical Review* 43: 291–310.

SEOWTEWA, ALEX
1971   Interview by C. G. Crampton and Richard Hart, Zuni, New Mexico, September 5. Typescript, Tape 993, Duke Indian Oral History Collection, University of Utah, Salt Lake City.

SHAPLIN, PHILIPPA D.
1971   *A Memento of the Hemenway Expedition.* Buried Treasures of the Peabody Museum, Harvard University, vol. 4.

SIMMONS, MARC
1968   *Spanish Government in New Mexico.* Albuquerque: University of New Mexico Press.

SIMPSON, JAMES H.

1850   "Journal of a Military Reconnaissance from Santa Fé, New Mexico, to
        the Navajo Country, Made with Troops under Command of Brevet
        Lieutenant Colonel John M. Washington, Chief of the Ninth Military
        Department, and Governor of New Mexico, in 1849." U.S. 31st Cong.,
        1st Sess., Sen. Ex. Doc. 64, pp. 55–168. Washington: Union Office.

1872   "Coronado's March in Search of the 'Seven Cities of Cibola' and Discus-
        sion of Their Probable Location." In *Annual Report of the Smithsonian
        Institution, 1869*, pp. 309–40. Washington: Government Printing
        Office.

SITGREAVES, L.

1853   *Report of an Expedition down the Zuni and Colorado Rivers.* U.S. 32nd
        Cong., 1st Sess., Sen. Doc. 59. Washington: Robert Armstrong.

SLATER, JOHN M.

1961   *El Morro, Inscription Rock, New Mexico: The Rock Itself, the Inscrip-
        tions Thereon, and the Travelers Who Made Them.* Los Angeles: Plan-
        tin Press.

SMITH, WATSON

1970   "Seventeenth-century Spanish Pueblos of the Western Pueblo Area."
        Smoke Signal (Tucson, Ariz.), no. 21.

SMITH, WATSON, AND JOHN M. ROBERTS

1954   *Zuni Law: A Field of Values.* Harvard University, Papers of the Pea-
        body Museum of American Archaeology and Ethnology, vol. 43, no. 1.
        Cambridge, Mass.: The Museum.

SMITH, WATSON, RICHARD B. WOODBURY, AND NATALIE F. S. WOODBURY

1966   *The Excavation of Hawikuh by Frederick Webb Hodge: Report of the
        Hendricks–Hodge Expedition, 1917–1923.* Contributions from the
        Museum of the American Indian, Heye Foundation, vol. 20. New York:
        Museum of the American Indian, Heye Foundation.

SPICER, EDWARD H.

1962   *Cycles of Conquest: The Impact of Spain, Mexico, and the United States
        on the Indians of the Southwest, 1533–1960.* Tucson: University of
        Arizona Press.

SPIER, LESLIE

1917a   "An Outline for a Chronology of Zuni Ruins." *Anthropological Papers
        of the American Museum of Natural History*, vol. 18, pt. 3, pp. 205–331.

1917b   "Zuñi Chronology." In *Proceedings of the National Academy of Sci-
        ences* 3: 280–83.

SQUIER, E. G.

1848   "New Mexico and California. The Ancient Monuments and Aboriginal and Semi-Civilized Nations. . . ." *American Review, a Whig Journal* 8: 503–28.

STERN, CHARLOTTE, AND OTHERS, EDS.

1959   *Historical Sociology: The Selected Papers of Bernhard J. Stern.* New York: Citadel Press.

STEVENSON, JAMES

1883   "Illustrated Catalogue of the Collections Obtained from the Indians of New Mexico and Arizona, in 1879, [and] from the Indians of New Mexico in 1880." In *Second Annual Report of the Bureau of Ethnology, 1880–81*, pp. 307–465. Washington: Government Printing Office.

1884   "Illustrated Catalogue of the Collections Obtained from the Pueblos of Zuñi, New Mexico, and Wolpi, Arizona, in 1881." In *Third Annual Report of the Bureau of Ethnology, 1881–82*, pp. 511–94. Washington: Government Printing Office.

STEVENSON, MATILDA COXE (TILLY)

1881   *Zuñi and the Zuñians.* Washington: [n.p.].

1890– Papers, 1890–1918. MSS, National Anthropological Archives, Smith-
1918   sonian Institution, Washington, D.C.

1904   "The Zuni Indians: Their Mythology, Esoteric Fraternities, and Ceremonies." In *Twenty-third Annual Report of the Bureau of American Ethnology, 1901–1902.* Washington: Government Printing Office.

1915   "Ethnobotany of the Zuñi Indians." In *Thirtieth Annual Report of the Bureau of American Ethnology, 1908–1909.* Washington: Government Printing Office.

SWANTON, JOHN R.

1952   *The Indian Tribes of North America.* Bureau of American Ethnology Bulletin no. 145. Washington: Government Printing Office.

TAFT, ROBERT

1943   *Artists and Illustrators of the Old West, 1850–1900.* New York: Charles Scribner's Sons.

TANNER, HENRY S.

1823   *New American Atlas Containing Maps of the Several States of the North American Union Projected and Drawn on a Uniform Scale from Documents Found in the Public Offices of the United States and State Govern-*

ments and Other Original and Authentic Information. Philadelphia: H. S. Tanner.

TEDLOCK, DENNIS ERNEST

1968   "The Ethnography of Tale-telling at Zuni." Ph.D. dissertation, Tulane University.

TELLING, IRVING

1952   "New Mexican Frontiers: A Social History of the Gallup Area, 1881–1901." Ph.D. dissertation, Harvard University.

1953   "Ramah, New Mexico, 1876–1900: An Historical Episode with Some Value Analysis." *Utah Historical Quarterly* 21: 117–36.

TEN BROECK, P. G. S.

1854   "Manners and Customs of the Moqui and Navajo Tribes of New Mexico." *In* Henry R. Schoolcraft, *Historical and Statistical Information Respecting the Indian Tribes of the United States*, 4: 72–91. Philadelphia: Lippincott, Grambo.

THOMAS, ALFRED BARNABY, ED. AND TRANS.

1932   *Forgotten Frontiers: A Study of the Spanish Indian Policy of Don Juan Bautista de Anza, Governor of New Mexico, 1777–1787; from the Original Documents from the Archives of Spain, Mexico and New Mexico.* Norman: University of Oklahoma Press.

1935   *After Coronado: Spanish Exploration Northeast of New Mexico, 1696–1727; Documents from the Archives of Spain, Mexico and New Mexico.* Norman: University of Oklahoma Press.

1941   *Teodoro de Croix and the Northern Frontier of New Spain, 1776–1783, from the Original Document in the Archives of the Indies, Seville.* Norman: University of Oklahoma Press.

THOMAS, BENJAMIN M.

1874–   Letters sent, December 2, 1874–April 13, 1883, Pueblo Agency, Bureau
1883   of Indian Affairs, Record Group 75, Archives Branch, Federal Records Center, Denver.

1877   "Fifth Annual Report as United States Indian Agent." In *Report of the Commissioner of Indian Affairs, 1877*. U.S. 45th Cong., 2nd Sess., House Ex. Doc. 1, 8: 557–58. Washington: Government Printing Office.

TIETJEN, GARY L.

1969   *Encounter with the Frontier.* Los Alamos, N. Mex.: the author.

TWITCHELL, RALPH EMERSON

1911– *The Leading Facts of New Mexican History.* 5 vols. Cedar Rapids,
1915   Iowa: Torch Press.

1914   *The Spanish Archives of New Mexico, Comp. and Chronologically
       Arranged with Historical, Genealogical, Geographical and Other Anno-
       tations.* 2 vols. Cedar Rapids, Iowa: Torch Press.

TWITCHELL, RALPH EMERSON, ED.

1925   *Old Santa Fe: The Story of New Mexico's Ancient Capital.* Santa Fe:
       New Mexican Publishing Corp.

TYLER, HAMILTON A.

1964   *Pueblo Gods and Myths.* Norman: University of Oklahoma Press.

TYLER, S. LYMAN

1952   "The Myth of the Lake of Copala and Land of Teguayo." *Utah Histori-
       cal Quarterly* 20: 313–29.

UNDERHILL, RUTH M.

1938   *First Penthouse Dwellers of America.* New York: J. J. Augustin.

1956   *The Navajos.* Norman: University of Oklahoma Press.

U.S. BUREAU OF INDIAN AFFAIRS

1858– *Annual Reports of the Commissioner of Indian Affairs, 1858–1919.*
1920   Published under various auspices usually as a report to the Secretary of
       the Interior. Washington: Government Printing Office.

U.S. BUREAU OF INDIAN AFFAIRS. PUEBLO AND ZUNI AGENCIES

1874– Letters sent, 1874–1917. MSS, National Archives, Record Group 75,
1917   Federal Records Center, Denver.

1874– Correspondence, 1874–1917. MSS, National Archives, Record Group
1917   75, Washington, D.C.

U.S. CENSUS OFFICE

1894   *Report on Indians Taxed and Not Taxed in the United States (except
       Alaska) at the Eleventh Census: 1890.* Washington: Government Print-
       ing Office.

U.S. DEPARTMENT OF INTERIOR

1885   "Zuni Indian Reservation in New Mexico and Arizona. Letter from the
       Secretary of the Interior Transmitting in Response to a Resolution of the
       House of Representatives . . . December 3, 1883." U.S. 48th Cong.,
       2nd Sess., House Ex. Doc. 11. Washington: Government Printing Office.

U.S. INDIAN CLAIMS COMMISSION

The Navajo Tribe of Indians. Docket no. 229. Proposed Findings of Fact in Behalf of the Navajo Tribe of Indians in Area of the Overall Navajo Claim. 6 vols. [n.p., n.d.].

U.S. WAR DEPARTMENT

1855– *Reports of Explorations and Surveys to Ascertain the Most Practicable*
1861 *and Economical Route for a Railroad from the Mississippi River to the Pacific Ocean, Made under Direction of the Secretary of War. . . .* 12 vols. in 13. Washington: A. O. P. Nicholson and others.

U.S. WORK PROJECTS ADMINISTRATION

1940 *New Mexico, a Guide to the State.* New York: Hastings House.

UTLEY, ROBERT M.

1967 *Frontiersmen in Blue: The United States Army and the Indian, 1848–1865.* New York: Macmillan Co.

VANDERWAGEN, ANDREW, AND ETTA VANDERWAGEN

1926 "At the Laying of the Cornerstone of the Mission Church at Zuni, N. M., Aug. 31–1926." MS, Gertrude VanderWagen Wall, Zuni, N. Mex.

VAN VALKENBURGH, RICHARD

1938 *A Short History of the Navajo People.* Window Rock, Ariz.: U.S. Department of Interior.

"A Visit to Zuni." Hartford, Conn. *Evening Press*, March 7, 1864. Reprinted in *Arizoniana*, vol. 1, no. 3 (fall 1960), p. 23.

VIVIAN, GORDON, AND PAUL REITER

1960 *The Great Kivas of Chaco Canyon and Their Relationships.* Santa Fe, N. Mex.: School of American Research.

VOGT, EVON Z., AND ETHEL M. ALBERT, EDS.

1966 *People of Rimrock: A Study of Five Cultures.* Cambridge, Mass.: Harvard University Press.

WAGNER, HENRY R.

1967 *The Spanish Southwest, 1542–1794: An Annotated Bibliography.* Los Angeles: Quivira Society. 2 vols.

1968 *The Cartography of the Northwest Coast of America to the Year 1800.* Reprint of the edition issued at Berkeley, 1937. Amsterdam: N. Israel.

WALLACE, EDWARD S.
1955   *The Great Reconnaissance: Soldiers, Artists and Scientists on the Frontier, 1848–1861.* Boston: Little, Brown and Co.

WALLACE, SUSAN E.
1888   *The Land of the Pueblos.* New York: John B. Alden.

WARD, JOHN
1868   "New Mexico Superintendency." *In* U.S. Department of the Interior, Commissioner of Indian Affairs, *Annual Report 1867*, pp. 189–213. Washington: Government Printing Office.

WASHINGTON, JOHN M.
1849   "Operations in New Mexico." *In* U.S. 31st Cong., 1st Sess., House Ex. Doc. 5, pp. 109–15. Washington: House of Representatives.

WEBER, DAVID J.
1971   *The Taos Trappers: The Fur Trade in the Far Southwest, 1540–1846.* Norman: University of Oklahoma Press.

WENGER, MARTIN
1959   "American Realist, Thomas Eakins." *American Scene* 2: 3.

WHEAT, CARL I.
1957–   *Mapping the Transmississippi West: 1540–1861.* 5 vols.: 1 (1957)
1963   *The Spanish Entrada to the Louisiana Purchase, 1540–1804*; 2 (1958) *From Lewis and Clark to Fremont, 1804–1845*; 3 (1959) *From the Mexican War to the Boundary Surveys, 1846–1854*; 4 (1960) *From the Pacific Railroad Surveys to the Onset of the Civil War, 1855–1860*; 5 (1963) *From the Civil War to the Geological Survey.* San Francisco: Institute of Historical Cartography.

WHEELER, GEORGE M.
1875   "Annual Report upon the Geographical Explorations and Surveys West of the One Hundredth Meridian, in California, Nevada, Nebraska, Utah, Arizona, Colorado, New Mexico, Wyoming and Montana." Appendix LL in *Annual Report of the Chief of Engineers for 1875.* Washington: Government Printing Office.

1879   *Report upon United States Geographical Surveys West of the One Hundredth Meridian.* Vol. 7, *Archaeology*, edited by F. W. Putnam. Washington: Government Printing Office.

1889   *Report upon United States Geographical Surveys West of the One Hundredth Meridian.* Vol. 1, *Geographical Report.* Washington: Government Printing Office.

WHIPPLE, A. W.

1856 "Report of Explorations for a Railway Route, near the 25th Parallel of North Latitude, from the Mississippi River to the Pacific Ocean." *In* U.S. War Department, *Reports of Explorations and Surveys to Ascertain the Most Practicable and Economical Route for a Railroad from the Mississippi River to the Pacific Ocean*, 3: 1–136. Washington: A. O. P. Nicholson.

WHIPPLE, A. W., THOMAS EWBANK, AND W. M. TURNER

1856 "Route near the Thirty-fifth Parallel, under the Command of Lieut. A. W. Whipple, Topographical Engineers in 1853 and 1854. Report upon the Indian Tribes, 1855." *In* U.S. War Department, *Reports of Explorations and Surveys to Ascertain the Most Practicable and Economical Route for a Railroad from the Mississippi River to the Pacific Ocean*, vol. 3, pt. 3. Washington: A. O. P. Nicholson.

WILKEN, ROBERT L.

1953 *Anselm Weber, O. F. M., Missionary to the Navaho, 1898–1921*. Milwaukee: Bruce Publishing Co.

WILLEY, GORDON R.

1966 *An Introduction to American Archaeology*. Vol. 1, *North and Middle America*. Englewood Cliffs, N. J.: Prentice-Hall.

WILSON, EDMUND

1956 *Red, Black, Blond and Olive: Studies in Four Civilizations: Zuñi, Haiti, Soviet Russia, Israel*. London: W. H. Allen.

WINSHIP, GEORGE PARKER

1896 "The Coronado Expedition, 1540–1542." *In* Bureau of American Ethnology, *Fourteenth Annual Report, 1892–93*, 1: 329–613. Washington: Government Printing Office.

WINSOR, JUSTIN, ED.

1884– *Narrative and Critical History of America*. 8 vols. Boston and New
1889 York: Houghton Mifflin.

WOODBURY, RICHARD B.

1956 "The Antecedents of Zuni Culture." *Transactions of the New York Academy of Sciences*, series 2, 18: 557–63.

WOODBURY, RICHARD B., AND NATALIE F. S. WOODBURY

1956 "Zuni Prehistory and El Morro National Monument." *Southwestern Lore* 21: 56–60.

WOODWARD, ARTHUR
1939   "Frank Cushing — 'First War-chief of Zuñi,' " *Masterkey* 13 : 172–79.

WORCESTER, DONALD EMMET
1947   "Early History of the Navaho Indians." Ph.D. dissertation, University of California, Berkeley.

WORMINGTON, H. M.
1961   *Prehistoric Indians of the Southwest.* 5th ed. Denver Museum of Natural History, Popular Series, no. 7. Denver: Denver Museum of Natural History.

WRIGHT, LYLE H., ED.
1946   *John Udell Journal, Kept During a Trip Across the Plains, Containing an Account of the Massacre of a Portion of His Party by the Mojave Indians in 1859.* Los Angeles: N. A. Kovach.

ZUNI PUEBLO. LAND GRANT PAPERS
1689–   Surveyor-General Records. Pueblo of Zuni, Case V. MSS, Santa Fe,
1854   N. Mex., U.S. Bureau of Land Management.

Index

Zuni roof construction

THE ZUNIS OF CIBOLA was set in Intertype Baskerville
with handset foundry Lydian display type.
Typography by Donald M. Henriksen
Printed by the University of Utah Printing Service
on Hopper Sonata paper.
Bound by Mountain States Bindery in Holliston Record Buckram.